BBC

Speakout

3RD EDITION

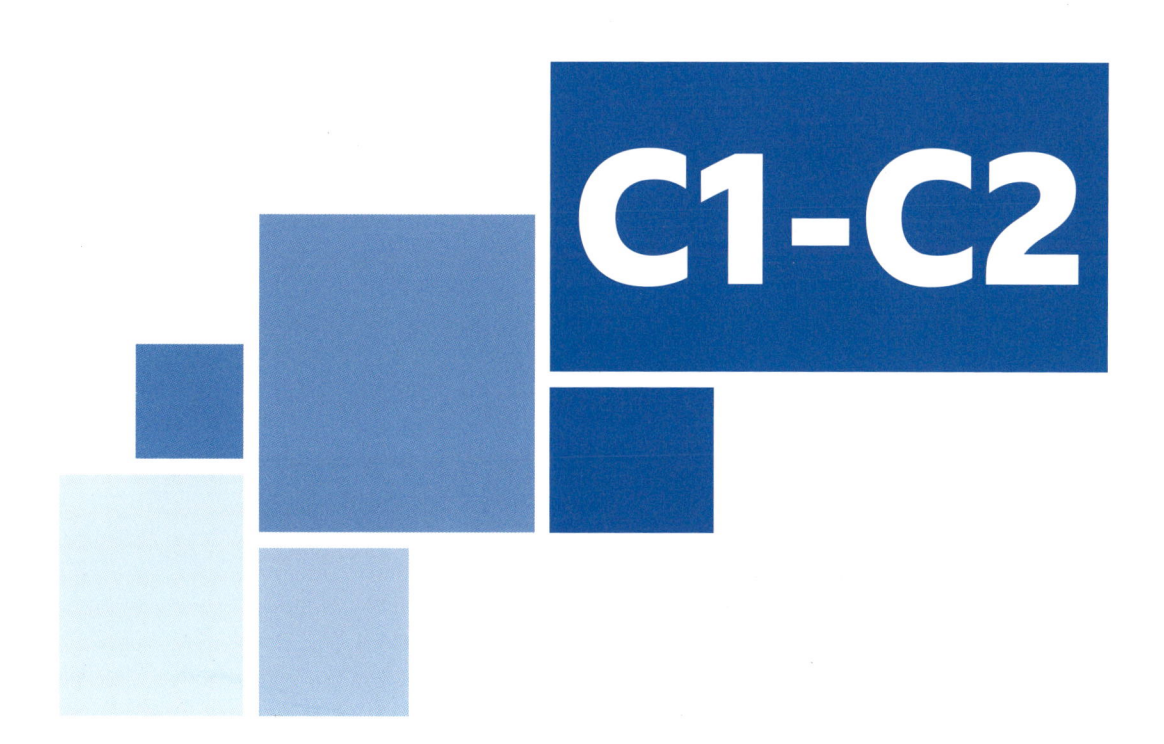

C1-C2

Workbook

Pearson Education Limited
KAO Two
KAO Park
Hockham Way
Harlow, Essex
CM17 9SR
England
and Associated Companies throughout the world.

pearsonenglish.com/speakout3e

© Pearson Education Limited 2023

All rights reserved; no part of this publication may be reproduced, stored in a retrieval system, or transmitted in any form or by any means, electronic, mechanical, photocopying, recording, or otherwise without the prior written permission of the Publishers.

First published 2023

Second impression 2023

ISBN: 978-1-292-40739-5

Set in BBC Reith Sans

Printed and bound by Neografia, Slovakia

Acknowledgements
Written by Damian Williams

Image Credit(s):
123RF.com: Andriy Popov 33, julief514 47, rawpixel 65, Sergii Koval 15;
Alamy Stock Photo: Eva-Camilla Swensen 64, Keenstock 11, PA Images 53, Zoonar GmbH 41; **Getty Images:** d3sign/Moment 55, David Schneider/iStock 29, FlamingoImages/iStock 21, gorodenkoff/iStock 25, millann/iStock 41, Tara Moore/Stone 49, tdub303/E+ 41, Tony Garcia/Photodisc 27, Xavier Lorenzo/iStock 49; **Shutterstock:** Al Clark 15, Christine Bird 10, Fanfo 15, Jacob Lund 18, Poring Studio 26

Cover Images: *Front:* **Getty Images:** Luis Alvarez, Maskot, MoMo Productions

CONTENTS

LESSON	VOCABULARY	GRAMMAR	PRONUNCIATION
1A pp4–5	describing attitudes; idioms	conditional forms	*if* in natural speech
1B pp6–7	collocations: education; compound nouns	nominal relative clauses	emphatic syllable stress
**1C	1D** pp8–9	creativity		polite intonation
2A pp10–11	describing the impact of an action; binomials	advanced ways of comparing	schwa /ə/
2B pp12–13	summarising verbs; multi-word verbs for reporting	reporting	using intonation to show contrasting opinions
**2C	2D** pp14–15	conventions/cultural heritage		expressing surprise and asking for reaction
REVIEW 1–2 pp16–17			
3A pp18–19	collocations: job searching	modal verbs and phrases	linking sounds in modal phrases
3B pp20–21	verb–noun collocations; metaphors	passives	word stress
**3C	3D** pp22–23	collocations: politics; politics		stress and intonation when paraphrasing
4A pp24–25	verb–noun collocations; adverb–adjective collocations	verb patterns	syllable stress in verb–noun collocations
4B pp26–27	collocations: needing and giving; adjectives to describe people	continuous and perfect aspects	stress in collocations featuring verbs with 'weak' meanings
**4C	4D** pp28–29	money and economy		chunking language
REVIEW 3–4 pp30–31			
5A pp32–33	collocations: first impressions; adjectives and adjectival endings	giving emphasis: inversion, clefting, tailing, fronting	stress while giving emphasis
5B pp34–35	spreading misinformation	participle clauses	intonation in participle clauses
**5C	5D** pp36–37	persuasion; adjectives to describe presentations		intonation: being persuasive
6A pp38–39	describing literature; describing books and films	narrative tenses review	intonation to show surprise/interest
6B pp40–41	reacting to poetry and song	adverbials	intonation to show contrast
**6C	6D** pp42–43	adjective–noun collocations: travel		informal phrases when telling anecdotes
REVIEW 5–6 pp44–45			
7A pp46–47	idioms for choices; connotation	omitting words	word stress in idiomatic phrases
7B pp48–49	ways of reading; idioms: books and reading	prepositional phrases	stress in phrasal verbs and dependent prepositions
**7C	7D** pp50–51	collocations: discussing issues		intonation when hedging and expressing reservations
8A pp52–53	idioms and collocations: skills and abilities; compound adjectives	noun phrases	linking consonants
8B pp54–55	adjectives to describe sensations and reactions; verbs to describe reactions	uses of *will* and *would*	contracted *will*
**8C	8D** pp56–57	well-being		intonation in sentences containing contrasting ideas
REVIEW 7–8 pp58–59			

CUMULATIVE REVIEW 1–4 pp60–61	CUMULATIVE REVIEW 5–8 pp62–63	CUMULATIVE REVIEW 1–8 pp64–67
AUDIOSCRIPTS pp68–77	**ANSWER KEY** pp78–93	

Lesson 1A

GRAMMAR | conditional forms
VOCABULARY | describing attitudes; idioms
PRONUNCIATION | *if* in natural speech

VOCABULARY

describing attitudes

1 **Choose the correct word to complete the sentences.**

1 The idea that failure creates opportunities really .... true for me.
 a calls **b** rings **c** strikes
2 To say all successful people are rich is a bit of a .... statement.
 a brushing **b** wiping **c** sweeping
3 What you said about your experience when travelling really struck a chord .... me.
 a for **b** to **c** with
4 The idea that we can learn from mistakes is spot ...., in my opinion.
 a on **b** in **c** off
5 Some of the things people believe about politicians are complete ....
 a fallacies **b** paradoxes **c** deviations
6 There's .... of truth in the idea, but it's not without its problems.
 a a component **b** an element **c** a segment
7 I hate the way the media just .... out these trite phrases all the time.
 a trot **b** run **c** spread
8 You can't say that. It's .... not true.
 a officially **b** patently **c** openly

idioms

2 **Choose the correct word or phrase to complete the sentences.**

1 I think I'm going to have to throw in the **towel** / **share** in this game. I just can't win.
2 I trained as a science teacher, but I decided to change **strides** / **tack** and teach geography.
3 Try not to get hung **up about** / **on about** the details. Remember the main aim.
4 The remarks about my performance are really starting to **knock** / **throw** my confidence.
5 The way he gets results really **flies** / **changes** in the face of conventional wisdom.
6 You're doing a great job and **giving** / **making** strides in our new market.
7 That's a great idea and one I can really go **along** / **on** with.
8 I've wanted to learn the guitar for ages, so this year I'm finally going to **go** / **give** it a go.
9 After a few weeks of working in sales, I realised I'm just not cut **out for** / **up for** it.
10 Believe me, I have my **fair** / **true** share of problems with the new system.

GRAMMAR

conditional forms

3 **The sentences below each have a mistake. Choose the best option to correct the mistake.**

1 If I to study journalism, I know I'd enjoy it.
 a I will **b** I was to **c** I were to
2 You can't go in there <u>if</u> you have permission.
 a without **b** unless **c** otherwise
3 I'll give it a go <u>as</u> you come with me.
 a as long as **b** condition **c** will
4 <u>Had if there</u> been even an element of truth in the theory, I might have taken it seriously.
 a If there hadn't **b** Had there **c** There had

4 **Complete the sentences with the words and phrases in the box. There are two extra items.**

| But for   Had you   If I   If I were to   Provided that |
| Should   Unless   Without knowing |

1 .... we can afford the rent, we'll take the place.
2 .... the support of my husband, I would never have written this book.
3 .... exactly what you want, I can't really help you.
4 .... tell him how I feel, do you think he'd understand?
5 .... you pay a deposit, we can't keep it for you.
6 .... we finish early, I'll let you know.

5 **Complete the second sentence so that it has the same meaning as the first sentence.**

1 If you don't take your ID, you won't be able to get in.
 You need ...., otherwise ....
2 If my teacher hadn't helped me, I would have failed the exam.
 But for ....
3 We can just take the next flight if we miss ours.
 Should ....
4 If you hadn't driven so slowly, we would have been on time.
 If it hadn't been for your ....
5 If you'd spent more time studying, you would have got better grades.
 Had you ....
6 If Lily were to prepare the meal, everyone would love it.
 Were ....

PRONUNCIATION

6 A 🔊 **1.01** | *if* in natural speech | Listen and complete the sentences with three words in each gap. A contraction counts as one word.

1 _____ any questions, just let me know.
2 _____ too expensive, let's do that course together.
3 _____ check the facts, they would believe it.
4 _____ now, we should make it.
5 _____ true for you, then it probably is.
6 _____ too difficult, let's give it a go.

B 🔊 **1.01** | Listen again and repeat.

READING

7 Read the introduction to the article and choose the best phrase to fill the gap.
   a Practice makes perfect
   b It doesn't matter as long as you do your best
   c If at first you don't succeed, try, try, try again

8 Read the article and choose the correct person.
   1 Who expresses a stronger opinion than the others?
   2 Who thinks success is unique for everyone?
   3 Who suggests that success is measurable?
   4 Who says that they always try their hardest?
   5 Who suggests people need to decide what will drive them first?
   6 Who talks about the effect of their success on other people?

9 Read the article again. Are the statements True (T) or False (F)?
   1 Roman thinks that many people don't understand what success means until they achieve it.
   2 Roman agrees with the conventional wisdom because in his own experience doing his best has been rewarding.
   3 According to Tod, the success of his company stems from using motivational statements.
   4 Tod thinks the idea that trying hard won't always work in the world of business.
   5 Isla thinks success for her personally isn't an easy thing to measure.
   6 Isla believes luck is important for success.

What does success really mean?

'_____', or so the conventional wisdom goes. But is this really true? Obviously, there are limits to what you can achieve on your own, and even with others, but can you feel a sense of success just by knowing that you've given it your all? Or, quite simply, does success mean that you've achieved what you originally set out to do, regardless of whether or not you've tried your hardest? We spoke to three successful professionals about what success means to them.

Roman Hughes, surgeon

I think the conventional wisdom is spot on for me. The whole idea of success is a very personal thing, and obviously, success means different things to different people. That's the key, I think. In order to be successful, you first need to define what that means to you. It's important to visualise yourself being successful at what you do and then give it your all. So, for some, it might mean wealth and all the trappings that come with it, like a big house and nice car, but for others, that vision just doesn't strike a chord. It's important to also have a clear understanding of what motivates you to succeed. For me, success means being able to enjoy what I do every day, so that it doesn't feel like work. I know that I'm in a privileged position, but I've worked hard to get here. So, in that sense, the conventional wisdom definitely rings true.

Tod Ibarra, founder of Roboxx

Doing your best is obviously important, and telling a child at a school sports day that taking part is more important than winning is probably wise. But in the adult world of business, the idea that all you need to succeed is to 'do your best' is absolute twaddle. Being successful is about getting results. If my team doesn't get results, my company won't survive. It's as simple as that. If I were to trot out trite inspirational phrases like 'just do your best' to my staff, then we wouldn't be where we are today. Success is a process whereby you do what you know works. And it's constantly changing. What brings results today might not tomorrow, so it's constantly under review and analysis. But to say nothing matters as long as you give it your all is just a complete fallacy.

Isla Boyer, author

My motivation for succeeding has always been about legacy. It might appear that being a successful author is a clear-cut thing to measure – you get your book published. But to me, it's more complex than that. By 'legacy' I'm talking about how people feel after they've read my stories. If the words have moved them in some way, then I know I've done my job, more so if that effect remains with them. To be successful, I think you have to be lucky and get a break at some point, but it's what you do with that luck that counts. I know I'll only leave that emotional legacy to my readers if I absolutely give it my all when writing. So, part of the conventional wisdom strikes a chord with me. And that's why I make sure I do my best – with every word I write.

Lesson 1B

GRAMMAR | nominal relative clauses
VOCABULARY | collocations: education; compound nouns
PRONUNCIATION | emphatic syllable stress

VOCABULARY

collocations: education

1 Choose the correct words to complete the advert.

> Here at Millfield Cross Community College, we are always ¹**striving / focusing** for excellence. With hundreds of different subjects on offer, you can be sure you'll be able to ²**foster / find** your own path. We pride ourselves on the fact that we ³**fulfil / maintain** rigorous standards in education in order to ⁴**deliver / fulfil** a quality curriculum in all fields. Whether you study face-to-face at the college or take one of our online courses, we ensure that we ⁵**develop / take** a nurturing environment while ⁶**fostering / focusing** on individuality, as we know that different people have different needs. So why not ⁷**find / take** the initiative today and see what we have on offer? It's the first step to ⁸**fulfilling / delivering** your true potential.

2 Complete the conversation using words from the box.

> complete fair individual good
> mutual nurturing quality rigorous

A: How are you finding your new teaching job, Ava?
B: I'm loving it! But school's different from when I was a student, I think. It used to be all about delivering a(n) ¹_____ curriculum. It was also more about maintaining ²_____ standards of teaching and learning.
A: And how is it different nowadays?
B: It's more about developing a(n) ³_____ environment, providing support and establishing ⁴_____ respect between students and staff. The idea is that by fostering ⁵_____ relationships, students will achieve more.

PRONUNCIATION

3 A 🔊 **1.02** | emphatic syllable stress | Listen and repeat each sentence exactly as you hear it.

B 🔊 **1.02** | Underline the stressed syllables in the phrases. Listen and check.

1 take the initiative
2 fulfil your potential
3 striving for excellence
4 a nurturing environment
5 rigorous standards
6 mutual respect
7 fostering good relationships
8 a quality curriculum

compound nouns

4 Complete the compound noun in each sentence. The first letter is given.

1 Our school offers a blended l_____ course which combines online and face-to-face study.
2 There are good things about working in a virtual learning e_____, but for me it's not as good as a physical classroom.
3 It took me nearly ten years to pay off my student l_____ after finishing university.
4 Nowadays, schools do a lot to develop the critical t_____ skills of younger students.
5 A joint venture between the company and college will provide free vocational t_____ for out-of-work adults.
6 The government has promised no increase in tuition f_____ for the next year.
7 When I was at school there was a lot of rote l_____ – we had to learn things by memorising them.
8 We do a lot of peer a_____ in English classes, where we review each other's work.
9 We're a private language school with external a_____ from the country's largest professional body.
10 On this course, half of our marks come from continuous a_____, and the rest from the final exam.

GRAMMAR

nominal relative clauses

5 Choose the correct word to complete the sentences.

1 I'd like to speak with you later, _____ you have a few minutes spare.
   a whatever   b whichever   c whenever
2 I like the new curriculum. It's _____ what these students need.
   a precisely   b when   c whatever
3 _____ other people think doesn't matter to me.
   a What   b When   c Where
4 This website shows _____ to study in a virtual-learning environment.
   a how   b who   c you
5 _____ gets the most points wins the game.
   a Whatever   b What   c Whoever
6 _____ we're looking for is a way to blend online and face-to-face learning.
   a Who   b What   c That

6

1B

6 Complete the conversation with one word in each gap.

A: What training would you like to do this year, Marcus? We have lots of training courses available, so ¹_____ you like the look of, we can sign you up for.

B: Well, I'd like to improve my sales technique, but I don't really know ²_____ to do in practical terms to achieve this. I think it would be really useful if I could shadow one of the senior sales reps, to get an insight into ³_____ they do things.

A: Right. Our advanced sales courses involve a placement with a senior sales rep for a couple of hours a week. The time isn't fixed, either. You go ⁴_____ it's convenient for both of you.

B: Oh, that's precisely ⁵_____ I meant. How do I enrol?

A: I'll email you the guidance document. It has all the sales courses available. ⁶_____ of them you choose, I'm sure you'll find it useful.

LISTENING

7 🔊 1.03 | Listen to the first part of a radio programme about STEM (science, technology, engineering and mathematics) education. Which topics (a–h) are discussed?

a the number of hours children spend at school
b the world of work
c skills that children need to develop at school
d the amount of homework students should have
e the integration of school subjects
f the use of technology in jobs
g children with special educational needs
h implementing this type of learning in schools

8 🔊 1.03 | Listen again and choose the correct option (a–c) to complete the sentences.

1 Kendra says that STEM learning began because children
   a weren't learning what they later needed in life.
   b didn't learn enough about technology.
   c were learning about jobs which don't exist.
2 STEM learning can teach skills which will be useful in
   a some jobs.
   b all jobs.
   c technical jobs.
3 The key idea that Kendra expresses about STEAM learning is that
   a it only focuses on part of the traditional curriculum.
   b it's a mixed curriculum.
   c it's different from other types of curriculum.
4 According to Kendra, adding the arts to STEM education to create the 'STEAM' model allows for a greater focus on
   a developing critical thinking.
   b communication skills.
   c developing creativity.

5 In order to implement STEAM education, educators need to
   a change their mindset.
   b focus more on knowledge.
   c work together more closely.
6 Key skills to develop in children include ones that
   a they wouldn't use in traditional education.
   b they don't yet have.
   c they already possess.

9 🔊 1.04 | Listen to the recording. Write what you hear. You will hear the sentences only once.

1 _____
2 _____
3 _____
4 _____

WRITING

note-taking and summary writing

10 Complete the summary of what you heard in Ex 8 with the correct form of the verbs in the box.

| accept begin cite compare |
| focus give go point |

In this extract about STE(A)M learning, the presenter, ¹_____ by outlining the aims of STEM education in general terms and introducing a specialist, Kendra Lewis. She ²_____ the skills children are traditionally taught with the skills they'll need in the future and ³_____ out that there's a mismatch between the two. She then ⁴_____ a description of STEM learning and ⁵_____ that education needs to go even further than that and integrate the arts into the model. She then ⁶_____ on the fact that many jobs in the future will be automated, and ⁷_____ on to say that a STEAM model of education will allow schools to develop skills in children that will set them apart from technology in terms of being able to do a job. She ⁸_____ creativity in problem-solving as one of those skills. Finally, she gives advice for educators wishing to implement a STEAM model and explains that the starting point should be integration, both between different disciplines and between different parts of the educational process.

11 🔊 1.05 | Listen to the next part of the programme. Make notes to include in a summary.

12 Use your notes from Ex 11 and the verbs from Ex 10 to write a summary of what you heard. Write 200–220 words.

Lesson 1C

HOW TO ... | manage interaction during a discussion
VOCABULARY | creativity
PRONUNCIATION | polite intonation

VOCABULARY

creativity

1 Choose the correct word to complete the sentences.
1 I wouldn't believe every word Jamie tells you – he has a rather **novel / fertile / intuitive** imagination.
2 We really need to think outside the **box / sky / hole** for this project and try something different.
3 A lot of my ideas are **sparked / fired / excited** by things I see in nature.
4 We're seeing a lot of **basic / raw / silent** talent enter the company, which is great.
5 I had a **spark / flash / light** of inspiration on the way to work this morning.
6 Olivia's come up with a **raw / contemporary / novel** idea for our promotion.

2 Complete the social media comments with the words in the box. There are two extra words.

blue   fertile   innate   inspiration
intuitive   outside   sparked   up

Tessa: Ugh, I'm completely out of ideas for my assignment! What does everyone do when they need new ideas?

Ezra: I drop everything and go for a walk. I almost always get a flash of ¹_____ when I try not to think about something. Walking in the park or just down the street, I find my ideas come completely out of the ²_____!

Bianca: I just ask my brother! He's got a(n) ³_____ talent for thinking ⁴_____ the box and coming ⁵_____ with novel ideas!

Chris: I try to relax, close my eyes, and go with my instinct rather than overthink it. I try to be ⁶_____ about these things.

How to ...

manage interaction during a discussion

3 🔊 1.06 | Listen to a radio discussion about creativity. Number the topics (a–f) in the order they are mentioned.
a the 'creative flow'
b sources of inspiration
c having ideas and carrying them out
d the time of day
e trying things out to see what works
f jumping in a river

4 🔊 1.06 | Match the phrase beginnings (1–7) with the endings (a–g). Listen and check.
1 If I can
2 Earlier you raised
3 Let me pick
4 If I can just bring
5 What I started
6 Going back to
7 As we

a come in here ...
b to say was ...
c mentioned before ...
d an important point ...
e what I was saying earlier ...
f up on that.
g Daisy back in.

PRONUNCIATION

5 🔊 1.07 | **polite intonation** | Listen and decide which sentences are said with polite intonation.
1 But surely it's not that simple.
2 But don't you think it's important to consider?
3 So you're saying we can draw ideas from anywhere.
4 Did you say 'a river'? What's that got to do with it?

SPEAKING

6 A 🔊 1.08 | Complete the discussion. Write one word in each gap. Listen and check.

A: To go back to my earlier ¹_____ about what exactly creativity is, can we add anything to our definition? To get the ball ²_____, let's start with Alison.
B: Well, I think there are two key concepts: novelty and value. Is it a new idea? Does it have value?
A: But, surely, an idea doesn't have to be completely new? Sorry, I didn't mean to ³_____ you off, Alison. But take the work of a biographer, for example. They're telling a story that's already there. The novelty comes from the way that they tell it. Sorry Alison, you were ⁴_____ ...
B: Not at all, you're right. That's where novelty plays a part, in how you turn ideas into reality.
A: I'd ⁵_____ to hear Chris's thoughts on this.
C: I completely agree. And value is important, too. Does your idea have value to other people? Obviously, everyone's different, and the more people it has value for, the more valuable it is.
A: Yes, and going back to ⁶_____ we were saying before, not all creative people are alike.

B 🔊 1.09 | You are A in Ex 6A. Listen and speak after the beep. Record the conversation if you can.

C Listen to your recording and compare it to Ex 6A.

D Repeat Ex 6B, without looking at the discussion in Ex 6A. Then repeat Ex 6C.

Speak anywhere Go to the interactive speaking practice

Lesson 1D

LISTENING | favourite teachers
READING | teachers who have made a real difference

LISTENING

1 🔊 **1.10** | Listen to three people describing their favourite teachers. Who gives these reasons for liking them: Ilsa (I), Brayden (B) or Joanna (J)?
1 their ability to create a 'safe space' in lessons
2 the amount of work they put into their job
3 their own enthusiasm for the subject

2 🔊 **1.10** | Listen again and choose the correct person.
1 Who says the teacher encouraged them to find answers for themselves?
2 Who says they weren't interested in the subject before they had this teacher?
3 Who says they found the subject difficult before they had this teacher?
4 Who talks about how the teacher created their own materials?
5 Who describes a situation in which the teacher made them think about things in a different way?
6 Who describes how the teacher created a positive atmosphere in the lessons?

READING

3 Read the article about two teachers who went above and beyond. Match the headings (a–c) with the paragraphs (1 and 2). There is one extra heading.
a Developing skills the right way
b The agreement
c The sounds of hope

4 Read the article again. Are the statements True (T) or False (F)?
1 Cateura smells bad.
2 Favio Chávez knew how bad things were for residents of Cateura before he visited.
3 Chávez asked businesses across the country to donate musical instruments.
4 Many children at Whitney Elementary School had a stable home life when Sherrie Gahn arrived.
5 Gahn asked local businesses to donate money.
6 Because of what Gahn did, the children became better students.

Going the extra mile

All of us can think of a significant teacher we've had. But, every now and then, a teacher comes along who astounds everyone by the lengths to which they are willing to go.

1 .... On the outskirts of Asunción, Paraguay's capital, sits the sprawling settlement of Cateura, home to around 250,000 families. The area is also home to the country's largest landfill site: a huge pile of rubbish discarded by the residents of the capital. There's no electricity or running water, and daily life is dominated by the overwhelming stench of the tip. For most people who live here, a meagre living is earned by searching the dump for recyclable material, which can then be sold for a few cents. When teacher, musician and environmental technician Favio Chávez visited the area as part of a state recycling project, he was shocked at the conditions these families were living in. Knowing the benefits that learning musical instruments can bring, he decided to start a project, teaching music to children in the area. But he had a problem: how to provide them with the musical instruments they needed. That's when he realised the answer lay all around them, in the rubbish. Enlisting the help of former carpenter Don Cola Gomez, they set about creating musical instruments from the material they found in the dump. Don has now made over 400 string instruments and 50 guitars, and, thanks to Favio's teaching skills, the children have formed what's become known as 'The Landfill Harmonic'. Using the instruments they've crafted, they regularly perform classical concerts and, for many, it has provided a new focus and opportunities.

2 .... When school principal Sherrie Gahn first arrived at Whitney Elementary School in Las Vegas, she was shocked at the conditions the children were living in outside school. Up to three-quarters of the children's families were living in motels and she even saw children eating packets of ketchup, because they were so hungry. That was when she made a deal with the parents: keep your children in school and I'll take care of everything else. She then set about launching a national campaign to raise funds by asking businesses and organisations across the country to donate money. She was so successful that one pop star even donated $100,000 in 2011, and then visited the school in 2013 and donated a further $150,000. Sherrie used the money to buy food and clothes for the children. She also paid for haircuts, dental treatment and, in some cases, even paid the families' rent. Children were given food packages to take home on a Friday to see the families through the weekend and she set up a 'clothes pantry' in one of the classrooms so that children could help themselves when they needed new clothes. The result was the establishment of a classroom dynamic where children could focus on the subjects at hand and not have to worry about what they were going to eat or wear. As a result, the students' scores in all subjects greatly improved.

Lesson 2A

GRAMMAR | advanced ways of comparing
VOCABULARY | describing the impact of an action; binomials
PRONUNCIATION | schwa /ə/

VOCABULARY

describing the impact of an action

1 Choose the correct words to complete the text.

A lot has been said about the recent renovation, or 'modernisation', of my local area. What was once a collection of decrepit old buildings is now a thriving cultural hub. The aim of modernising the area was to help raise its cultural ¹**figure** / **profile** by ²**facilitating** / **facing** cultural development, and the improvements to local buildings and streets were expected to ³**bring** / **take** long-term benefits to the wider area. The problem with modernisation, however, is that it is often led by the private sector and, as new businesses move in, they often do more harm ⁴**as** / **than** good for the residents. In our area, for example, it's had a ⁵**destructive** / **detrimental** effect on local people's standard of living because of soaring cost of rent, forcing many out of the area. Those who manage to stay end ⁶**off** / **up** having to pay a lot more than they used to.

2 Complete the conversation using words from the box.

> boost   detrimental   facilitate   harm
> profile   showcase   stuck   tangible

A: What do you think of our city's bid to become the new 'City of Culture', Esra? Do you think it will have any ¹_____ benefits?

B: Yes. Giving the cultural life of the city a ²_____ is always a good thing.

A: I'm not so sure. I worry that it might do more ³_____ than good. They plough all this money into new theatres, exhibitions and stuff and when the moment's passed, we end up ⁴_____ with things local people don't need.

B: Yes, but, at the same time, we get to ⁵_____ the best of our local talent. And that can only be a good thing.

binomials

3 Complete the binomial in each sentence.

1 In the end, we grew tired of the hustle and b_____ of city life and moved to the country.
2 We tend to find that, by and l_____, it's more expensive to live in a larger city.
3 Buy a travel pass if you're going to be out and a_____ exploring all day.
4 Increased tourism is part and p_____ of being a 'City of Culture'.
5 We made mistakes in the project, but you live and l_____, don't you?
6 The solutions to the problems aren't cut and d_____ – they're quite complex.

4 Complete each sentence with a binomial using one word from each box.

> first   give   make   peace   slowly   sooner

> break   foremost   later   quiet   surely   take

1 I like a bit of _____ after a stressful day at work.
2 _____, we need to ensure everyone has a decent quality of life.
3 We can't fail. The success of this project really is _____ for us.
4 It won't happen overnight, but _____, we will start to see some tangible benefits.
5 It's not urgent, but _____ we're going to have to decide what to do with the city's open spaces.
6 The project will cost €5 million, _____.

GRAMMAR

advanced ways of comparing

5 Choose the correct word to complete the sentences.

1 This part of the city is _____ like where we live – nice and quiet.
   a bit   **b** rather   **c** lot
2 You _____ have picked a better location than this, right next to the station.
   a wouldn't   **b** can't   **c** couldn't
3 Living in the suburbs is _____ near as expensive as living in the city centre.
   a anywhere   **b** nowhere   **c** much
4 It's not so much a City of Culture _____ a City of Traffic!
   a as   **b** than   **c** like
5 This bag is _____ like the other one.
   a lot   **b** little   **c** nothing
6 The new café isn't a _____ on the old one.
   a variance   **b** patch   **c** nowhere

10

PRONUNCIATION

6 A 🔊 2.01 | schwa /ə/ | Complete the sentences with the missing words. Listen and check. What vowel sound do the missing words have in common?

1 This chair's nowhere near .... comfortable .... my old one.
2 This feels .... lot like being at home.
3 You can't drive any faster .... you are.
4 I think she's more upset .... angry, really.
5 This hill is nothing like .... steep .... I expected.

B 🔊 2.01 | Listen again and repeat.

READING

7 📄 Read the dictionary entry and answer the questions. Use no more than three words for each answer.

1 What's another name for 'twin towns'?
2 Is it a national or an international relationship?
3 What is their objective sometimes (apart from cultural understanding)?
4 When did twin towns in their contemporary form start?

twin town [n]

a twin town, or 'sister city', is a town or city with a legal or social connection with one or more towns in a different country or countries. The aim of having these ties is to develop cultural understanding and in some cases, trade. Such cultural ties have a long history, but the modern idea as we know it came about during the mid-20th century.

8 Read the article again. Choose the best answer to each question.

1 In the first paragraph, how does the writer suggest many people feel about twin towns?
  a largely uninterested
  b friendly towards the residents
2 What was the original thinking behind the creation of twin towns?
  a as a way of preventing immediate conflict in Europe
  b as a way of avoiding long-term conflict
3 What is special about Rome and Paris?
  a they are twinned with other cities
  b they see their connection as unique and equal
4 Why does the writer include information on shared industrial heritage?
  a to show how little relevance some town-twinning has in the modern world
  b to show how some cities became twinned
5 What benefit of educational ties does the writer mention?
  a creating new opportunities to travel
  b providing extra qualifications

Do cities really need siblings?

Travel round the UK and, upon arriving in most towns, you're likely to see a sign which says something along the lines of 'Welcome to [*town*]. Twinned with [*exotic-sounding place you've never heard of and have no intention of finding out about*]'. But what exactly does it mean for a town to be 'twinned' with another town in some far-off place?

At the end of World War II, the prevalent thought across the world was 'never again'. In order to see off the threat of future wars, many famous organisations were created to build stronger links between nations that had previously been at war with each other, such as the United Nations (UN). A perhaps lesser-known way of forging links between areas was that of twin towns, also known as sister cities. This was intended as a way of opening up lasting channels of communication between cities after years of conflict between warring nations. One of the most famous of these was between Coventry (UK) and Dresden (then in East Germany), both of which had suffered devastation from bombing campaigns during the war. Similarly, in 1956, the two previously warring cities of Paris and Rome became exclusively twinned. This sisterhood of great cities carries the motto, 'Only Paris is worthy of Rome; only Rome is worthy of Paris.'

Many now question the need for twinned towns, especially in today's hyperconnected world. It could be argued that the ties have little relevance for people who live in the towns and cities. Most people have never even visited their town's sibling or even know where it is. Another reason two cities might be linked is a shared industrial heritage. For example, Sunderland in the north of England is twinned with Saint-Nazaire in France, due to their historical ties in the maritime and ship-building industries. But, decades on, much has now changed in these industries. So, is there much point in them being twinned?

Part of the answer may come through education. Famous university towns have often been twinned for that very reason. Oxford and Cambridge have been twinned with other notable university cities such as Szeged (Hungary), Heidelberg (Germany) and Grenoble (France). When places link in this way, it has tangible benefits for young people, such as exchange programmes where teenagers get to visit the other town and stay with a family.

The fresh perspectives that this can bring can only be good for young people. But mostly, especially in light of recent world events, any links we can build between nations are more than welcome.

Lesson 2B

GRAMMAR | reporting
VOCABULARY | summarising verbs; multi-word verbs for reporting
PRONUNCIATION | using intonation to show contrasting opinions

VOCABULARY

summarising verbs

1 Choose the correct word to complete the sentences.
1 Despite describing the intense challenges involved in translating, she _____ that it is a very rewarding job.
   a maintained   b echoed   c illustrated
2 James _____ his point with an example from his own experience.
   a pondered   b called   c illustrated
3 Despite praising the project's achievements so far, he _____ there was still a lot of work to do.
   a echoed   b questioned   c accepted
4 During the meeting, Nigella _____ the issue of staff cutbacks.
   a commented   b raised   c voiced
5 We're here today to _____ our concern about the development plans.
   a call   b voice   c accept
6 When I came in this morning, Anna _____ on my new jacket.
   a commented   b voiced   c accepted
7 My boss _____ whether the project was really delivering enough.
   a raised   b commented   c questioned

2 Complete the summarising sentences with the correct form of the verbs in the box.

| acknowledge   call   cite |
| echo   ponder   question |

1 'International companies spend millions on translation services.'
   She _____ the fact that international companies spend millions on translation services.
2 'Yes, I understand you're having a lot of problems with the new system.'
   He _____ the difficulties with the new system.
3 'Today we're going to try and imagine what life was like in the 1600s.'
   In history class yesterday, we _____ what life was like in the 1600s.
4 'Yes, I completely agree with you that AI can be useful in the workplace.'
   I _____ her point about AI in the workplace.
5 'I'm not sure just throwing money at it is going to improve the situation.'
   He _____ whether increased funding would improve the situation.
6 'We need better regulation of the film industry.'
   The minister _____ for better regulation of the film industry.

multi-word verbs for reporting

3 Choose the correct words to complete the text.

A few months ago, I read that an organisation to help deaf people was calling ¹**to** / **for** more people to learn sign language. I have a friend who works with deaf children, communicating through sign language. He instantly talked me ²**into** / **to** signing up for a course. I enjoyed learning it and I'm now able to reel ³**off** / **out** quite a few sentences in sign language. Anyway, last week he tipped me ⁴**out** / **off** that a signing position was available where he works, and filled me ⁵**in** / **up** on what I needed to do to apply for it. I handed my application in and he backed me ⁶**up** / **on**, saying what a fast learner I was. So now it's fingers crossed that I get an interview – quite literally!

GRAMMAR

reporting

4 The sentences below each have a mistake. Choose the best option to correct the mistake.
1 Marie <u>explored</u> her boss to take fast action.
   a implored   b imploring   c exploring
2 He asked <u>are</u> subtitles were available.
   a about   b whether   c do
3 The rules <u>profess</u> that no photography is allowed.
   a echo   b stipulate   c acknowledge
4 <u>Accord</u> to this article, many people use subtitles.
   a Accordingly   b Accorded   c According

5 Complete the summary of a radio programme with the correct form of the words in the box.

| able   call   claim   confidence |
| echo   need   opinion   point |

A really interesting programme ¹_____ for TV channels to make subtitles more widely available, after a study ²_____ that most people who use subtitles are not hearing impaired. Chris Morgan, who works in film-making, ³_____ this claim and was ⁴_____ that subtitling would become universally available soon. In his ⁵_____, the rise in the use of subtitles was down to more people watching TV on smart devices, particularly in public. Other people on the programme ⁶_____ out that subtitles helped them understand accents more easily. A representative from a video streaming service questioned their ⁷_____ to apply subtitles universally, but accepted the ⁸_____ for them to be more available.

12

PRONUNCIATION

6 A 🔊 **2.02** | using intonation to show contrasting opinions | What is the function of the second part of the sentences? What happens to the intonation? Listen and check.

1 I always watch TV with the subtitles on, but my husband prefers watching without them.
2 His teacher thinks translation apps aren't very good, but Connor finds them quite useful.
3 While Scarlett thought writing subtitles would be quite easy, her boss knew this wasn't the case.

B 🔊 **2.02** | Listen again and repeat.

LISTENING

7 🔊 **2.03** | Listen to an interview with a subtitler. Number the challenges in the order they are mentioned.

a creative synthesis
b space restrictions
c audiovisual rhythm conservation
d time restrictions
e reading flow conservation

8 🔊 **2.03** | Listen again. Are the sentences True (T) or False (F)?

1 Lisa usually works as a translator.
2 She believes her work is more challenging than that of a translator.
3 The first thing she needs to consider is how the text will look on screen.
4 The speed at which an actor speaks can determine how difficult subtitling is.
5 Subtitlers have to transcribe the exact words that the speaker says.
6 They have to take into account the personality of the speaker on screen.
7 Each line of the subtitles must be a complete unit of meaning.
8 The main aim of subtitling is for the viewer not to notice them.

WRITING

an informative summary

9 A 🔊 **2.04** | Listen to an interview with a voiceover artist and make notes to answer the questions.

1 What kinds of things does a voiceover artist record for?
2 How does a voiceover artist find work?
3 What are the pros and cons of this job?

B Read the blog (A) and the advertisement (B). Add to your notes from Ex 9A and answer these questions.

1 What is a typical working day like?
2 What skills does a voiceover artist need?

10 Use your notes to write an informative summary of the work of a voiceover artist. Write around 220 words.

2B

A My name's Deanna Pope and I'm a professional voiceover artist. If you've ever listened to an audiobook, radio advertisement or watched an animated movie, then chances are you've heard my voice. I really enjoy what I do. It's a great way to earn a living, but it can be demanding at times. This is my typical day.

Morning

I usually get up at 8 a.m. It's important for me to set a routine and stick to it to be able to manage and keep on top of the different tasks I need to do. I try to do non-vocal tasks first in order to to 'wake up' my voice rather than do any recording with my 'morning voice'. So I answer emails, send invoices to clients, that kind of thing. I download any scripts for auditions that I like the look of.

Afternoon

I head upstairs to my studio and start recording. First, I record my auditions. I usually spend the first hour of work every day on these. I like to think of them as a sort of investment into future work. It's important to do them well in advance of deadlines so I can take your time with them and record them in a relaxed voice. If I rush them in order to meet a deadline, it will show, and I might not get work. After that, my voice will feel warmed up and I'm ready to work on my main clients' jobs. I get through a lot of water as it's vital to stay hydrated, otherwise I risk damaging my voice.

Evening

After dinner, I like to go for a walk. It's a great way to rest my voice before the next day's work ... and get some much-needed exercise after being at home all day!

B

Voiceover artist

We are looking for a voiceover artist to record commentary for a series of radio adverts for a travel company. We are particularly interested in people with the following skills:

- the ability to understand the intent behind what you're reading
- reading fluency
- the ability to work to strict deadlines
- a good sense of timing

For the audition script and to submit your audition recording and CV, please click here.

Lesson 2C

HOW TO ... | maintain and develop interaction
VOCABULARY | conventions/cultural heritage
PRONUNCIATION | expressing surprise and asking for reaction

VOCABULARY

conventions/cultural heritage

1 Complete the conversation using words from the box.

> commonplace deeply frowned irrespective
> long-standing peculiar rooted stereotypical

A: How was your work trip to China, Alissa?
B: Great. I must say though, they do business differently there. For one thing, lateness isn't just ¹_____ upon. It's actually normal to get to a meeting around fifteen minutes early.
A: That's interesting.
B: And business cards are still ²_____ there, and they're designed really ornately, almost like a power symbol. Also, everything follows strict rules of seniority. It's a ³_____ convention to find the most senior person and greet them first. Then, during the meeting, you have to address them first, ⁴_____ of whether they're the right person to speak to. But the most ⁵_____ thing for me was the small talk. It's all personal questions like, 'How old are you?' and 'How much do you earn?'

2 Choose the correct words to complete the sentences.
1. Many people associate the British with drinking tea, but that's just a belief about **stereotypical** / **irrespective** behaviour. Coffee is popular, too.
2. It's important to respect other people's cultural beliefs, **peculiar** / **irrespective** of whether you agree with them.
3. My husband's family has a deeply **standing** / **rooted** heritage dating back centuries.
4. It's a long- **standing** / **holding** tradition in our family to have a party on someone's birthday.
5. Didn't you think it was a bit **commonplace** / **peculiar** the way he didn't say anything?
6. Informal language in a business letter is generally frowned **upon** / **down**.

How to ...

maintain and develop interaction

3 🔊 2.05 | Listen to a discussion about politeness. Who does these things: Nigel, Stacey or Wanda?
1. describes a situation where they were at fault
2. thinks that, without manners, nobody would be polite to each other
3. describes a situation where someone apologised to an object
4. concedes that people sometimes take politeness too far
5. differentiates between polite language and polite behaviour
6. talks about speaking to people they don't know

4 🔊 2.05 | Choose the correct words to complete the sentences. Listen again and check.
1. **And** / **But** surely it's good to be polite like that?
2. I **bring** / **take** your point.
3. You **give** / **make** a good point.
4. **Fair** / **Just** enough.
5. That's a relevant **point** / **decision**.
6. You're looking at things the wrong **side** / **way** round.

PRONUNCIATION

5 A 🔊 2.06 | **expressing surprise and asking for reaction** | Match the sentence beginnings (1–4) with the endings (a–d). Listen and check.

1. But surely it's good
2. But surely that's the
3. But surely that's not
4. But surely you don't

a. best way to behave?
b. to be polite like that?
c. believe that?
d. a bad thing?

B 🔊 2.06 | Listen again and repeat.

SPEAKING

6 A 🔊 2.07 | Complete the discussion with the phrases (a–f). Listen and check.

a. good point   c. but surely   e. a flaw
b. fair enough   d. coming from   f. strong views

A: I think it's fair to say that people's personalities are influenced by their culture.
B: I think there's ¹_____ in your argument there. People's personalities are made up of lots of things, not just culture.
A: No, no, I'm not saying that at all. I'm just saying that it's one of the influences, not the only one.
B: ²_____. I see what you mean. ³_____ other things are much more important. The experiences you have, education, for example.
A: Yes, but I think culture has a bigger impact than many people realise. The language, the way family is regarded, these are all part of culture.
B: I think I get where you're ⁴_____. I guess these are things which affect us at a young age and seem less important as we get older.
A: You make a ⁵_____. The less relevant something is to us as we get older, the less aware of it we become, I guess.
C: It's clear you both have ⁶_____ on this.

B 🔊 2.08 | You are B in Ex 6A. Listen and speak after the beep. Record the conversation if you can.

C Listen to your recording and compare it to Ex 6A.

D Repeat Ex 6B, without looking at the conversation in Ex 6A. Then repeat Ex 6C.

Speak anywhere Go to the interactive speaking practice

Lesson 2D

LISTENING | traditional British food
READING | street food

LISTENING

1 🔊 **2.09** | Listen to a podcast about British food. Match the names of the food (1–3) with the photos (A–C).
1 Welsh Rarebit
2 Irish Champ
3 Clootie Dumpling

2 🔊 **2.09** | Listen again and choose the correct word to complete the statements.
1 The presenter thinks traditional English food is **popular** / **unpopular** round the world.
2 Rabbit **is** / **isn't** part of Welsh Rarebit.
3 Dylan's modern take on the dish is using a different kind of **bread** / **cheese**.
4 People usually eat Irish Champ **on its own** / **with something else**.
5 A Clootie Dumpling is named after **its ingredients** / **the way it's baked**.
6 Every year, people take part in a **festival** / **competition** in Avonbridge.

READING

3 Read the article about street food. Choose the reasons (1–9) given for the popularity of street food.
1 low expenditure
2 an easy business to get into
3 good quality
4 cleanliness
5 authenticity
6 vendors as stakeholders in their business
7 a new take on traditional dishes
8 comfort
9 how easy it is to buy

4 Complete the sentences with words and phrases from the article. Use no more than three words in each gap.
1 You can purchase .... from a vehicle in the USA.
2 Far back in Greek history, ... were a street food.
3 The low cost of street food encourages people to taste a wider variety of ....
4 Being able to watch the food being cooked gives people peace of mind about ....
5 Many street vendors offer you the chance to .... something before you buy it.
6 The writer suggests you can have a complete meal made up of dishes from .... of the world.
7 The final explanation that the writer mentions for why people like street food is ....

Why is street food so popular?

Whether you're eating fried rice in a street stall in Indonesia or fish tacos from a food truck in California, street food is universally popular. It has a long history, right back to ancient Greece where vendors sold small fried fish (though some Greek philosophers frowned upon the practice). A vast array of culinary delights are available to eat anywhere. So why is it so popular?

The first, most obvious answer is the cost – or lack of it. Vendors generally have low start-up and running costs compared to a traditional restaurant, which means they can pass this on to customers. And when things are cheaper, you're likely to try more different types of food than you normally would, meaning a more enjoyable experience (assuming you like what you try).

Quality is often better with small, independent street food vendors, too. There are a number of reasons for this. First and foremost, you can watch your food being cooked. This gives people peace of mind when it comes to hygiene concerns, and the fact that the vendors know they're being watched means they're cooking to the best of their ability. Many street-food vendors allow you to sample their wares, which means you might try something you normally wouldn't. Usually street food-vendors are the owners of their business, so making sure you enjoy the quality of their food is part of their livelihood.

Traditional brick-and-mortar restaurants often only sell one type of cuisine, such as Italian or Chinese. Although, when you visit a street-food market, it's possible to have a three-course meal from three different parts of the globe, all in one place. This wide variety also leads to innovations in food, whether it's a fusion of different cuisines, such as Japanese sushi, tacos or Indian pies, or completely new types of food or drink.

Another reason why street food is so popular is its convenience. In today's busy world, you can grab a meal and eat it on the go. Or you can hang around with friends while you eat. Whatever your preference, it's clear that street food is something to be celebrated, and will be for years to come.

1–2 REVIEW

GRAMMAR

1 Use the prompts to write sentences using conditional forms. Use the correct form of the verbs in brackets.
1. If I / (know) / about / dress code, / I / (dress) / smartly.
2. Unless you / (check), / you / (not have) / the full picture.
3. But / my parents' support, / I / (not go) / university.
4. If I / (be) / go out tonight, / I / (regret) it tomorrow.
5. Had you / (study) more, / you / (pass) / the exam.
6. We / (be) / there on time / providing / we leave early.

2 Complete the conversation with the words in the box. There are two extra words.

> exactly   how   this   what   whatever
> whenever   who   whoever

A: ¹_____ takes on the head-of-year role is going to have a tough job.
B: I know, they'll need to know ²_____ to implement the new curriculum.
A: That's ³_____ what I mean. It seems to me that ⁴_____ you want to do, the curriculum restricts it.
B: Yes. It doesn't matter ⁵_____ you think about teaching. You just need to follow the plan set out for you.
A: You see, ⁶_____ is what I feared would happen when they first introduced it.

3 📄 The sentences below have a mistake. Choose the best option to correct the mistake.
1. The new system is <u>no</u> like the old one. It's better.
   a nowhere   b nothing   c none
2. The sequel was easily as exciting <u>than</u> the first film.
   a like   b is   c as
3. It wasn't so much a picnic <u>like</u> a festival.
   a is   b as   c than
4. I'm more excited <u>like</u> worried about the trip.
   a than   b like   c as

4 Choose the correct words to complete the text.

People working in the translation industry last night were ¹**hopeful / regretful** that new legislation would be passed safeguarding their rights. According ²**from / to** Alissa Webb, president of the National Association of Translators, workers have seen an erosion of their rights in recent years. She ³**professed / acknowledged** that the industry has become more competitive, thus reducing pay levels and benefits, but ⁴**implored / claimed** industry leaders to respect workers' rights. In doing so, she ⁵**questioned / cited** the example of one of the association's members who had seen his salary reduced by ten percent in real terms. MP Ruth West ⁶**echoed / pointed out** these concerns and questioned the industry's ⁷**able / ability** to regulate itself sufficiently, saying that things ⁸**will / have** to change.

VOCABULARY

5 Complete the sentences with a word from each box.

> complete   ring   spot   struck   sweeping   vacuous

> chord   comments   fallacy   on   statement   true

1. This is exactly what we need. Your idea is _____ _____.
2. What Julia said about the boss really _____ a _____ with me.
3. The idea that being rich makes you happy is a _____ _____, in my opinion.
4. At work we have these posters on the walls with _____ _____ which are supposed to motivate us.
5. Something about his excuse for being late doesn't _____ _____ with me. I think he's lying.
6. To say that all unemployed people are lazy is a bit of a _____ _____!

6 Complete the sentences with one word in each gap.
1. It's no use getting hung _____ over small mistakes.
2. Her methods may fly _____ the face of conventional wisdom, but she gets results.
3. To be honest, I'm close to throwing _____ the towel right now.
4. Go on, give it a go, you've got _____ to lose.
5. After having to deal with rejection after rejection, I realised I just wasn't cut _____ for life as an actor.
6. The company is _____ strides in developing new, eco-friendly technology.

7 Complete the text with the words in the box.

> blended   critical   nurturing   path
> potential   rigorous   tuition   virtual

I really like the university where I study. We study through ¹_____ learning, so part of our study is in a ²_____-learning environment, and part of it is face-to-face, on campus. The staff at the university maintain ³_____ standards in teaching, developing a ⁴_____ environment to help us fulfil our ⁵_____. In all lessons, they encourage us to use ⁶_____ thinking to question what we learn and find our own ⁷_____ in the subject. I guess that's why the ⁸_____ fees are so high!

16

REVIEW 1–2

8 Choose the correct words to complete the sentences.
1. Using her **fertile** / **novel** imagination, she created some of the most popular books of the decade.
2. We really need to think outside the **talent** / **box** with this project. Anything goes, really.
3. He just showed up on my doorstep, completely **in** / **out of** the blue.
4. That art exhibition really **sparked** / **flashed** my imagination.
5. James just oozes **raw** / **fresh** talent.

9 Complete the sentences with one word in each gap. The first letter is given.
1. Teachers should lead students towards understanding something, rather than feeding them the a_____ .
2. Talk me t_____ your ideas for the assignment and I'll help you.
3. I always try to a_____ my teaching to suit individual learners' preferences.
4. I had an amazing geography teacher at school who was able to inspire me on a personal l_____ .
5. Teachers have to take students' different needs and styles of learning into a_____ .

10 Choose the correct option (a or b) to complete each sentence (1–6).
1. Training is needed to facilitate
2. Investment in the sector will have tangible
   a. benefits for all concerned.
   b. the development of our employees.
3. The conference is a fantastic opportunity for us to showcase
4. The article should help raise
   a. the best of our talent.
   b. the cultural profile of our town.
5. All too often a city ends up stuck
6. Sometimes publicity can have a detrimental
   a. with buildings they have no use for.
   b. effect on the city's profile.

11 📄 Choose the correct word to complete the sentences.
1. It's mainly a true story, give _____ take a few small details.
   a. and   b. or   c. but
2. Trams are a great way to travel when you're _____ and about in the city.
   a. in   b. out   c. across
3. Thanks for coming to the meeting. I'll try to keep it as _____ and sweet as possible.
   a. short   b. long   c. small
4. Self-defence is _____ and parcel of training to become a police officer.
   a. bit   b. piece   c. part
5. Attendees will be able to _____ and choose which stands they want to visit.
   a. pick   b. select   c. take
6. Keep practising, then _____ but surely you'll become a good player.
   a. fast   b. quickly   c. slowly

12 Complete the text with the correct form of the verbs in the box.

acknowledge   echo   fill   illustrate   raise   reel

Last night there was a TV programme on about the work of dubbing specialists. To start, the presenter ¹_____ the fact that dubbing has not always been successful in the past, and ²_____ off countless examples where this has been the case. However, the industry has come a long way over the last few decades. There was an interview with a professional dubber, who ³_____ the issue of the need for people who provide voiceovers to have a deep understanding of the character. To ⁴_____ his point, he said that as part of the process he'll meet with both the writer and the actor who will ⁵_____ him in on the necessary details. The presenter then ⁶_____ this point and went on to describe other methods they use.

13 Choose the correct words to complete the sentences.
1. Most people have a **deeply rooted** / **commonplace** cultural heritage that they're proud of.
2. We offer equal opportunities for advancement, **irrespective of** / **peculiar to** your background.
3. The film was characterised by **stereotypical** / **deeply-rooted** characters and a tired storyline.
4. Too much vanity is usually **looked** / **frowned** upon in most cultures.
5. While English is used around the world, bilingualism is also **long-standing** / **commonplace**.
6. This type of tree is **stereotypical** / **peculiar** to this region.

14 Choose the correct options (a–c) to complete the text.

Looking to try new and interesting food? Well, Camden Food Market is the ideal place to go. From the moment you enter, the ¹_____ smells and hustle and bustle of the market create a(n) ²_____ on your senses. From the Mexican ³_____ on Indian food to Peruvian soups which expertly ⁴_____ flavours, you're bound to find ⁵_____ cuisine in every corner.

1. a. topped   b. intriguing   c. inquisitive
2. a. attack   b. hit   c. assault
3. a. give   b. take   c. try
4. a. stir   b. have   c. fuse
5. a. unique   b. equal   c. the same

17

Lesson 3A

GRAMMAR | modal verbs and phrases
VOCABULARY | collocations; job searching
PRONUNCIATION | linking sounds in modal phrases

VOCABULARY

collocations: job searching

1 Complete the conversation using words from the box.

> change identify jeopardise leave
> play search spread warrant

A: How is the search for a new analyst coming along, Ben? Do any of those CVs ¹_____ a second look?

B: Nothing outstanding yet, I'm afraid. This one here is able to ²_____ his strong selling points for the job, but I've had a look on some of his social media, and he tends to ³_____ a slightly problematic digital footprint.

A: How so?

B: He appears to have very strong political views and uses social media to ⁴_____ the word about them.

A: I see what you mean. That will definitely ⁵_____ his chance of success. OK, well, keep looking.

2 Complete the sentences with one word in each gap.

1 Hayley used the conference as a way to meet people and spread the _____ that she was looking for work.
2 A cover email is a good way to highlight your strong _____ points for a prospective employer.
3 Don't get involved in arguments online. You shouldn't leave a problematic digital _____ if you're looking for a job.
4 There are several things that can jeopardise your chances of _____ in a job application.
5 A strong introduction, aimed directly at the job you're applying for, can help your application warrant a _____ look.
6 Have you seen this job advert? I think it plays to your particular _____.

GRAMMAR

modal verbs and phrases

3 Choose the correct words to complete the text.

Job searching in the digital age

Twenty-odd years ago, the idea that you could find a job by sitting at your computer seemed totally ¹**unimaginable / crucial**. But nowadays it's absolutely ²**inevitable / essential** that you make use of digital tools to help find that perfect job. For example, it's a good idea to include the many different types of software that you're ³**likely / capable of** using. Most employers prefer to hire people who have ⁴**an aptitude / a given** for using tech (and it's ⁵**a requirement / guaranteed** for certain jobs). It's also a good idea to search for yourself online, as any company you apply for is ⁶**undoubtedly / bound** to search for you, too. Remember, too, that a CV doesn't have to be a typed document these days. You ⁷**can / may** well have a website or, depending on the type of job you're applying for, there's ⁸**the odds / a chance** they may ask you for a video introducing yourself.

4 Choose the correct word to complete the sentences.

1 The company might be _____ for a new department manager soon. You should apply.
   a looked   b look   c looking
2 It's _____ unlikely that you'll hear back from them before the end of the week.
   a highly   b bound   c strong
3 I think it's _____ that Darren will get the marketing job.
   a in all probability
   b a chance   c a given
4 We're not _____ to eat at our desks, but everyone does.
   a likely   b supposed   c given
5 It's _____ that we find someone to cover for Anya before she goes on maternity leave.
   a highly   b imperative   c capable
6 I would _____ that lots of people will apply for this job.
   a guess   b need   c odds

18

3A

PRONUNCIATION

5 A 🔊 **3.01** | **linking sounds in modal phrases** | Listen and complete the sentences with one word in each gap. Notice how these words are linked to the previous one.

1 The **odds** .... that you'll be promoted.
2 Malia's **bound** .... be late for the meeting.
3 It's **guaranteed** .... succeed.
4 In .... probability, we're not going to get funding.
5 I'm **capable** .... completing it myself, thank you.

B 🔊 **3.01** | Listen again and repeat.

LISTENING

6 🔊 **3.02** | Listen to a presentation about the future of job searching. Choose the three trends that are mentioned.

1 increasing use of mobile devices for job searching and application
2 increasing use of computer programs to select candidates
3 job searching becoming more like online shopping
4 the decreasing need to relocate to a new area in order to get a job
5 job seekers developing their own brand
6 innovative ways to make new contacts

7 🔊 **3.02** | Listen again. Choose the correct option (a or b) to complete the sentences.

1 The speaker mentions the number of applicants a company received
   a to show how popular the available jobs are.
   b to highlight the necessity for some form of automation in the selection process.
2 An advantage of candidates talking to AI is that
   a it is much cheaper for employers when hiring.
   b employers can spend more quality time with applicants in person.
3 An effect of the 'consumerisation' of job hunting is that companies will need to
   a post adverts for jobs on multiple platforms.
   b treat applicants in a similar way to their customers.
4 Smart searches for particular jobs may well mean
   a an applicant considers a different job to the one they were looking for.
   b companies have fewer applicants to shortlist for interview.
5 The main point the speaker makes about building an online brand is that
   a you'll need to create your own website.
   b it's something you'll need to work on continuously.

WRITING

a cover email/letter

8 Read the cover email. Are the statements True (T) or False (F)?

The writer has:
1 **avoided** contractions.
2 **avoided** colloquial language.
3 **avoided** formal verbs and phrases.
4 **clearly outlined** why he is writing.
5 **included** specific examples of the skills required.
6 **met** all the requirements in the advertisement.

Sales and marketing executive

Sentyx property services

We are looking for a sales and marketing executive to join our expanding team. This is a full-time, permanent role. Main duties will include:

- maintaining and developing relationships with existing clients.
- liaising with potential customers with a view to expanding our client base.

Requirements:

- degree in marketing or a related field.
- relevant sales and/or marketing experience (at least five years preferred).
- a proven track record in meeting sales targets.
- teamworking and communication skills.

Send your CV and cover email to James Wilkley at info@sentyx.com

---

Hi James

Hope you're well. I really like the look of this job and I've heard great things about your company.

I've got a degree in marketing and have worked in the sales role I'm in now for five years, so I think I fit the bill! I'm also good at working in a team and great at communicating – all my colleagues and clients say so. That's why I'd be good at the job.

I'm afraid I haven't updated my CV for a while, but I can send it if you agree I'm a good fit for the job.

Let me know by email if you'd like to see me.

Bye for now,

Chris

9 Rewrite the cover email in a more formal and appropriate style. Write 200–220 words.

Lesson 3B

GRAMMAR | passives
VOCABULARY | verb–noun collocations; metaphors
PRONUNCIATION | word stress

VOCABULARY

verb–noun collocations

1 Complete the sentences with one word from each box.

> aggravate   alleviate   boost   ease   engender
> exacerbate   strengthen

> bonds   boredom   distrust   divisions   morale
> problem   stress

1 Breaking down big projects into smaller tasks can really help _____ those _____ levels.
2 Keeping your video turned off a video call can sometimes _____ _____ among others.
3 The differences of opinion between staff members only served to _____ _____ between them.
4 You need to rest. Too much exercise will only _____ the _____ with your knee.
5 Regular staff meet-ups outside working hours can help to _____ _____ between team members.
6 This year's end-of-year bonus has certainly helped to _____ _____ across the department!
7 I actually look forward to meetings at work because they _____ the _____ of sitting at my desk for most of the day.

metaphors

2 Choose the correct word to complete the sentences.

1 You need to _____ down the language you use when speaking to clients.
  a wet   b flood   c water
2 I've got so much work on at the moment, I'm finding it hard to keep my _____ above water.
  a head   b nose   c self
3 Don't be such a wet _____. Come out with us after work.
  a blanket   b cover   c tap
4 It seems my screen only _____ during the most important meetings!
  a ices   b freezes   c pours
5 I get my best ideas first thing in the morning. That's when my creativity really _____.
  a pours   b flows   c streams
6 When do you think the information about the new changes is likely to _____ down from senior management?
  a water   b flow   c trickle

PRONUNCIATION

3 A ◆ 3.03 | **word stress** | Listen and mark the stressed syllables.

1 morale   5 boredom
2 exacerbate   6 alleviate
3 divisions   7 engender
4 aggravate   8 distrust

B ◆ 3.03 | Listen again and repeat.

GRAMMAR

passives

4 Choose the correct words to complete the sentences.

1 The office **got** / **had** broken into last night. It was very distressing.
2 At the last management meeting, **they were** / **it was** decided not to continue with the project.
3 Something **must** / **needs** be done about the unreliable internet connection.
4 Have you **had** / **been** your computer upgraded by the company?
5 I hate not **being** / **be** respected in this position.
6 Not **to have been** / **are being** shown how to use the system properly is poor practice.
7 There's still a great deal **learnt** / **to be learnt** about remote working.
8 All employees should **to be** / **have been** provided with company laptops.
9 Using company computers to go on social media **has** / **is** prohibited.
10 I'm **having** / **being** some new software installed on my computer by IT at the moment.

5 The sentences below have a mistake. Choose the best option to correct the mistake.

1 The game has been cancelling because of the bad weather.
  a is cancelling
  b has been cancelled
  c has cancelled
2 I need to get my cut hair before my job interview on Thursday.
  a get my hair cut
  b get cut my hair
  c my hair cut
3 The CEO will say to be thinking about leaving the company.
  a is saying   b is said   c said
4 I hate not be consulted before changes are implemented.
  a no being   b not am being   c not being

20

3B

READING

6 Read a blog post and an article about working from home. Which points (a–c) do both texts include?
  a Your choice of clothes can affect your productivity.
  b A lack of distractions means you get more done.
  c The food you eat is important.

7 Match the statement with a text (A or B).
  1 The writer describes how people around other people can sometimes have a bad effect.
  2 The writer describes a way to start the day.
  3 The writer mentions personality types.
  4 The writer says that people spend more time working when they're at home.
  5 The writer gives some advice about the workspace.
  6 The writer says that some types of interaction can be more effective when working remotely.
  7 The writer discusses the benefits of learning to manage time better.

8 Read texts A and B again and answer the questions.
  1 Which has more direct interaction with the reader?
  2 Which text has more of a planned structure?
  3 Which uses more colloquial or idiomatic language?
  4 Which text uses more complex language and sentence structures?

A What I've learnt about working remotely

If you follow my blog, you'll know that for the last four months I've been working for a computer software company that bills itself as totally online. I have to say I'm enjoying it no end. It's taught me a fair few things about how best to manage my time, so I thought I'd share them with you. The first thing I realised when working from home is that I don't need to dress up for the office every day. Big plus! Except, I soon started to realise that if I do dress up for the office every morning it really motivates me to get started and put my work 'hat' on (changing it from my home 'hat'), and helps me focus on my work more easily. It also means I'm ready to go in case my boss springs a video call on me at short notice. Something else dawned on me in those first few weeks – I was ending each day feeling absolutely drained. I had a comfortable place to work (in front of a big window overlooking the park – always work near a window if you can: another top tip! – there was none of the dreaded commute, so why was I feeling so done-in at the end of each day? Then it hit me – it was down to the very fact that I didn't have those interruptions. The fact that I was so focused and able to concentrate meant I was working much harder. So I started using a timer to force myself to take a break every thirty minutes, no matter what I was doing. I felt much better at the end of each day.

B Some myths about working from home

To those who have never worked remotely before, it may conjure up images of an employee at home, sitting on the sofa while they idly scan their laptop screen. But the reality of working from home is very different. Here we expose some myths about it.

Firstly, there's the idea that anyone can work from home. While this is technically and physically true, it's been shown that people with emotional stability and good self-discipline work best at home. Of course, these qualities aren't easily quantifiable. It doesn't mean that people who don't possess them should stay in the office, but they need more support when working from home.

Another common fallacy is that working from home is easier. That there are fewer distractions from other people so you can focus better and get your work done more quickly, leaving you free for the rest of your day to go and sit in the park or whatever else takes your fancy. While many people do find they can focus and concentrate more easily at home (assuming they're alone), they often find they end up working longer hours in order to fill the day. This can end up having a detrimental effect on their work–life balance as they find it hard to ease those stress levels.

There are some health advantages of working from home, however, as people do often find they have more time to exercise. There is also the benefit of being able to prepare their own food at home, which means they're more likely to eat fresh food rather than grabbing something 'to go' on the way to work.

Employers sometimes worry that working from home can be bad for morale and employees' well-being, as most people need daily face-to-face social interaction. But not all social interaction is healthy (think of the crowded daily commute). Another worry is that meetings won't be as productive if people are video-calling from a non-work environment. But this really isn't true, as, when working remotely, people often feel more of a need not to waste each other's time. This is especially the case if people are meeting across different time zones and it's very late (or early) for some colleagues.

However you feel about working from home, it's true that it's not right for everyone: but the reality is, it is here to stay.

Lesson 3C

HOW TO ... | check understanding by paraphrasing and summarising
VOCABULARY | collocations: politics; politics
PRONUNCIATION | stress and intonation when paraphrasing

VOCABULARY

collocations: politics

1 Choose the correct word to complete the sentences.
1 We must make every effort to **enforce** / **eliminate** / **tackle** the new regulations once implemented.
2 The new company policy is aimed at **shaping** / **encouraging** / **allocating** diversity in the workforce.
3 We must **stand** / **enforce** / **eliminate** discrimination at all levels of society.
4 Our party aims to **sit** / **fight** / **stand** up for those unable to do so for themselves.
5 We are currently working to **shape** / **size** / **figure** policy to reduce overall emissions.
6 The government needs to **allocate** / **encourage** / **eliminate** more resources to improving transport infrastructure.

politics

2 Complete the text with the words in the box. There are two extra words.

| ballot | cast | constitution | exit | head |
| hereditary | liberal | manifesto | spin | wing |

Two political systems: the UK and the US

In many ways, the political system of the UK is similar to the system in the US. Both systems have two major political parties which (in theory, at least) each represent the left and right ¹_____ of the political spectrum. Each party produces a ²_____ which outlines their main policies going into a general election. And each system uses ³_____ polls on the night of the election to give an indication of which way it's going to go. But there are some big differences. In the US system, the ⁴_____ of state is a president who is elected through an electoral college system, whereby party representatives ⁵_____ votes, while in the UK, it's a(n) ⁶_____ monarch who is largely ceremonial. Another important difference is that America has a (famously) written ⁷_____, which supersedes all political components of the system. In the UK, it is unwritten, and built from a series of laws over time. One thing rings true for both systems, however. All party leaders like to ⁸_____ any defeat into something that makes them look good!

How to ...

check understanding by paraphrasing and summarising

3 🔊 3.04 | Listen to an interview with a politician. Are the statements True (T) or False (F)?
1 Lucy Bishop says that new workers are not well-enough qualified.
2 She thinks educators need to rethink their approach.
3 She wants more focus on business in education.
4 She wants 'work skills' to be better integrated into existing school subjects.

4 🔊 3.05 | Listen to the recording. Write what you hear. You will hear the sentences only once.
1 _____
2 _____
3 _____
4 _____

PRONUNCIATION

5 🔊 3.05 | **stress and intonation when paraphrasing** | Listen and repeat the sentences from Ex 4. Focus on the stress and intonation, and any pauses you hear.

SPEAKING

6 A 🔊 3.06 | Complete the conversation with one word in each gap. The first letter is given. Listen and check.

A: I was really impressed with Lucy Bishop's interview. Her skills initiative sounds like a great idea.
B: So, in other ¹w_____, you think it will solve all the problems in industry?
A: Ha, no, not at all. ²W_____ I said was I think it's definitely going to be a force for good, especially in helping to tackle inequalities.
B: Am I ³r_____ in thinking inequality is simply caused by people not having the right skills?
A: No, you've ⁴g_____ it all wrong. But it's still a major contributory factor.
B: Let me ⁵r_____ that. Surely other things are more important. Like good quality housing.
A: OK, let me ⁶p_____ it another way. This new initiative is important, but it's one of many important factors.
B: Absolutely. ⁷That's e_____ what I mean.

B 🔊 3.07 | You are B in in Ex 6A. Listen and speak after the beep. Record the conversation if you can.

C Listen to your recording and compare it to Ex 6A.

D Repeat Ex 6B, without looking at the conversation in Ex 6A. Then repeat Ex 6C.

Speak anywhere Go to the interactive speaking practice

Lesson 3D

LISTENING | an internship
READING | a perfect workspace

LISTENING

1 🔊 **3.08** | Listen to a conversation between two people about an internship. Number the topics in the order they are mentioned.

a choosing the right company
b clothes and behaviour
c managing your workload
d researching the company
e going over what you've learnt
f not getting some things right
g confidential information
h watching someone work

2 🔊 **3.08** | Listen again and choose the correct option (a or b) to complete each statement.

1 Harry says an internship is only a good thing to do
   a if it's at the company you want to work for in the future.
   b if it's the type of job you want to do in the future.
2 He warns that at the wrong company you might
   a end up doing minor jobs.
   b end up doing nothing.
3 The first thing he had to do when he started his internship was
   a some paperwork.
   b manage sensitive information.
4 In meetings with the supervisor, they
   a just focused on that week.
   b focused on that week and the future.
5 Harry thinks an intern
   a is a proper member of staff.
   b isn't a proper member of staff.
6 At the start of his internship, Harry wanted
   a to appear easy to work with.
   b to appear easy to make friends with.
7 Harry thinks errors are
   a important to avoid.
   b important to develop.

READING

3 Read the article about creating the perfect workspace. Match the topics (a–h) with the paragraphs (1–6). There are two extra topics.

a Think about free time at work.
b Consider what people eat.
c Brighten up the working day.
d Consider health and wellness.
e Make travel easier.
f Limit meetings.
g Think about time not spent at work.
h Make it comfortable.

Six steps to creating the perfect workspace

Most employers know that a good workspace is important for the health and well-being of their staff. Having a sound corporate social responsibility policy and shared values among staff is important. But how can we improve the social aspect of work through the physical environment and the activities we carry out?

¹ .... This isn't about having colourful sofas and beanbags to lounge around on, but the simple things which are often overlooked, like modern, clean bathrooms and a well-equipped shared kitchen. Employees should have sufficient space and the capacity to allow them to personalise their own space, too. They might want to bring in family photos or a house plant, for instance.

² .... Some studies suggest that different hues promote different styles of work: blue and green are associated with creativity, for example, and red is connected to promoting careful concentration. Whether you buy into all that or not, natural light is important, as well as avoiding too much glare or shadow.

³ .... There are many aspects to this, such as providing access to fresh fruit and the option of standing desks. You could even run a weekly competition to see who used the stairs instead of the lifts the most.

⁴ .... Although open-plan offices allow for freer communication, it's important to provide quiet spaces where staff can go when they need to concentrate or just have some quiet time. Some companies even provide 'nap rooms.' Leisure areas, with table tennis and other games, are useful as spaces to spend breaks or blow off steam.

⁵ .... While often thought of as a necessary evil, they're rarely as productive as people think. And unless everyone's fully involved, it's going to be wasting time that could be much better spent. Setting a strict time limit at the start can make sure nobody gets too side-tracked. Think twice before scheduling one – could everything be communicated by an email?

⁶ .... Some corporations have been experimenting with the idea of unlimited days off. At first glance this sounds ludicrous. But the caveat is that the work still needs to get done on time. And, so far, they've been finding that people are actually taking less time off as a result. It seems that most people have a sense of duty, and knowing that they don't need to be in the office helps them work more productively when they are.

4 Read the article again. Are the statements True (T) or False (F), according to the writer?

1 Workers should be able to make their workspace their own.
2 Different colours help different ways of thinking.
3 There isn't much employers can do to promote health.
4 Sometimes employee isolation is necessary.
5 When it comes to meetings, less is more.
6 People work less when they don't have to.

Lesson 4A

GRAMMAR | verb patterns
VOCABULARY | verb–noun collocations; adverb–adjective collocations
PRONUNCIATION | syllable stress in verb–noun collocations

VOCABULARY

verb–noun collocations

1 Choose the correct word to complete the sentences.
   1 I wanted to know how much my car weighs simply to _____ my curiosity.
      a satisfy **b** raise **c** back
   2 This is more than just a job to me. I'm _____ my ambition.
      a serving **b** pushing **c** pursuing
   3 How are we going to _____ funding?
      a push **b** raise **c** fuel
   4 This new discovery will also _____ science and progress.
      a raise **b** serve **c** back
   5 What most _____ your motivation?
      a fuels **b** backs **c** realises
   6 When he finally reached the summit, Jack had _____ his dream.
      a pushed **b** fuelled **c** realised

2 Complete the text with the correct form of the verbs in the box.

   back fuel pursue push raise realise satisfy

Community pioneers

Shocked by rising food and fuel prices last year, Jake and Lisa Hartwell wondered what they could do to help the poorest in their community. To ¹_____ their curiosity, they spoke to local people on social media and came up with the idea of a community garden in an area of their town not being used for any purpose. ²_____ by the motivation to help people struggling financially, they approached the council to ask them to ³_____ the project. Council approval was swift, but they were told they'd need to ⁴_____ their own funds for the garden. This they eventually did, but it wasn't easy. They really had to ⁵_____ the limits in approaching local businesses and more well-off residents, but they eventually got the funds they needed. And more than that, they ended up with an army of volunteers to dig, plant and toil. For the Hartwells, this was more than just aiming to do something for the community. They were ⁶_____ an ambition. Finally, when summer came, and the food and flowers were grown, they had ⁷_____ their dream.

PRONUNCIATION

3 A 🔊 4.01 | syllable stress in verb–noun collocations | Listen and mark the syllables in the collocations in bold given the main stress.
   1 We need to think about how to **raise funding**.
   2 Who's going to **back our project**?
   3 I've always wanted to **pursue my ambition**.
   4 Wow, they're really **pushing the limits**!
   5 It's interesting, but I don't see how it **serves science**.
   6 I just wanted to **satisfy my curiosity**, really.

   B 🔊 4.01 | Listen again and repeat.

adverb–adjective collocations

4 Choose the correct words to complete the sentences.
   1 Channelling funds into conservation programmes is **blindingly / infinitely** preferable to space exploration, in my opinion.
   2 The government has **ludicrously / vehemently** high expectations of the success of the project, in my view.
   3 It is expected that energy costs will become **gravely / significantly** cheaper over the next year.
   4 It was **blindingly / significantly** obvious from the start that they weren't going to succeed.
   5 One of the most **immediately / wildly** important issues in today's world is climate change.
   6 Many staff were **blindingly / vehemently** opposed to the introduction of the new scheme.
   7 Many **infinitely / wildly** inaccurate speculations about the president appeared on social media.
   8 If you think raising funding for the venture will be easy, then you're **blindingly / gravely** mistaken.

GRAMMAR

verb patterns

5 Choose the correct word or phrase to complete the sentences.
   1 I can't come out tonight, I've got too much work _____.
      a do **b** doing **c** to do
   2 You can't put off _____ to her about the issue any longer.
      a talk **b** to talk **c** talking
   3 Sorry I'm late, I stopped _____ to the boss on my way in.
      a to speak **b** speaking **c** speak
   4 How far are we willing _____ with this?
      a to go **b** go **c** going
   5 It'd be a waste of resources for any more money _____ on this old machine.
      a is spent **b** to be spent **c** to spend
   6 Since _____ his arm in the summer, he hasn't been able to play tennis.
      a to hurt **b** hurt **c** hurting

READING

6 Read the text and answer the questions. Use no more than three words for each answer.

25th Innovation in Technology conference

This year, Massachusetts will be host to the conference, and the theme is 'Pioneers in technology.' You are welcome to submit proposals for talks or apply to be an exhibitor.

Last year in Philadelphia was a resounding success, with over 20,000 attendees and 800 tech companies taking part.

As well as exhibitors, we are featuring several keynote speakers on topics as varied as intelligent automation and the growth of the 'metaverse'.

1 If someone wants to speak at the conference, what do they need to do?
2 Where was the previous conference?
3 Apart from the growth of the 'metaverse', what other subject is mentioned?

7 Read the article about the pioneers of tech. Match the innovations (1–3) with the purposes (a–e). There are two extra functions.

1 a human-robot interface
2 an air hub
3 self-healing concrete

a It will reduce maintenance costs.
b It helps people with physical disabilities.
c It can reduce energy costs.
d It makes driving easier.
e It provides relief for people who are ill.

8 Read the article again. Are the statements True (T) or False (F)?

1 Scientists in Switzerland are using brain-reading technology for the first time.
2 The brain-reading software can be used by anyone.
3 The software functions more effectively after it's been used many times.
4 The hub being built in Coventry will be for professional vehicles at first.
5 The hub will be powered by electricity.
6 Self-healing concrete will be made up of three 'living' elements.
7 The concrete can help clean the air.

The pioneers of tech

Technology has long provided solutions to many problems humanity faces, and right now several pioneers are pushing the limits to ensure that continues. Three key areas in which technology serves science are health, transport and construction.

Technology which can read human brainwaves isn't new, but researchers at the Swiss Federal Institute of Technology Lausanne (EPFL) have developed software to connect the human brain with a robot arm. The aim here is to afford tetraplegic patients, who can't move their upper or lower body, the ability to engage more easily with the world around them. At the moment, it's limited to relatively simple movements like picking up a cup, but the potential is vast. The user wears an EEG (electroencephalogram) cap, which reads brain signals and then converts them to the physical movements of the robot arm. This technology is a long way off from being universally developed, as everyone's brain signals are different. This is further complicated by the fact that the brain often focuses on several things at the same time. However, the software developed by the team features a form of AI that learns how to distinguish different signals as it goes on, learning the correct functions over time. And this is, of course, immediately important to those with restricted physical movement.

Another pioneering development, this time in the world of transport, comes from a British company called urban-Air Port Ltd. They're building a hub for delivery drones and flying taxis, and say that it will ease congestion caused by delivery cars and vans on the ground. In the future, they have plans for electric Vertical Take-Off and Landing aircraft (eVTOLs) which can ferry passengers into and out of the city, much like current 'Park and Ride' schemes which use buses. The whole hub and its vehicles are powered by hydrogen and are carbon neutral with zero emissions. In fact, it doesn't need to be connected to the national energy grid at all.

And, finally, to construction. Using a mixture of sand, gel and bacteria, a pioneering team from the University of Colorado in Boulder have developed a type of 'living concrete'. This is able to bear a heavy load, but it can also heal itself. So, if it gets cracked, the living element inside is able to repair the damage. This is highly important as concrete is the second-most consumed material on Earth, after water. It also means it can be easily recycled. And it's not just the self-healing which makes this a super-material. It can also draw in dangerous toxins from air pollution, as well as be made to glow, providing a cheap form of street lighting at night.

Lesson 4B

GRAMMAR | continuous and perfect aspects
VOCABULARY | collocations: needing and giving; adjectives to describe people
PRONUNCIATION | stress in collocations featuring verbs with 'weak' meanings

VOCABULARY

collocations: needing and giving

1 Complete the conversation using words from the box.

> day effect ends foot
> hand patch place word

A: I love this new community app. Have you seen it?
B: No, what is it?
A: So, what you do is put in your location, and it connects you with your neighbours. Now if anyone's going through a rough [1]............, perhaps finding it hard to make [2]............ meet, you can give them a helping [3]............
B: That sounds great. I imagine it has a knock-on [4]............ of bringing people together.
A: Exactly. But to work best it needs everyone to connect, so I'm going to spread the [5]............ where I live!

2 Complete the text with one word in each gap.

A couple of years ago I was going through a bit of a [1]............ patch. I was on my own and had lost my job, so I was finding it hard to make ends [2]............. Most days it was a struggle simply to [3]............ the day. I knew I had to do something to break out of the cycle, so one day I started volunteering at a local food bank to give others a [4]............ hand. Not only did it feel good to break out of the situation, but it had the [5]............-on effect of lifting my spirits and giving me a purpose in life. Now, I just want to [6]............ the word and encourage others to do the same!

adjectives to describe people

3 Match the adjectives in the box with the descriptions (1–8).

> aloof appreciative compassionate
> conscientious enterprising intuitive
> resourceful selfless

1 When I was going through a rough patch, my friend Jamie called me every day.
2 Chandra's always looking for new ways to make money, and he's usually successful!
3 Elsa never takes an interest in what I'm doing.
4 She's always so thankful when I do something for her, even if it's something minor.
5 Gavin always seems to know how I'm feeling.
6 My dad can use what's to hand to make things.
7 I think Mia's a bit of a perfectionist, she always wants to do her work to the best standard.
8 Cate's always doing things for others. Sometimes I wish she'd do something nice for herself.

PRONUNCIATION

4 A 🔊 **4.02** | **stress in collocations featuring verbs with 'weak' meanings** | Listen and mark the most stressed word in the collocations in bold.

1 Can you help me **spread the word** about our organisation?
2 Some mornings I just don't feel like I can **face the day**.
3 Some people in society struggle to **make ends meet**.
4 Why not **give them a helping hand**?

B 🔊 **4.02** | Listen again and repeat.

GRAMMAR

continuous and perfect aspects

5 Choose the correct words to complete the sentences.

1 The charity **had been looking** / **had looked** for innovative ways to raise money for a long time by that point.
2 She **lives** / **'s living** with her parents for the time being while she waits for her new flat to be ready to move into.
3 I'm exhausted. I **'ve been helping** / **'ve helped** out at the food bank all evening and I still have a lot of work left to do.
4 By the end of the year we will **have received** / **receive** thousands of donations.
5 The government **has finally implemented** / **has finally been implementing** their plan after several months of delays.
6 I think I **'ve lost** / **'ve been losing** my keys. I usually put them in my bag, but they're not there.
7 When I woke up, I realised I **forgot** / **'d forgotten** to turn off the lights.
8 I **'ve had** / **'ve been having** jackfruit a few times. It's very nice.

4B

6 The sentences below each have a mistake. Choose the best option to correct the mistake.

1 This time tomorrow <u>we'll volunteer</u> at the local charity sale.
   a we were volunteering
   b we'll be volunteering   c we've been volunteering
2 I sent her the documents last Tuesday, so she <u>was receiving</u> them by last Friday.
   a 'll have received
   b 's received   c 's been receiving
3 Back in 2009 <u>we've driven</u> around South America.
   a we'll have driven
   b we're driving   c we were driving
4 Has anyone <u>been seeing</u> my glasses?
   a have seen
   b seen   c see

LISTENING

7 🔊 4.03 | Listen to an interview with two charity workers. Which two ideas do they discuss?
   a social media 'challenges' set up to support charities
   b software which allows you to see how donations are used
   c finding investors to help small businesses
   d using comedians to help raise awareness

8 🔊 4.03 | Listen again. Are the statements True (T) or False (F)?
1 Caleb made the app in response to people asking about the charity's activities.
2 He has always worked for the charity.
3 Caleb thinks using the app makes people revisit the charity.
4 He's not sure whether people like the app.
5 ImpactVest was established ten years ago.
6 The charity aims to connect people in richer and poorer countries.
7 Investors have to invest a minimum amount.
8 ImpactVest aims to make investment more personal.

WRITING

write an informal review of a product or service

9 A Read the review of a charity app and choose the best title (a, b or c).
   a Keeping track of your donations.
   b A ping for a pound.
   c Spending money wisely.

Have you ever made a donation to charity, only to wonder what exactly the money is being spent on? It's not that we don't trust charities to use the money wisely, but sometimes it can feel like the money goes into a dark vacuous 'pool' of doing good. Wouldn't it be nice to see the human face of what our compassion achieves?

This app, provided by the charity ScotKids, does exactly what it says on the tin. Unlike other charities which post the occasional success story on their website or social media, this app allows you to track – in real time – exactly where your money goes.

The way it works is simple. When you make a donation to the charity, it's given a tracking number (much like when you post a parcel). Whenever some or all of that money is spent, you get pinged in the app and it shows precisely what it's being used for. If it's being used to help someone directly, you can read about them and what they need.

There are so many other apps which claim to be making a difference, but this one really does, in ways which you can see. I wholeheartedly recommend this app for people who want to not only make a difference, but also see the effects of lending a helping hand in human terms.

B Read the review again and number the topics (a–e) in the order they appear.
   a an explanation of how it works
   b a short summary of the benefits
   c engaging the reader
   d a recommendation
   e what makes it unique compared to other products

10 Write an informal review of the ImpactVest charity from Ex 8. Write 220–240 words.

Lesson 4C

HOW TO ... | present survey results
VOCABULARY | money and economy
PRONUNCIATION | chunking language

VOCABULARY

money and economy

1 Choose the correct word to complete the sentences.
1 Quite frankly, your _____ model isn't working.
   a business   b economy   c profit
2 These are the sorts of things which can _____ customer loyalty.
   a ride   b fly   c drive
3 Economics is based on the idea that the world has _____ resources which therefore need to be managed.
   a infinite   b finite   c unlimited
4 Do we truly live in _____ economy?
   a a sharing   b an umbrella   c a customer
5 Many types of business fall under these _____ terms.
   a raincoat   b hooded   c umbrella
6 Green industries aim to align the _____ of business and the environment.
   a possibilities   b incentives   c profits

2 Match the sentence beginnings (1–6) with the endings (a–f).
1 In order to survive, companies need to provide on-demand
2 We do what we can to help the community, but we're still essentially a profit-
3 I need to set up a website that can manage online
4 A major part of the sharing economy is collaborative
5 The fall of the regime opened up lots of new investment
6 There are lots of new zero-

a opportunities for those willing to take the risk.
b consumption.
c access to their products or services.
d waste incentives around at the moment.
e driven business.
f transactions. Can you help?

How to ...

present survey results

3 🔊 **4.04** | Listen to part of a presentation of the results of a survey into the idea of compulsory community service for 16-year-olds. Choose the best summary.
a Most people are completely in favour of the idea.
b Most people are partially in favour of the idea.
c Most people are against the idea.

4 🔊 **4.04** | Complete the sentences with one word in each gap. Listen again and check.
1 On the _____, most respondents tended to agree with some form of compulsory community service ...
2 _____ said that, many people expressed a concern that this shouldn't go too far.
3 _____ cite one example, one respondent stated that this should by no means include military service.
4 Generally _____, though, most people thought community service was a good idea in principle.
5 Their interest _____ reflected the fact that they feel young people should do more to help strengthen local communities.
6 Our _____ was simply that this idea is perceived as a positive thing.

PRONUNCIATION

5 A 🔊 **4.05** | **chunking language** | Listen and mark where the natural pauses occur.
1 Having said that, many people expressed a concern that this shouldn't go too far.
2 To cite one example, a respondent stated that this should by no means include military service.
3 Generally speaking, though, most people thought community service was a good idea.

B 🔊 **4.05** | Listen again and repeat.

SPEAKING

6 A 🔊 **4.06** | Complete the extract from a presentation with one word in each gap. Listen and check.

When asked if they would make use of young volunteers, **the overall** [1]_____ was one of enthusiasm. **To** [2]_____ **one example**, an elderly respondent stated that she would welcome help collecting her medication from the chemist. [3]_____ **illustration of this** was a respondent who said he would like to see young people out picking up litter during school hours. **Their interest presumably** [4]_____ the fact that not only would they appreciate the help, but it would be useful for the young people themselves. **One** [5]_____ **speculate that** they believed young people would learn the value of community relationships. **The consensus** [6]_____ **to be** that this idea would be good for everyone.

B 🔊 **4.07** | You are the speaker in Ex 6A. Listen and say the phrases in bold after the beep. Record yourself if you can.

C Listen to your recording and compare it to Ex 6A.

D Repeat Ex 6B, without looking at the script. Then repeat Ex 6C.

Speak anywhere   Go to the interactive speaking practice

Lesson 4D

LISTENING | an endangered species
READING | a conservation success story

4C | 4D

LISTENING

1 🔊 **4.08** | Listen to a documentary. What is a vaquita?
   a a cow   **b** a porpoise   **c** a dolphin

2 🔊 **4.08** | Listen again and answer the questions.
   1 Which are longer, male or female vaquitas?
   2 What are cetaceans?
   3 Where does the vaquita live?
   4 What does it eat?
   5 What industry is to blame for vaquitas being endangered?
   6 How many were there in 1997?
   7 How many are thought to exist today?
   8 What happened to the female that was captured?

READING

3 Read the article quickly. Was the project successful?

4 Read the article again and choose the correct option (a or b) to complete the sentences.
   1 The writer was surprised by the fact that
      a the bird was in a city.
      b the bird caught a mouse.
   2 In the past, people didn't like red kites because
      a of the waste they produced.
      b of how they looked.
   3 The British country they were safest in during medieval times was
      a Scotland.
      b Wales.
   4 Flying in birds on a plane
      a had never happened before.
      b had taken place before, elsewhere.
   5 The population of the birds first started to increase
      a thanks to people in London.
      b because of the transport network.
   6 One in ten red kites in the world
      a are in Britain.
      b are outside Britain.

The Rise of the Red Kite

Typing in my office in a quiet English town, I look out of my window and see a magnificent bird high up in the sky. As I'm marvelling at its beauty and grace, all of a sudden it swoops down and catches a mouse in its talons. Wondering what a bird of prey is doing in such an urban environment, I watch it as it glides away again, and that's when I realise what it is – a red kite!

The red kite has had a troubled history in Britain. In medieval times they were very unpopular, largely because they ate carrion (dead, rotting animals). Their fearsome appearance also created an impression of them as harbingers of doom. King James II of Scotland even went so far as to say they should be 'killed wherever possible'. In Wales, however, they were seen as useful, because of the way they got rid of carrion and other rubbish, so they were afforded some protection over the next hundred years.

By the turn of the twentieth century, their numbers had dwindled to just a few breeding pairs in Wales. But all that changed in July 1990, when concerns that they were set to disappear from the UK forced conservationist groups to take immediate action. That came in the unprecedented form of flying in thirteen birds from Spain on a jet. These birds were introduced in the Chiltern valley, in the centre of England. Not only did they survive the journey, but they went on to thrive. From their new home, they started to spread out westwards along the corridor of the M40 motorway, feeding on carrion found there.

From there they spread out across the whole country. In 2006 came the first sighting in London, and now there are more than 10,000 red kites in Britain. Nowadays, they're a common sight for millions of people in the UK.

This is the story of the world's most successful reintroduction project – a truly magnificent and awe-inspiring creature that has gone from being on the brink of extinction in Britain to numbers there now forming nearly ten percent of the world's population. In fact, it's been so successful that it's inspired the possibility of reintroducing other animals, such as eagles in the south of England and beavers throughout the UK.

29

3-4 REVIEW

GRAMMAR

1 Put the words in the correct order to make sentences.

1 given / he'll / that / It's / the / a / job / get / .
2 that / It / unimaginable / fire / her / seems / totally / they'd / .
3 trainers / supposed / We / work / at / to / aren't / wear / .
4 sorted / This / be / needs / immediately / to / out / .
5 the / phone / the / That / have / on / must / client / been / .
6 we'll / tonight / The / are / odds / get / that / homework / .

2 Choose the correct word to complete the sentences.

1 It is **thinking** / **thought** / **be thought** that the writer lived here when he was a boy.
2 I'm **have** / **had** / **having** my bike repaired today.
3 I hate **being** / **be** / **been** talked to like that.
4 I **got** / **were** / **had** knocked off my bike this morning.
5 All these reports by tomorrow? It can't **do** / **be done** / **being done**!
6 Not **to have been** / **to have to be** / **have been** told about the party is the worst thing.

3 Choose the correct words to complete the text.

¹**Solve** / **Solving** local issues is usually the job of a council, and while most councils are committed to ²**do** / **doing** what they can, limited resources mean that they are often unable ³**to fix** / **fixing** everything. Enter Community Start, an organisation which works with local volunteers with the purpose of ⁴**to engage** / **engaging** local residents to help out. They basically persuade local people ⁵**to get** / **getting** involved with things like fence repairs and managing community gardens. Many residents are willing ⁶**to pull** / **pulling** together to carry out this work, and quite often they enjoy it!

4 Complete the sentences with the correct form of the verbs in brackets. Use contractions where possible.

1 I .... (never, try) Thai food, but I'd like to!
2 For several months in 2015, I .... (live) in China.
3 This time tomorrow, we .... (travel) by plane to Argentina.
4 I .... (be) at home since this morning and nobody's called.
5 By the time it's completed, I .... (work) on this project for nine months.
6 Sheila .... (wait) for over an hour by the time we arrived.

VOCABULARY

5 Choose the correct words to complete the sentences.

1 It's important to look for a job which **plays** / **works** to your strengths.
2 Some things you do online can leave a problematic digital **fingerprint** / **footprint**.
3 Lying in a job application can **jeopardise** / **spread** your chances of success.
4 When you put together your CV, you need to identify your strong **buying** / **selling** points.
5 As an employer, what sorts of things on a CV make it **warrant** / **guarantee** a second look?

6 Complete the text with the words in the box.

alleviate   aggravate   boost
engender   exacerbate   strengthen

Thinking of encouraging your staff to work from home? Maintaining regular contact is important, but don't overdo it as this may ¹............... distrust, and if workers feel like they're being micro-managed, it will only ²............... the problem. At the same time, the opposite course of action can ³............... existing divisions, too. You need to strike a balance by having regular 'catch-up' meetings. They can help ⁴............... any boredom and ⁵............... bonds between team members. You can also help ⁶............... morale by encouraging staff to take time out during the day to do something relaxing.

7 Complete the sentences with one word in each gap. The first letter is given.

1 I hate it when I'm on a video call and the screen f............... – I lose track of the conversation.
2 I'm so busy at work at the moment, I'm struggling to keep my h............... above water.
3 I like my boss, but he can be a bit of a wet b............... at times. He doesn't seem to like us having fun.
4 Typical, I'm off work for one day and my inbox is f............... with emails when I get back!
5 Information from management doesn't appear to be t............... down to the rest of us at the moment, does it?

8 Complete the sentences with the verbs in the box.

allocate   encourage   enforce   shape   tackle

1 Our aim is to seek out and .... inequalities wherever we find them. They can't be ignored.
2 This government is doing everything it can to .... the regulations.
3 What is happening now will .... our party's policy in the future.
4 The council needs to .... more resources to road repairs.
5 What more can we do to .... diversity?

REVIEW 3–4

9 Choose the correct word to complete the sentences.
1. The **exit / entry / outside** polls appear to suggest that the government are going to retain power.
2. Most countries in the world have an elected **master / top / head** of state.
3. Union bosses are usually elected by secret **election / ballot / choice**.
4. My mum has very liberal political **views / sees / looks** in general.
5. The written **restitution / institution / constitution** of the USA is probably the world's most famous.
6. The party has recently published its new **manifest / manifesto / manual**.

10 Complete the sentences with one word in each gap. The first letter is given.
1. It's great to work with people who s_____ the same values as me.
2. I couldn't work from home. I really like the social a_____ of working in an office.
3. I don't ever see myself leaving my current f_____ of work
4. Shania had to leave her job in the end, citing the t_____ work culture that had developed.
5. The company has a sound financial f_____, and can afford to go through a brief difficult period.

11 Complete the sentences with the words in the box. There are two extra words.

| back   fuel   pursue   push |
| raise   realise   satisfy   serve |

1. It's more than just a promotion, I've finally managed to _____ my dream!
2. The boss is meeting potential investors to try and get them to _____ our project.
3. What methods can we use to _____ funding for the expedition?
4. Some companies are really trying to _____ the limits of space exploration.
5. It's an amazing feat, but does it really _____ science and progress?
6. I've decided to leave my job and _____ my ambition of becoming a writer one day.

12 Choose the correct words to complete the sentences.
1. The committee is **vehemently / incredibly** opposed to the new housing development.
2. The price of fuel at the moment is **wildly / ludicrously** high.
3. The answer should be **amazingly / blindingly** obvious to experts in the field.
4. This version is **gravely / significantly** cheaper than the previous one.
5. Claims that the sector is failing are **wildly / infinitely** inaccurate.
6. If you think you can get away with cheating, then you're **gravely / vehemently** mistaken.

13 Complete the email with one word in each gap. The first letter is given.

Listen, I know the company is going through a bit of a rough ¹p_____ at the moment, but we really need to think about giving the research and development department a helping ²h_____. It's vital that we think long-term here, and investing in further research will have a positive knock-on ³e_____ in allowing us to improve the quality of our products. At the moment, they're finding it difficult to make ends ⁴m_____ and may have to lose valuable staff. I know some of them are suffering greatly and find it difficult to even ⁵f_____ the day a lot of the time. If you could sanction just a two percent increase in their budget next year, I'll spread the ⁶w_____. Letting them know will really boost morale.

14 Choose the correct words to complete the text.

I like to think I'm a ¹**selfless / conscientious** person who always tries to do my best at work. My brother can seem quite ²**aloof / appreciative** when it comes to work matters (I don't think he really likes his job at all). My mum is very ³**intuitive / compassionate**, she really cares about other people. My dad has his own business and is very ⁴**enterprising / appreciative**, he's always coming up with new money-making ideas. He's also very ⁵**resourceful / selfless** at home, forever making things out of old bits of wood. My sister's a very ⁶**aloof / intuitive** person, who always seems to know how you're feeling.

15 Complete the sentences with the words in the box.

| finite   profit   transactions   umbrella   zero |

1. No matter how much good the company does for the community, it is essentially a _____-driven entity.
2. We're a _____-waste restaurant. For example, all the oil we use is recycled into fuel.
3. There are several types of business which fall under these _____ terms.
4. We need to remember that we're dealing with _____ resources, not an unlimited supply.
5. Online _____ account for around forty percent of our business.

16 Choose the correct words to complete the sentences.
1. Unless immediate action is **made / taken**, the species may die out.
2. Illegal fishing has **grave / sad** impacts on the local dolphin population.
3. What's needed is a **global / world** assessment of marine life.
4. Sadly, the species is **fixed / set** to disappear very soon.
5. The lack of conservation means this animal is on the **brink / top** of extinction.

31

Lesson 5A

GRAMMAR | giving emphasis: inversion, clefting, tailing, fronting
VOCABULARY | collocations: first impressions; adjectives and adjectival endings
PRONUNCIATION | stress while giving emphasis

VOCABULARY

collocations: first impressions

1 Choose the correct words to complete the social media posts.

Kaylie Reid I'm starting a new job tomorrow and I expect people will be sizing me ¹**up / down** when they meet me for the first time. What's the best way to make a good first impression? Any tips?

Rob Teller Keep in mind that anything you say or do will ²**make / have** a bearing on how you're perceived for the rest of your time there. If you tell any lies about yourself or try to ³**project / protect** a certain image, then this may lead to problematic ⁴**preconcepts / preconceptions** further down the road. So don't try to ⁵**taint / adopt** the mannerisms of the people around you. Just be yourself.

Becka Becks Try to ⁶**establish / adopt** an immediate rapport with people you meet by asking them lots of questions about themselves and showing an interest in what they say. If you can get on people's good sides as soon as you meet them, it will have a ⁷**lasting / long** effect.

Matt Lane Be careful not to judge people by their appearance, background or accent. These things can sometimes ⁸**taint / establish** our impression of people without us realising it.

adjectives and adjectival endings

2 Choose the correct words to complete the sentences.
1 Despite his **dishevelled / implausible** appearance at work, he looked very smart at the event.
2 I felt quite **bereft / industrious** when Liberty left the company. She was one of my best friends.
3 Don't be so **distinctive / gullible**, it's clearly a scam.
4 Guy has a **self-deprecating / unfavourable** sense of humour which makes him instantly likeable.
5 The collared dove has a **pompous / distinctive** white band around its neck.
6 You need to update your antivirus software, otherwise you're **susceptible / unapproachable** to attacks.
7 We can't agree to such **unfavourable / dishevelled** terms in the contract, I'm afraid.
8 People would believe you more if you didn't tell such **susceptible / implausible** stories.

3 Complete the conversation using words from the box.

| disconcerting industrious pompous reassuring |
| successive unapproachable unintelligible unperturbed |

A: How's the new job going, Liz?
B: It's OK. The people in my team are generally nice, which is obviously ¹_____. All, that is, except for one guy, Marcus. He's just really ²_____, a real know-it-all. And he's really ³_____ most of the time. You just can't speak to him.
A: Oh, that's somewhat ⁴_____.
B: I know. But I'm ⁵_____ by it because, as I said, the rest of the team are nice.

GRAMMAR

giving emphasis: inversion, clefting, tailing, fronting

4 The sentences below have a mistake. Choose the best option to correct the mistake.
1 She made a really good impression, the new boss made.
   a the new boss make
   b the new boss
   c the new boss did make
2 That new guy, he where's from?
   a from where he's
   b where's he from
   c he's where from
3 I hate what most is not getting credit for something.
   a What most I hate
   b I hate most what
   c What I hate most
4 We're going to stay where, I have no idea.
   a Where are we going to stay
   b Where we're going to stay
   c We're where going to stay

5 Complete the second sentence so that it means the same as the first using the words in brackets.
1 My wife's brother is an electrician and she can give you his work number. (brother's)
   My wife, _____ and she can give you his work number.
2 My workload last month was so heavy that I didn't have any free time. (was)
   So heavy _____ that I didn't have any free time.
3 I love the team spirit in my new job. (about)
   What _____ is the team spirit.
4 That was the best film I've seen in ages. (was)
   It _____, that film.
5 Jan took your mug, not me. (who)
   It _____, not me.

5A

PRONUNCIATION

6 A 🔊 **5.01** | stress while giving emphasis | Listen and mark the word with the main stress in each sentence.
1. What I hate most is when people lie to me.
2. Under no circumstances should you attempt to lift this without help.
3. It felt like the longest ever, that meeting.
4. That customer you were talking to, what did she want?
5. All I needed was a bit more time.
6. When I'm going to have time to finish this, I have no idea.

B 🔊 **5.01** | Listen again and repeat.

READING

7 Read the article about first impressions and number the topics (a–d) in the order they are mentioned.
- a an example of how first impressions can be wrong
- b how quickly first impressions are formed
- c using your face to create a good impression
- d the image people try to project in public

Can you judge a book by its cover?

It never really sat quite right with me, the old saying, 'never judge a book by its cover'. If that was true, then why do publishers put so much effort into designing eye-catching covers? But, of course, this was my overly literal mind not instantly grasping the fact that this was meant to be a metaphor for not judging people by the first impression you get when you meet them.

Like it or not, first impressions are instant, subconscious, and have a lasting effect. As implausible as it sounds, some research indicates that we make up our mind about a person's character in around a tenth of a second of meeting them for the first time. We unwittingly size them up by their posture, eye gaze, tone of voice, body language and facial expressions. In a world which is becoming ever more aesthetic, appearance counts. If we see something we don't like, it taints our impression.

That's not to say that this is a good thing, or that we're not often mistaken. Judging people by their appearance is problematic for a number of reasons. People tend to wear a 'mask' in public, especially in a more formal work setting, depending on their role. They try to project themselves in a certain way, even adopting mannerisms that they believe will help them succeed. My wife's sister, she's got a very high-powered job and she does just this. At work she manages a department, and often has a rather stern, serious manner. But whenever we meet up socially, she's one of the kindest, friendliest people I know. She has a self-deprecating humour that really warms you to her. But if you met her at work, you'd think the opposite.

I also remember my mother had her 'phone voice' which she used when answering the phone. This was a much posher version of her true tone of voice.

8 Read the article again and choose the correct options (a or b) to answer the questions.
1. Why does the writer describe first impressions as 'subconscious'?
   - a to suggest they're involuntary
   - b to suggest they happen instantly
2. What is meant by the phrase 'In a world which is becoming ever more aesthetic'?
   - a People place more importance on how they feel.
   - b People place more importance on what things look like.
3. What does the writer mean by 'People tend to wear a mask in public'?
   - a People often choose clothes based on what they think other people want to see.
   - b People often act differently in private to when they meet others.
4. Why does the writer mention monkeys?
   - a to inform us of a human trait
   - b to inform us how monkeys behave
5. What does the last paragraph tell us about how the writer feels about judging people?
   - a we should never do it
   - b there's a time and a place for it

At times, it was hilarious when, after the caller introduced themselves and she realised it was a friend or family member, she instantly slipped back into the English she normally used, without thinking!

Whether it's possible to judge a person on first impressions or not, people do. So how can we make a good first impression? One obvious way is by dressing appropriately, but other less conscious ways in which we project an image are also important, like our facial expressions. A lot of our expressions come from our eyebrows. In monkeys, raised eyebrows are a sign of aggression, but with us it's the opposite. Raised eyebrows are friendly and inviting. Smiling, we know, is also important, but remember that people can spot a fake smile from a mile off. It can be hard to control some facial expressions when you're nervous, so, before an interview, it's a good idea to do some facial warm-up exercises to ensure you appear as relaxed as possible.

Summing up, 'never judge a book by its cover' is perhaps not the best advice, as people do it in a split-second and without thinking. Outside of situations like job interviews, 'never judge at all' for me is the best advice.

Lesson 5B

GRAMMAR | participle clauses
VOCABULARY | spreading misinformation
PRONUNCIATION | intonation in participle clauses

VOCABULARY

spreading misinformation

1 **Choose the correct words to complete the sentences.**
  1 The story **got / went** viral in a matter of hours.
  2 It's hoped that the news will **make / sway** public opinion in favour of the government.
  3 It's been shown that fake stories **escalate / distort** much more quickly than true ones.
  4 Be careful what you read online – conspiracy theories **quash / abound**.
  5 What can I do to **boost / distort** my self-esteem?
  6 It was largely true, but some of the details had been **swayed / embellished**.

2 **Choose the correct word to complete the sentences.**
  1 Despite attempts by the group to .... information, most people know the truth.
     a dissuade **b** sway **c** distort
  2 That video I posted has gone ....!
     a popular **b** viral **c** virus
  3 We're all guilty of .... the details a bit when we tell an anecdote.
     a embellishing **b** spreading **c** escalating
  4 We need to .... the rumour.
     a sway **b** quash **c** distort
  5 Why would you help to .... a story like that, when it's clearly untrue?
     a escalate **b** sway **c** boost
  6 Everyone wants to .... their own self-esteem on social media.
     a distort **b** escalate **c** boost

3 **Complete the text with the words in the box.**

  | abound boost distort embellish |
  | escalates go quashed sway |

  There are several reasons why people might spread misinformation online. A false story might come from a bot, a piece of software designed to change the context or ¹............... information, perhaps to ²............... public opinion for political gain. There are also trolls, people who want to cause other people distress or simply ³............... their own self-esteem. But often it's unintentional. People might unwittingly spread a rumour online (or even ⁴............... the details). They might see a headline that they agree with and feel the need to try and make it ⁵............... viral. The worst scenario is when a celebrity believes a story without checking its facts and shares it. The story then ⁶..............., conspiracy theories ⁷............... and it can be shared thousands of times before the rumour is ⁸................

GRAMMAR

participle clauses

4 **Choose the correct word or phrase to complete the sentences.**
  1 Having .... caught out before, Ben didn't believe the scam.
     a be **b** been **c** being
  2 .... by the desire to succeed, Kyra gave it her very best.
     a Having motivated
     b Motivated
     c Motivating
  3 The payment .... to the contractor was too little, too late.
     a sent **b** sending **c** having sent
  4 .... carefully, your writing will be much better in quality.
     a Having **b** Planning **c** Planned
  5 The two old friends greeted each other, ... each other tightly.
     a hug **b** hugged **c** hugging
  6 Georgiou had no way of contacting us, ... his phone.
     a having lost **b** losing **c** having losing

5 **Complete the sentences with the correct form of the words in brackets.**
  1 .... (forget) how to play the piano, Marsha decided to have lessons in later life.
  2 The train .... (approach) platform 4 is the 9.18 service to London Euston.
  3 .... (design) by Carlos, the new format looks great.
  4 Williams is the obvious choice for captain, ... (have) so much experience.
  5 .... (run) all the way through the airport, she just made her flight.
  6 .... (cook) on a low heat for twenty minutes, the flavour really comes out.

PRONUNCIATION

6A 🔊 **5.02** | **intonation in participle clauses** | Complete the sentences with one word in each gap. Listen and check.
  1 Having .... the game, the team walked off the pitch miserably.
  2 .... an experienced salesperson, Talita knew how to win customers round.
  3 Produced by Paul Simmons, the film .... a roaring success.
  4 .... shut my computer down, I remembered that I needed some important files from it.

B 🔊 **5.02** | Listen again and repeat the sentences, paying attention to the intonation.

LISTENING

7 🔊 **5.03** | Listen to a radio programme about scams. Which two of scams (a–c) are discussed?

a Someone makes you transfer funds to another account.
b Someone takes control of your bank account.
c Someone uses some facts about you to get money.

8 🔊 **5.03** | Listen again. Are the statements True (T) or False (F) according to what you hear?

1 Scammers aren't getting any more sophisticated.
2 With authorised push payments, someone tells you you've already been conned out of money.
3 Targets for authorised push payments include people about to move.
4 Dorian says that banks have systems in place against scammers, so you don't need to worry.
5 He also suggests buying things from websites you haven't used before.

9 🔊 **5.04** | Listen to the recording. Write what you hear. You will hear the sentences only once.

1 _____
2 _____
3 _____
4 _____

WRITING

a report

10 Complete the report with the words in the box.

| aim consensus few cited minimise |
| large on points proportion worrying |

11 Write a report on the effects of a social media presence for businesses. Use the ideas below. Write 250–300 words.

+ Customers expect it nowadays.
+ It can help the company's image.
+ Direct interaction with customers.
+ They can promote new products or services.

− It must be monitored constantly.
− Complaints can be amplified.
− It must be managed skilfully to avoid poorly timed or worded posts.

> We've had to invest a lot in ensuring the account is kept updated at all times in response to comments about information being out of date.
> Pat Barkman, CEO NuTech

> There's been positive feedback on posts where we've shown how we support the local community.
> Darshana Fallon, local councillor

A report into the potential positive and negative effects of social media in the workplace

Introduction

The ¹_____ of this report is to summarise the positive and negative effects of social media in the workplace, based on the findings of a survey of 100 employees in five different companies. It will go ²_____ to offer recommendations on how companies can ³_____ any negative effects.

Positive effects

There was a clear ⁴_____ among those interviewed that using social media in the workplace helps boost staff morale. A commonly ⁵_____ reason was that it affords people the opportunity to take regular breaks throughout the day. Instead of heading outside or to the break room, they are able to have a brief rest from work at their desks. A ⁶_____ people said this actually made them feel more productive. A significant ⁷_____ of those interviewed also stated that it helps build strong relationships at work, which helps them work better as a team.

Negative effects

On the other hand, a surprisingly ⁸_____ number of respondents described what happens when social media goes wrong. According to the survey, an irresponsible comment, perhaps made when angry, can quickly go viral and disrupt workplace relationships quite significantly. Or, worse, it can cause jealousy among employees. A ⁹_____ number of employees cited examples of colleagues spreading rumours and distorting information about others which caused huge rifts in the office.

Recommendations

After considering these ¹⁰_____, I recommend that employers should be advised to draw up a strict code of conduct about the use of social media for employees to adhere to.

In addition, employees should be advised to:

- follow the code of conduct provided by their employer.
- make use of social media to build relationships at work.
- not respond to negative comments (if they feel compelled to comment negatively, they should instead walk away from their desk and return later when calm).

I believe that social media in the workplace has more positive than negative effects and so should be allowed, but with strict guidelines.

Lesson 5C

HOW TO ... | use persuasive techniques in presentations
VOCABULARY | persuasion; adjectives to describe presentations
PRONUNCIATION | intonation: being persuasive

VOCABULARY

persuasion

1 **Complete the advert with the verbs in the box. There are two extra verbs.**

> bolster   bring   come   convince
> gauge   go   own

Got an idea you want to sell? Our presenting course will equip you with the skills you need to ¹_____ the room and ²_____ people round to your way of thinking. This two-day course will help with skills such as how to:
- ³_____ the audience's reactions.
- ⁴_____ across as knowledgeable.
- ⁵_____ people of your credibility.

adjectives to describe presentations

2 **Choose the correct word to complete the sentences.**
1 That was a _____ talk. I didn't learn much.
   a mediocre   b captivating   c pertinent
2 I really liked the _____ way the speaker got us thinking about our own lives.
   a muddled   b subtle   c inappropriate
3 That was a really _____ explanation of what could have been said in a few words.
   a cogent   b assured   c long-winded
4 The talk was good overall, though the speaker got a bit _____ towards the end.
   a muddled   b subtle   c cogent
5 She's a really good speaker, with a(n) _____ and confident manner.
   a stiff   b self-effacing   c assured
6 That was truly _____. I didn't want it to end!
   a muddled   b captivating   c long-winded
7 Unfortunately, his body language is quite _____.
   a stiff   b captivating   c pertinent
8 I thought what he said at the end of the talk was a bit _____ given the audience.
   a expressive   b inappropriate   c stiff

How to ...

use persuasive techniques in presentations

3 🔊 **5.05** | **Listen to part of a presentation. Which activity (a–e) does the speaker NOT do?**
   a ask the audience to visualise success
   b describe an audience's reactions
   c use a simile
   d describe feelings of nervousness
   e talk about the benefits of the course

4 🔊 **5.05** | **Complete the extracts with one word in each gap. Listen again and check.**
1 To be _____ honest, you couldn't do better than taking one of our courses ...
2 ... and say things _____, 'That was awesome!'
3 ... you'll feel _____ a cat that's just got a big old plate of cream.
4 ... no last-minute panic ... no cold sweats ... _____ fear of forgetting what you're going to say.
5 _____ only will you be able to present more calmly, you'll also be more likely to sell your idea.
6 So what are you waiting _____?
7 You'll be cool, _____ and collected.

5 **Match the sentences in Ex 4 with the persuasive techniques (a–g).**
   a direct speech   e repetition
   b persuasive phrases   f negative inversion
   c a rhetorical question g the rule of three
   d a simile or metaphor

PRONUNCIATION

6A 🔊 **5.06** | **intonation: being persuasive** | **Listen and decide if the intonation rises or falls on the words (1–3).**
   You'll be ¹cool, ²calm and ³collected.

B 🔊 **5.07** | **Listen and repeat the sentences.**
1 The software is robust, reliable and rapid.
2 Our product is cool, creative and captivating.
3 The walk is barefoot, bewildering and beautiful.
4 The film is magnificent, mysterious and magical.

SPEAKING

7A 🔊 **5.08** | **Listen and complete the presentation with two words in each gap.**

Today I'd like to tell you about virtual reality games. Perhaps you've played them with the kids, or with friends. But ¹_____ for a moment the benefits they could bring to the workplace. ²_____ would VR games be a good way to let off steam, but they could also help build strong bonds between members of your team. If it were up ³_____, and I ran a company, I would definitely give them a try. VR games can be seen as a huge opportunity and a ⁴_____ when it comes to the team-building exercises you can do without anyone needing to leave the office. So come on, what have you been ⁵_____? VR is a way to get your staff doing something ⁶_____ and creative.

B **Practise saying the presentation in Ex 7A. Pay attention to your intonation. Record yourself if you can.**

C **Listen to your recording and compare it to Ex 7A.**

Speak anywhere Go to the interactive speaking practice

Lesson 5D

LISTENING | describing role models
READING | how to be a positive influence

LISTENING

1 🔊 **5.09** | Listen to two people describing their role models. Which types of role model (1–5) to they describe?

1 a teacher
2 a friend's mother
3 a life coach
4 a family member
5 a colleague

2 🔊 **5.09** | Listen again and answer the questions.

Which person (Cora, Ed or both) says:
1 they felt like others didn't want them around?
2 they immediately had a connection when they first met their role model?
3 their role model liked them immediately?
4 how their role model dealt with difficulties?
5 they did things they didn't think they had the ability to do?
6 they weren't the best person to do something?
7 they want to be like their role model?
8 they still contact each other occasionally?

READING

3 Read the article about being a positive influence and match the headings (a–g) with the paragraphs (1–6.) There is one extra heading.

a Listen to people
b Maintain a positive attitude
c Be careful with your praise
d Keep an eye out for good things
e Lead by example
f Be genuine
g Be nice rather than right

4 Read the article again. Are the statements True (T) or False (F), according to the writer.

1 The writer suggests big problems are usually smaller than they appear at the time.
2 Setting small targets is only important for you.
3 Leading by example can help others see things are possible.
4 The supermarket manager's actions made him unpopular with staff.
5 Pretending to be someone else makes other people feel comfortable.
6 Not agreeing with someone doesn't mean you shouldn't listen to them.
7 When someone succeeds, you should make their success feel important.
8 Many people are able to persuade others to come round to their point of view in arguments where they both have strong opinions.

Six ways to be a positive influence on others

¹_____ This can be hard when we're susceptible to the trials and tribulations of daily life, but there are two ways to keep up your outlook. On the one hand, when faced with problems, try to keep things in perspective and look at the whole picture. The other way is to set yourself small, achievable goals every day or week. Achieving these will put you in a good frame of mind, which will rub off on others.

²_____ Not only will this avoid claims of hypocrisy, or 'Do as I say, not as I do', but you'll also be demonstrating that things can actually be done. When I was younger, I worked in a supermarket on the shop floor. One of our managers would always 'muck in' at busy times. I think everyone admired him for doing that.

³_____ If you try to be something or someone you aren't, it might make other people suspicious. This isn't positive. What's positive is working out what unique skills and knowledge you have, and amplifying them. This is essentially what social media influencers do.

⁴_____ Not just to hear what they say, but also to pay attention to what they're not saying. This makes people feel like you're genuinely paying attention and trying to empathise with how they feel. Even if you don't agree with what they say, the act of hearing them will make them feel like what they're saying is important.

⁵_____ Pay attention to people's actions and when you notice something that's been done successfully, compliment them and make a bit of a song and dance about it. What you want, here, is for others to feel like you are invested in their success; that when they succeed, it makes you feel good. Moreover, having experienced your enthusiasm, others may well seek out your opinion in the future.

⁶_____ It's so easy to get drawn into arguments over something you feel passionately about. (This is especially so with the partial anonymity afforded by social media.) But, in arguments over a polarising issue, how often does one side actually 'win' and convince the other? That's not something I've ever experienced. Rather than confront someone else's opinion head-on, which will probably result in negative feelings on both sides, show you understand their point of view or concern and offer yours.

Lesson 6A

GRAMMAR | narrative tenses review
VOCABULARY | describing literature; describing books and films
PRONUNCIATION | intonation to show surprise/interest

VOCABULARY

describing literature

1 Choose the correct word to complete the sentences.
   1 Having grown up in Johannesburg, the setting of the book really .... with me.
      a revolved   b devoted   c resonated
   2 It's about the Second World War, seen .... the eyes of a young boy.
      a about   b by   c through
   3 The author has a .... following, who won't be disappointed with her latest title.
      a revolved   b devoted   c set
   4 This classic .... many serious issues.
      a deals   b addresses   c resonates
   5 His latest novel .... new ground in how the plot unfolds.
      a breaks   b plunges   c devotes
   6 It's set against the .... of a war.
      a backdrop   b following   c ground

2 Complete the plot summary with the correct form of the words in the box.

   | devote   plunge   resonate   revolve   see   set |

   Kraken by China Miéville
   This fantasy novel is ¹............... against the backdrop of a dark and mysterious London as ²............... through the eyes of an employee of the British Museum of Natural History. One morning, he arrives at work to discover a huge giant squid has vanished overnight. Straight away, he's ³............... into a magical world which ⁴............... around a secret squad of the police, several religious cults and supernatural and criminal groups. Having lived in London, the ideas in the book ⁵............... with me when I read it. The author has a ⁶............... following and this book is one of the reasons for that.

describing books and films

3 Choose the correct words to complete the quotes.
   1 'This book is a **sheer / debut** delight to read.'
   2 'An exciting detective story in the **grip / style** of the Sherlock Holmes novels.'
   3 'Ingeniously **riveted / plotted** twists and turns leave the reader on the edge of their seat.'
   4 'It **grips / twists** the reader at every turn of the page.'
   5 'This was a truly **fiendish / riveting** page-turner.'
   6 'A first-class **sheer / debut** novel from this exciting new author.'
   7 'The ending was **fiendishly / ingenious** clever.'

GRAMMAR

narrative tenses review

4 The sentences below have a mistake. Choose the best option to correct the mistake.
   1 We were all sitting around calmly chatting when suddenly we <u>were hearing</u> a huge crash.
      a 'd heard   b heard   c 'd been hearing
   2 So, in walks Clara and she just sits down and <u>wasn't saying</u> a word to any of us!
      a doesn't say   b hadn't said   c had said
   3 We <u>talked</u> about the book in the past, but I think she'd forgotten that day.
      a talk   b were talking   c 'd talked
   4 I met Charlie while I <u>live</u> in Saudi Arabia.
      a lived   b was living   c had lived

5 Choose the correct words to complete the text.

   Up until a year or so ago, I ¹**'d been steadily getting / steadily got** through my self-devised list of books to read, albeit it very slowly. I ²**was liking / liked** to read at night when I ³**went / had been going** to bed as a way of getting to sleep. Every night ⁴**followed / was following** the same, familiar pattern: while my eyes ⁵**had gently run / were gently running** across the page from left to right, no matter how gripping the storyline, I ⁶**was feeling / felt** myself falling into the soft embrace of sleep. It was only when I ⁷**woke / was waking** up (often with the book in question on my face) that I realised I ⁸**fell / had fallen** asleep and not made any significant progress with the story. Nowadays, I don't even bother to pick up my book when I go to bed.

PRONUNCIATION

6 A 🔊 6.01 | **intonation to show surprise/interest** | Listen to the sentences. What happens to the stress and intonation on the parts in bold?
   1 He thinks he's going to have an easy day, **but it's actually the worst of his career**.
   2 When he arrives at the museum, **the squid is nowhere to be seen**.
   3 He thinks she loves him, **but actually she's in love with another**.
   4 After all the twists and turns in the story, **we find out it was Edmonson all along**.

   B 🔊 6.01 | Listen again and repeat.

6A

READING

7 Read the article. Are the statements True (T) or False (F)?
1 You should build the story around something readers will learn.
2 A good framework for a story gives you freedom to play about with the timeline.
3 Some confusion on the part of the reader is inevitable.
4 Before you have an idea for a story, spend time developing characters.
5 You should stick to writing things you know about.
6 You can always find time to do some writing.

8 Look at the extracts in the article (1–6). Choose the option (a or b) which best describes what the author means when using the underlined word or phrase.
1 a A good story is needs to be built with care.
  b A good story should take a long time to write.
2 a The writers deal with the different stages of the process successfully.
  b They avoid dealing with too many things.
3 a The author writes a lot of popular books.
  b The author has a lot of experience they can use.
4 a The reader expects you to get to the main events quickly.
  b The reader has made a personal investment by choosing your book to read.
5 a Readers will be able to recognise, feel and identify with the situations.
  b Readers will be surprised, excited and entertained by the situations.
6 a You don't need to be writing your very best story.
  b You don't need to be writing your most successful story.

WRITING

a review

9 Match the review features and techniques (1–5) with the examples (a–e).
1 an engaging introduction
2 some interesting information about the story
3 direct and rhetorical questions to involve the reader
4 use of a variety of adjectives and modifiers to help convince the reader of your opinion
5 a summary of your opinion and a reason for reading

a The story itself is absolutely amazing and quite brilliant.
b It's London, but not as you know it.
c It's well worth a read. It'll open up a whole new world to you that you never knew existed.
d This fiendishly clever tale is set against the backdrop of a murky underworld.
e And who do you think they meet at Earl's Court? That's right, it's the Earl himself!

10 Write a review of a book or film you think others should read or watch. Write 250–300 words.

What makes a good creative writer?

[1]<u>Crafting</u> a good story that captivates readers is a skill as old as humankind itself. The ability to imagine another world from that of the day-to-day is, for us, an innate ability. But creative writing is so much more than the ability to imagine things. A good story must be carefully constructed so that it resonates with people and addresses our fundamental emotions. [2]**So how do good creative writers <u>work through</u> this process?**

The first thing to do when building a story is decide on what your core message is. Whether it's your debut novel or you're [3]a <u>seasoned author</u> with a devoted following, there has to be something learnt in the story, whether that's a lesson in life or a resolution to a conflict. Having this clear message at the forefront of your mind creates a powerful building block upon which to start the process.

From this starting point, you can then begin to build the structure of your story. Remember that, when writing, you don't have to begin at the start. You can start to relay the narrative from the middle, or even the end. But a clear structure will allow you to do so without confusing the audience. And that is to be avoided at all costs. [4]**Bear in mind that the reader has <u>allowed you to make use of their time</u>**, and so if your offering is too difficult to follow, they'll just give up.

Once you've got the message and structure in place, it's time to explore your characters and scenarios. The key here is visualisation. Try to imagine yourself in their situation clearly. This will allow you to empathise with your characters [5]**and create situations which really <u>resonate with</u> your target audience**. This will also afford you a deeper understanding of the meaning of your narrative.

Don't be afraid to break new ground. Try writing in a different genre than you are used to, or from another perspective. You might want to try telling a tale as seen through the eyes of an insect, for example. Or set it against a backdrop you're completely unfamiliar with. I was always told to write about what I know, but there's no harm in throwing in a few surprises for your reader. This will help maintain their attention and hopefully keep them gripped until the end.

The difference between a successful creative writer and an unsuccessful one is most usually that the latter doesn't actually get round to writing, claiming they 'don't have the time' or whatever … It's easy to build short bursts of writing into your daily schedule. For example, when you have your morning coffee, instead of browsing your emails or checking the headlines, write for twenty minutes. [6]**You don't have to be working on your <u>masterpiece</u>**, you could just be writing down what you can remember about last night's dream. This is a very healthy habit to get into and, before you know it, you'll be turning out hundreds of words a day.

Lesson 6B

GRAMMAR | adverbials
VOCABULARY | reacting to poetry and song
PRONUNCIATION | intonation to show contrast

VOCABULARY

reacting to poetry and song

1 Choose the correct words to complete the sentences.

1 A lot of punk music was very **melancholic / confrontational**. It was like the singers were looking for a fight.
2 The tune in this song is so **simplistic / melodic**, it's truly a pleasure to listen to.
3 The poem serves as a **poignant / punchy** reminder of the horrors of poverty.
4 Shakespeare wrote a **rousing / melodic** speech for the king to give to his soldiers before the battle.
5 A lot of old-fashioned rock songs are quite **confrontational / simplistic** in musical terms, but very catchy nonetheless.
6 Her new album is a(n) **emotionally charged / rousing** collection of songs about her recent break-up from her husband.
7 That piece is so **melancholic / melodic** it always brings tears to my eyes.
8 The poem is full of short, **punchy / confrontational** lines which really have an effect on you.

2 Complete the conversation using words from the box.

| back   conjures   find   identify |
| lift   nothing   reduce   relate |

A: I love this song. I ¹_____ it so blissfully melodic and beautiful to listen to. It takes me ²_____ to my school days, when it was really popular, and ³_____ up images of long, lazy summer days.
B: Really? It does ⁴_____ for me, if I'm honest. I mean, it's a good song, I just can't find anything to ⁵_____ to in it.
A: OK, I'll put something else on, then!

3 Match the sentence beginnings (1–6) with the endings (a–f).

1 That song is so sad it always reduces
2 Listening to the poet recite his poem conjured
3 I can relate
4 Listening to music on my way to work always lifts
5 I always identify
6 It's a popular song, but personally it does

a up images of his impoverished childhood.
b nothing for me.
c my mood. It's a great way to start the day.
d with musicians who have had a difficult journey through life.
e me to tears!
f to most of her music.

GRAMMAR

adverbials

4 Choose the correct word or phrase to complete the sentences.

1 The musician is being taken to court after his new song was found to be _____ similar to one released by another musician.
  a utterly   b remarkably   c widely
2 This work is _____ brilliant!
  a fairly   b quite   c very
3 I'm _____ irritated by her refusal to work with us.
  a inextricably b absolutely c somewhat
4 _____, he asked for a pay rise even though his work has been terrible this year!
  a Difficult   b Unbelievably c Strange as
5 I _____ recommend this book of poetry, it's fantastic.
  a thoroughly b distinctly   c fairly
6 What she said in the meeting was _____ inappropriate.
  a heavily   b remarkably   c totally
7 The ideas in the two songs are _____ linked to each other.
  a utterly   b thoroughly   c inextricably
8 The exam was _____ difficult, but not too hard. I think I passed.
  a quite   b really   c absolutely

5 Match the sentence beginnings (1–8) with the endings (a–h).

1 I distinctly
2 She's remarkably
3 We were slightly
4 The documentary we watched last night was quite
5 I can only spare you five minutes, it's absolutely
6 To my
7 It soon became perfectly
8 I fully

a hectic here today.
b healthy for someone in her 90s.
c amused by the fact that he got what he deserved.
d clear that the speaker didn't know much about music.
e appreciate that you're busy, but this won't take long.
f remember you saying you were going to help me out.
g fascinating and we learnt a lot about the music industry.
h horror, I realised I'd forgotten my key.

PRONUNCIATION

6 A 🔊 **6.02** | intonation to show contrast | Listen to the sentences. Does the intonation rise or fall on the words in bold?

1 Some people **love their work** and some people **hate it**.
2 Some days he's quite **unwell** and others he's remarkably **healthy**.
3 Last week was absolutely **hectic**, but this week it's relatively **quiet**.
4 The meaning of songs can be quite **complex** or perfectly **clear**.

B 🔊 **6.02** | Listen again and repeat.

LISTENING

7 🔊 **6.03** | Listen to an interview with two members of a band. Which photo shows the band?

8 🔊 **6.03** | Listen again and tick (✓) the things they discuss.
1 how the presenter feels about their music
2 succeeding in the music industry
3 the band's biggest hits
4 how the band got together
5 communicating with the fans
6 relationships between band members
7 the songwriting process
8 their future plans

9 Listen again and choose the correct options.
1 Kyle thinks it's important for a band
   a to have the right opportunities.
   b to work hard.
   c to find the right sound.
2 Luke thinks that, when starting out, a band needs
   a to practise a lot.
   b to play the same music as other bands.
   c to study the competition carefully.
3 They started the band after they found out
   a a mutual friend wanted to start one.
   b they could both play musical instruments.
   c they both liked the same kind of music.
4 Kyle makes the point that
   a it's important for musicians to know each other's style of playing.
   b making good music is about the right connection between musicians.
   c everyone has to work as hard as each other.
5 Luke says the musicians in a band should
   a do things together outside rehearsal time.
   b respect each other's social commitments.
   c do things for each other.
6 Luke says they started out by
   a writing their own music.
   b playing other people's music that they liked.
   c playing other people's music for them.
7 Kyle writes
   a all of the music.
   b none of the songs.
   c the majority of the songs.
8 Kyle says that the band as a whole
   a find it easy to make music.
   b find it difficult to find the time when they can all rehearse together.
   c often have conflicting ideas.

10 🔊 **6.04** | Listen to the recording and write what you hear. You will hear the sentences only once.
1 ....
2 ....
3 ....
4 ....

Lesson 6C

HOW TO ... | tell an anecdote
VOCABULARY | adjective–noun collocations: travel
PRONUNCIATION | informal phrases when telling anecdotes

VOCABULARY

adjective–noun collocations: travel

1 Match sentence beginnings 1–10 with endings a–j.
   1 I learnt a lot about indigenous
   2 From Corcovado you get amazing panoramic
   3 First-class passengers can enjoy opulent
   4 The trail winds its way through primeval
   5 I looked out of the train window at the undulating
   6 In this state, quintessential
   7 The Nakasendo Trail is a legendary
   8 If you want to try truly authentic
   9 We visited several exquisitely
   10 Chile is surrounded by soaring

   a forests and beautiful scenery.
   b preserved villages when we travelled to Vietnam.
   c journey between Kyoto and Tokyo.
   d culture on our trip through the rainforest.
   e views of all of Rio de Janeiro.
   f hills of the countryside.
   g small-town diners abound.
   h mountains, which have long served as a defence.
   i dining throughout the entire journey.
   j cuisine, then visit the street market.

2 Choose the correct word to complete the sentences.
   1 The **rugged / well-appointed / dense** mountains overlook the city.
   2 We explored the **well-appointed / barren / rambling** trail over the hills and it was beautiful.
   3 The journey is made difficult by the **barren / dense / rugged** forest you have to pass through.
   4 The **barren / rambling / rugged** coastline of Croatia, with its cliffs is beautiful in the summer.
   5 The hotel overlooks a **dense / pristine / well-appointed** beach with golden sands.
   6 We passed miles and miles of empty, **dense / rambling / barren** landscape on the way here.

How to ...

tell an anecdote

3 6.05 | Listen to an anecdote about travelling to another city and number the events in the order they happened.
   a She left work.
   b A stranger approached her at the bus station.
   c Her friends from another city called.
   d She asked a stranger for help.
   e She realised the bus wasn't going to the airport.
   f She realised the mistake she had made.
   g She packed her bag for the weekend.

4 6.05 | Complete the sentences with one word in each gap. Listen again and check.
   1 They were _____, 'It's easy, you can get a cheap flight over on Friday night after work, …'
   2 I wasn't that sure about travelling to somewhere even newer, you know what I _____?
   3 _____, I hadn't really thought about this part of the journey, …
   4 It was one of _____ moments when you realise you've made a mistake …
   5 … _____ stranger came rushing up to me.

PRONUNCIATION

5 A 6.06 | **informal phrases when telling anecdotes** | Listen and decide if the phrases in bold are said faster. Then listen again and repeat.
   1 I always like to be active on holiday – climbing, cycling, running, **stuff like that**.
   2 She turned round and **she was like**, 'Why don't we rent a car?'
   3 It was **sort of** smooth and chocolatey.

SPEAKING

6 A 6.07 | Complete the anecdote with the words in the box. Listen and check.

   like (x2)   know   sort   stuff   this   those

   A few years ago, I was on holiday with a friend in Turkey, and one day he suggested we hire a car and see a bit of the countryside and mountains, ¹_____ like that. I wasn't sure at first, but then he was ²_____, 'Come on, it'll be an adventure.' So, we went into town and found ³_____ little car rental place. We told them where we wanted to go and the guy working there suggested we hire this ⁴_____ of mini jeep thing. We agreed. It wasn't long before we were racing along beautiful rugged country roads, and it really was truly beautiful, you ⁵_____ what I mean? Gradually, the road started to twist and turn, and climb up a hill. We got to this one corner and started to really climb the hill, but it just got steeper and steeper, and the car got slower and slower, until it came to a stop. It was one of ⁶_____ moments when you start to panic, and, as I felt the car engine grind, I was ⁷_____, 'Do you know what? I think you need to get out, sorry!' So, my friend hopped out and I was able to get the car under control and move it. After that, we turned around and went back. That was enough adventure!

B Practise saying the anecdote in Ex 6A. Pay attention to your pronunciation. Record yourself if you can.

C Listen to your recording and compare it to Ex 6A.

Lesson 6D

LISTENING | the future of design
READING | a short history of toys

LISTENING

1 🔊 **6.08** | Listen to a podcast about design. What conclusion do they draw at the end?
   a Designers in the future will have less work.
   b Designers in the future can do more work.
   c The design process will be a lot slower.

2 🔊 **6.08** | Listen again and match the people/things (1–6) to their description (a–f).
   1 Mandy Baker   4 Designers
   2 Managers   5 The design process
   3 AI   6 The podcast presenter

   a will be able to create huge numbers of designs.
   b is a designer.
   c is an expert in design.
   d will be able to diversify their roles.
   e will become much faster.
   f will manage and shape something rather than make something from new.

READING

3 Read the article about the history of toys. Match the summaries (a–e) with the paragraphs (1–5).
   a Self-preservation motivated their design.
   b The ingredients of a lasting design.
   c The first known toys.
   d The pros and cons of more complex systems.
   e Toys as a way of copying adult behaviour.

4 Read the article again and choose the correct option (a or b) to complete the sentences.
   1 Some of the oldest toys imitated
      a living things.
      b vehicles.
   2 The toys mentioned from China all
      a involved movement.
      b had complex designs.
   3 In paragraph 2, the writer suggests that children
      a inherently wanted to become soldiers.
      b were being 'trained' as soldiers.
   4 The industrial revolution led to the production of
      a more complex toys.
      b more traditional toys.
   5 The writer suggests that imitative play
      a has had an enduring effect on design.
      b allowed parents to teach their children things.
   6 The writer thinks that simple designs
      a encourage children to be creative in the way that they play with certain types of toy.
      b coupled with the creativity of children's minds has made certain types of toys last longer.

A short history of toys

[1] What was your favourite toy when you were a child? Kids have always played with toys, from simple, static objects to complex toys with several moving parts. In fact, toys that imitate humans and animals have been found which date back nearly five thousand years. The first written mention of a toy was about a yo-yo, made from wood or metal, in Greek, from 500 BCE (though we know Chinese children were playing with yo-yos much earlier than that). Another design classic is the kite, which we know children in China were also playing with nearly 5,000 years ago. Later, around 2500 BCE, children from better-off Indian families were playing with brass and bronze horses and elephants.

[2] How did this need to play with objects come about? And what influenced the design of toys? It seems one factor was the need for early human cultures to defend themselves. So, a simple stick might have been used as a precursor to using a real weapon such as a spear. By the time of the Middle Ages, these war-based toys became increasingly sophisticated and included toy soldiers and weapons.

[3] The Industrial Revolution launched a new era in toy production, and we started to see more complex toys with moving parts. This eventually led to such sophisticated moving toys as train sets. This was the age of wheels, swings, pendulums and springs. Sadly, however, one lasting effect of the Industrial Revolution has been the development of toy production on a massive scale, more recently using modern, easily moulded materials such as plastic, resulting in fewer high-quality, classically designed toys.

[4] Most toys, whether simple and traditional or modern and complex, arise from a desire to imitate (on the part of the child) or instruct (on the part of the parent). Imitative play gave rise to some of the designs which haven't changed their essential shape even up to today. The doll, for example, or – more recently – the teddy bear. And what of the humble ball? This is perhaps the most ancient of toys, and one school of thought suggests it originally had instructional value since a sphere has special significance in many religions and religious ceremonies.

[5] Whatever the toy and whatever its purpose, there do appear to be certain very simple toy designs which have pervaded numerous cultures through time, right up to the present day: toy weapons, balls, dolls, animals. And perhaps it's this very simplicity of design, when combined with the magical endless imagination of children, that has made them so popular through the ages.

5-6 REVIEW

GRAMMAR

1 Put the words in bold in the correct order to complete the sentences.
1 **misinformation / source / we / the / of / the** don't yet know.
2 **really / I / what / is / hate** not being believed.
3 **popular / this / it's / very / world / the / round** news website.
4 **this / which / it / story / was** started the rumours.
5 **need / we / all / is** a bit more time.
6 **where / you / that / shared, / article / did** you find it?

2 Rewrite the sentences with participle clauses.
1 Kevin knew the rumour was false, but he spread it anyway.
   Knowing ....
2 I read a book last week. It was fascinating.
   The book ....
3 We've discussed the matter at length and we've agreed it's not viable.
   Having ....
4 Sonja wasn't convinced by the story, so she decided to check it.
   Not ....
5 The article was written by Liam. It later proved to contain falsehoods.
   Written ....
6 The onions taste best when fried slowly.
   Fried ....

3 📄 Choose the correct word or phrase to complete the sentences.
1 We **talked / 'd talked / were talking** about the book when the lights suddenly went out.
2 I **'d been working / worked / was working** in the garden all morning, so by lunchtime I needed a rest.
3 What **had you done / were you doing / do you do** when you found out about Jackie?
4 We **hadn't even started / weren't even starting / didn't even start** working on the project when it was cancelled.
5 Coleen **wasn't knowing / hadn't been knowing / didn't know** Tunde before they met at the party.
6 So, yesterday, I'm having my coffee break when the manager **was walking / had walked / walks** in and starts shouting at everyone.

4 Complete the sentences with the words in the box.

| difficult   distinctly   fully |
| horror   perfectly   utterly |

1 It was .... clear to everyone in the room that she was lying.
2 All the performers were .... exhausted.
3 To my ...., I realised I'd lost the tickets.
4 I .... remember locking the door when I left earlier.
5 I .... appreciate your circumstances, but this is still unacceptable.
6 .... as it is to credit, the story is true.

VOCABULARY

5 Match the sentence beginnings (1–5) with the endings (a–e).
1 A person's accent can sometimes taint
2 Do you ever find yourself sizing
3 Creating a good first impression can have a lasting
4 Do you sometimes adopt the
5 I often try to project

a effect on your career.
b a certain image during a job interview.
c up someone when you first meet them?
d mannerisms of other people?
e our impression of them without us realising it.

6 Complete the sentences with the correct adjectival form of the words in the box.

| disconcert   dishevel   industry |
| reassure   intelligence   perturb |

1 Misha puts her success down to the fact that she's so .... and hard working.
2 I found her strange behaviour .... and didn't know how to react.
3 What he said was completely .... – I couldn't understand a word.
4 I was really stressed out about work when her calm, ... words made me feel a lot better.
5 His .... appearance suggested that he hadn't got much sleep the night before.
6 They were completely .... by the shouts and boos and continued to perform.

7 Choose the correct words to complete the sentences.
1 The minister's speech was enough to **embellish / sway** public opinion in the government's favour.
2 It seems that false stories are more like to **go / escalate** viral than true ones.
3 We often use social media as a way of **boosting / spreading** our own self-esteem.
4 During the enquiry, he was found to have **abounded / embellished** a lot of the details.
5 Have you ever knowingly **distorted / spread** information and given someone the wrong impression about something?

8 Complete the text with the verbs in the box.

| bolster   bring   come |
| convince   gauge   go   own |

Delivering an effective presentation is not so much about what you say as how you ¹................ across. If you really want to sell an idea and ²................ people round to your way of thinking, then you need to ³................ people's reactions and react accordingly. In this way, you'll be able to really ⁴................ the room and ⁵................ people of your credibility. You don't need to ⁶................ to extraordinary lengths – a few small techniques can help ⁷................ your professional image over time.

REVIEW 5–6

9 Choose the correct words to complete the conversation.

A: What did you think of the webinar?
B: I thought it was a bit ¹**mediocre / captivating**, to be honest. And it was very ²**pertinent / long-winded**. It didn't need to go on for an hour.
A: Yeah, I agree. She had a very ³**stiff / expressive** manner which wasn't easy to watch.
B: She got really ⁴**muddled / cogent** towards the end, when she couldn't answer those questions, too.
A: It's a shame because at the start, she seemed quite ⁵**assured / muddled** in what she was saying, like she really knew her stuff.
B: And I thought her comments about people who work in IT were ⁶**inappropriate / subtle**. There was no need for that, really.

10 Match the words and phrases in bold in the sentences (1–6) with the meanings (a–f).

1 I'm not **susceptible to** flattery.
2 Guy's father had been a police officer and it looks like he'll **go down the same path**.
3 Lily **handles herself** really well in front of an audience.
4 When I was growing up, my parents always used to **have an open house** for all my friends.
5 I always **aspire to** reach the top.
6 **Career-wise**, I'd love to work with animals.

a behave in a particular way
b in terms of a profession
c do a similar job/have a similar career
d have a home where visitors are always welcome
e likely to be influenced by something
f desire and work towards achieving something

11 Choose the correct words to complete the sentences.

1 I also had a difficult childhood myself, so his biography really **revolved / resonated** with me.
2 The book **addresses / plunges** several key issues related to the crisis.
3 It's a comedy **seen / set** against the backdrop of 1950s Berlin.
4 The film **breaks / revolves** new ground.
5 The author already has a **devoted / set** following.

12 Complete the review with the words in the box.

| debut   fiendishly   grips   plotted   riveting   sheer |

The Pact by Sharon Bolton

This ¹_____ page turner is a story about a group of friends about to venture to university when a game goes horribly wrong. They then make a pact which later comes back to haunt them. It's ingeniously ²_____ and a ³_____ delight to read. From the very beginning, it ⁴_____ the reader, who is left guessing right up to the end as to what the outcome will be. Though not Bolton's ⁵_____ novel, it breaks new ground and is ⁶_____ clever from start to finish.

13 Choose the correct words to complete the song review.

The Way of the Wind is the ¹**emotionally / simplistically** charged new song from the duo Lebanon. The deeply ²**melancholic / melodic** words to the song describe the singer's heartbreak after losing a loved one. Beautifully expressed, it ³**conjures / creates** up images of a time well spent with that person before they left. I have to say their previous songs did ⁴**anything / nothing** for me, really, but I can really ⁵**identify / relate** to the beautiful lyrics, which actually ⁶**increased / reduced** me to tears the first time I heard them!

14 Match the sentence beginnings (1–6) with the endings (a–f).

1 Enjoy opulent
2 I watched the undulating
3 From the hotel, you can take in panoramic
4 We went hiking through these primeval
5 Set against the backdrop of the soaring
6 The market is the best place to try authentic

a hills zoom past as I looked out of the train window.
b mountains, the tiny village seemed dwarfed.
c dining at our five-star restaurant.
d local cuisine.
e views of the surrounding area.
f forests every day on holiday.

15 Complete the conversation using words from the box.

| beach   buildings   farmhouse   forest furniture   mountains   room   town |

A: How was your holiday, Marcia?
B: Great, thanks. We stayed in this big old rambling ¹_____ in the middle of a dense ²_____. We had a really well-appointed ³_____ there, which was nice and modern.
A: Sounds lovely. And what did you get up to?
B: Well, we went and sat on a pristine ⁴_____ every day – it was backed by these rugged ⁵_____. Such a sight!

16 Match the phrases in bold (1–5) with meanings a–e.

1 The company designs **cutting-edge** technology.
2 The practical application of AI in a diverse range of areas has only really **come about** recently.
3 The design has helped **launch a new era** in emissions-free transport.
4 These early designs were **far removed from** the technology as we know it today.
5 It was decades before the technology was **bettered**.

a very different to
b the most advanced
c start a new time period
d improved upon
e happened

Lesson 7A

GRAMMAR | omitting words
VOCABULARY | idioms for choices; connotation
PRONUNCIATION | word stress in idiomatic phrases

VOCABULARY

idioms for choices

1 Complete the text with the words in the box.

> dig   quandary   second   sit
> sleep   spoilt   take   umming

Nowadays, we're often ¹_____ for choice in pretty much everything we do, whether it's ²_____ and ahhing over what sandwich to buy for lunch or being in a ³_____ over who to vote for in the next election. And sometimes we're pressured into making decisions so we ⁴_____ the path of least resistance, then later have ⁵_____ thoughts and even regret our decision. But I think it's OK to ⁶_____ on the fence sometimes, isn't it? Rather than have someone force you into making a decision you don't want to, just ⁷_____ your heels in and take time to ⁸_____ on it and give it proper consideration.

PRONUNCIATION

2 A 🔊 **7.01** | **word stress in idiomatic phrases** | Listen and underline the syllable with the main stress in the phrases in bold.

1 I don't want to **sit on the fence**.
2 It's time to stop **umming and ahhing**.
3 You need to **dig your heels in**.
4 It's easy to just **take the path of least resistance**.
5 I'm **in a bit of a quandary** over this.
6 Ooh, we're really **spoilt for choice**!

B 🔊 **7.01** | Listen again and repeat.

connotation

3 📄 Choose the correct word to complete the sentences.

1 Turn the lid _____-clockwise to open it.
   a dis   **b** anti   **c** post
2 I don't really _____ to the view that we have too much choice these days.
   a agree   **b** concur   **c** subscribe
3 I grew up in quite a(n) _____ village.
   a isolated   **b** alone   **c** confined
4 Let's order take-_____ tonight.
   a over   **b** away   **c** up
5 Andrea's got quite a lot of _____ with management.
   a punch   **b** clout   **c** pull
6 Ben's _____ upon a new career in journalism.
   a setting   **b** travelling   **c** embarking

4 Replace the words and phrases in bold with the correct form of the words and phrases in the box.

> anti   confront   embark upon
> out   subscribe to   vex

1 Our company's **going ahead with** a new project.
2 I **concur with** the view that everyone should have the freedom to choose.
3 **Faced** with the choice, I'd buy the cheaper one.
4 The pandemic continues to be a **worrying** problem.
5 We usually run round the track **counter**-clockwise.
6 I'll pick up some take-**away** on my way home.

GRAMMAR

omitting words

5 📄 Choose the correct word or phrase to complete the sentences.

1 _____ nice, being able to work the hours you want to.
   a Is   **b** Must it be   **c** Must be
2 _____ amazing, you have to see it.
   a Film's   **b** Film has   **c** Film
3 The people _____ in the lift are waiting to be rescued.
   a were trapped   **b** are trapped   **c** trapped
4 The time _____ look forward to is the spring.
   a I most   **b** most   **c** most I
5 _____, I'm afraid.
   a Bad is news   **b** Bad news   **c** Is bad news
6 _____ decided what you're going to have yet?
   a You have   **b** Are you   **c** You

6 Match the sentences with omitted words (1–7) with the types of omission (a–g).

1 Film went on way too long.
2 The house I grew up in was very small.
3 Not spoken to Allie for ages.
4 People caught shoplifting will be prosecuted.
5 Matt thinks he's going to get a promotion soon.
6 You doing anything after work?
7 Didn't wake till ten!

a a missing pronoun and auxiliary
b a missing subject
c a missing article
d missing *that*
e a missing auxiliary
f a missing relative pronoun
g a missing relative pronoun and auxiliary

READING

7 Read the article about decision-making and number the techniques (a–d) in the order they are mentioned.

a making a list of pros and cons of each idea
b a process with different steps
c a technique designed to save time
d grouping ideas that are linked in some way

8 Read the article again. Are statements True (T) or False (F), according to the writer?

1 Decision-making techniques are only for work situations.
2 In the seven-step model, we need to examine each of our ideas carefully.
3 Affinity diagrams are drawn on a piece of paper.
4 The aim of affinity diagrams is to limit the options to choose from by grouping them together.
5 Cost/benefit analysis is useful for big decisions.
6 Heuristics is good for finding exact solutions.

9 Read the article again and answer the questions.

Which technique:

1 considers the relationships between ideas?
2 is good for if you just need to get the decision made?
3 involves first defining the situation?
4 might include looking at past decisions?
5 includes consideration of the decision once it's been carried out?
6 requires you to look at two sides of each option?

10 Read the article again. Which techniques (1–7) does the writer use to engage directly with the reader?

1 rhetorical questions
2 humour
3 imperatives directed at the reader
4 directly addressing the reader
5 predicting the reader's response
6 using everyday examples
7 using *we* to share the process they are describing

It's time to get off the fence!

Decisions, decisions, eh? It's no fun being indecisive or – worse – being around someone who's indecisive. Everything takes ages when they're umming and ahhing, and you invariably end up making the wrong decision for them. But it doesn't have to be like that. In the world of business, managers often have to make several complex decisions under time pressures. It's inevitable, therefore, that they've developed a range of useful techniques to help the process. Now, you might be thinking, 'Yes, but deciding what to have for dinner isn't as important as how to allocate thousands of pounds,' and you might be right, but that doesn't mean we can't apply those techniques in our daily lives. So, what are some of these techniques?

First is the **seven-step model**: recognise, research, generate, evaluate, select, implement and review. You begin by recognising that a decision needs to be made. When deciding what to have for dinner, we might feel hungry, or just be planning ahead to the evening. Next we need to do our research. This might involve ambling around the supermarket to see what's on offer, looking up a recipe online, or just asking the others in your household what they fancy. This is linked to the next step, generating multiple solutions, or suggestions in our case. Then we need to evaluate each option. This might involve ideas such as 'Yes, but we had chicken yesterday, I fancy something different tonight'. Finally, we get to select the option based on our evaluation ('Yay! Pizza!'), and implement it (we cook the pizza). The final stage is to review what has happened ('That was delicious' or 'Won't have that again').

Another useful decision-making technique when we're in a quandary is what's called an **affinity diagram**. Let's say it's a relative's birthday coming up, and you need to decide what to do. Quite simply, what you do is write all your ideas on separate sticky notes or cards, and stick them to a wall or a board. The next step is to think about how they might be linked and organise them into groups accordingly, e.g. the preferences of the person, timing, location, cost, etc. The idea behind this is that when you're spoilt for choice and have many different options, you can organise them into sense groups, which lead you more easily towards making a decision.

You may also have heard of **cost/benefit analysis**, which can be useful in our daily lives, especially if we're looking to make a large purchase such as a new car. For this, think about all your options and make a list for each one of the costs (not just monetary, but also considerations such as 'Is it big enough for the family?' etc.). Then list the benefits (fuel economy, upkeep, etc.). This can lead you to a decision, or at least rule out the options which aren't viable.

For more complex decisions or problems that need to be solved, especially when you don't have the time to sleep on them, you can make use of **heuristics**. This involves making decisions that are good enough, though possibly not the best. It's a flexible technique, but isn't as precise or effective as other models. In some cases it may just be a case of thinking 'Well, that option didn't work last time, so let's go with the next one'.

Lesson 7B

GRAMMAR | prepositional phrases
VOCABULARY | ways of reading; idioms: books and reading
PRONUNCIATION | stress in phrasal verbs and dependent prepositions

VOCABULARY

ways of reading

1 Complete the conversation using words from the box.

cast   dip   flick   plough
pore   scrutinise   skim   skip

A: Can I ask you to ¹_____ a quick eye over my essay?
B: Sure, no problem. Let me see … well there's a problem with that first sentence, for a start.
A: OK, I didn't mean for you to ²_____ it or ³_____ through it all! Just quickly ⁴_____ it to see if I'm on the right track.
B: Ha, OK. I won't ⁵_____ over it then!

2 Choose the correct words to complete the sentences.
1 I like spending time in book shops, **perusing** / **casting** what's on offer.
2 I couldn't wait to find out what happens, so I **dipped** / **skipped** to the end.
3 I've been reading **about** / **up** on new clean energy initiatives recently.
4 I've read this book many times, but I still like to **dip** / **skim** into parts of it now and then.
5 I've **pored** / **ploughed** over the company literature, but still haven't found much out about it, to be honest.
6 I usually **skim** / **skip** articles quickly before deciding if I want to read them more carefully.
7 I never properly read magazines, just **dip** / **flick** through them, really.
8 Can you **cast** / **pore** an eye over my work and see if it's OK, please?

idioms: books and reading

3 Complete the text with the missing words. The first letter is given.

I've always been a ¹b_____, a real ²d_____-hard book lover. There's just nothing I like more than to ³c_____ up with a good book and a cup of coffee. Even if the book is quite ⁴h_____-going, I can close myself off from the world and get ⁵l_____ in it. When I was young, people always used to say, 'He's always got his ⁶n_____ in a book', and I'd read long books from ⁷c_____-to-cover in a matter of days. Even when I have to ⁸h_____ the books to revise for an exam, I don't mind.

GRAMMAR

prepositional phrases

4 The sentences below have a mistake. Choose the best option to correct the mistake.
1 Good planning is essential <u>on</u> good writing.
  a for   b at   c about
2 We decided <u>not</u> getting a new car in the end.
  a from   b away   c against
3 At the risk <u>on</u> sounding naive, what exactly is the problem here?
  a to   b for   c of
4 The thought <u>on</u> going back to work on Monday always ruins my Sunday evenings.
  a of   b about   c at
5 We're fully committed <u>for</u> implementing the necessary changes.
  a at   b on   c to
6 Our company is definitely <u>on</u> an advantage in terms of market share.
  a at   b in   c around

5 Match the sentence beginnings (1–8) with the endings (a–h).
1 There's absolutely no justification
2 I'm conscious
3 Elliot had been out
4 Most people would benefit
5 These clients are crucial
6 There's just no chance
7 I'm mindful of
8 You can pick what you want, within

a of work for some time when he got the job.
b limits, of course.
c for the success of the company.
d in law for the company's tactics.
e of the fact that we've only got ten minutes left.
f how little money we have left in the budget.
g from more training in their jobs.
h of them coming to an agreement.

PRONUNCIATION

6 A 🔊 7.02 | **stress in phrasal verbs and dependent prepositions** | Listen to the phrases. Which of the words in bold is stressed in each phrase?
1 Don't just **skip to** the end!
2 No need to **obsess about** it.
3 Do you **give in**?
4 This will help **protect** you **against** illness.
5 We need to **set aside** some time to talk.
6 I'm going to **comment on** this article.

B 🔊 7.02 | Listen again and repeat.

LISTENING

7 🔊 **7.03** | Listen to a radio programme about reading or listening to books. What is the conclusion at the end?

   a Reading books is more beneficial.
   b Listening to audiobooks is more beneficial.
   c They are both beneficial.

8 🔊 **7.03** | Listen again. Are the statements about reading (R) or listening to (L) stories, or both (B)?

   1 People don't always like to admit they do it.
   2 It involves remembering things.
   3 It is good for your brain in terms of understanding what happens in the story.
   4 Think about what the characters are feeling.
   5 You can do other things at the same time.
   6 It's easier to focus on the story.
   7 It's not easy to get back to where you lost focus.
   8 It uses higher-level brain activity.

9 🔊 **7.04** | Listen to the recording. Write what you hear. You will hear the sentences only once.

   1 ....
   2 ....
   3 ....
   4 ....

WRITING

a blog post

10 Read the blog post. Which of these things are given as arguments for (F) teaching grammar, and which of them are given as arguments against (A)?

   1 learning other languages
   2 the importance of vocabulary
   3 expressing ourselves accurately
   4 'lecturing' students
   5 developing the mind
   6 level of teacher's knowledge

Do we need to teach grammar at school?

Do you know the difference between a prefix and a suffix? Or how to construct a noun phrase? The chances are, if you went to school in the UK between 1960 and 1988, you don't. During and since this time, grammar has gone out of and come back into fashion in UK schools. In the sixties, a time of wild educational experiments, educators felt that you didn't need to be able to name grammatical structures in order to be able to speak a language. Quite right, too. I went to school in the early 1980s, at a time when we learnt nigh on zero grammar, and I like to think (though others might disagree) that I can speak and write perfectly clearly. However, grammar was reintroduced into the curriculum in 1988 as the eventual result of a report, originally published by the government in the 1970s, which had cited high levels of illiteracy in England and Wales.

But do we really need to teach grammar if it has no bearing on our ability to communicate effectively? Well, supporters would argue that it does exactly that, and that a lack of knowledge of grammar can hinder our ability to relay our message clearly. They also point towards the argument that it helps bolster other skills, such as comprehension, reading and writing skills, social interaction, and even thinking skills. They argue that a good knowledge of the meta-language of grammar also helps us when it comes to learning other languages.

The problem with reintroducing the teaching of grammar to children is that teachers who went to school during the 1970s or 1980s lack grammatical knowledge, and are finding themselves ill-equipped to teach it. While perhaps not an excuse to avoid teaching it, this is not only adding additional pressure to their workload, but it's not uncommon to see long, teacher-led 'lectures' on how to describe language using grammatical terms. Personally, I believe that some grammatical knowledge is useful, but more important is to learn the lexis and lexical structures of English. Collocations, fixed and semi-fixed phrases, these types of things, are far more useful in getting your message across.

11 📝 Read the question and write your response. Write a blog post of around 200 words.

> 'Employers should provide training in spelling and grammar to their employees.'

Do you agree or disagree with this statement? Why or why not?

Lesson 7C

HOW TO ... | hedge an opinion and express reservations
VOCABULARY | collocations: discussing issues
PRONUNCIATION | intonation when hedging and expressing reservations

VOCABULARY

collocations: discussing issues

1 📝 Choose the correct word to complete the sentences.

1 Opinions are _____ divided about wild animals in urban areas.
   a hotly   **b** deeply   **c** patently
2 Sorry, I was _____ oblivious to the fact you were on the phone.
   a completely   **b** absolutely   **c** actively
3 It seems _____ obvious to me that it's a good thing.
   a strictly   **b** deeply   **c** patently
4 The topic of conservation is _____ debated.
   a coldly   **b** completely   **c** hotly
5 The rules here are _____ enforced.
   a strictly   **b** deeply   **c** completely
6 Masha has become _____ involved in the cause.
   a patently   **b** actively   **c** hotly

How to ...

hedge an opinion and express reservations

2 🔊 **7.05** | Listen to a discussion about zoos and number the ideas (a–e) in the order they are mentioned.

   a the scientific study of animals
   b teaching people about protecting species
   c hunting animals illegally
   d watching animals in the wild
   e zoos are old-fashioned

3 🔊 **7.05** | Choose the correct words to complete the extracts. Listen again and check.

1 Well, **maybe** / **might** it's just me, but I'm not really a fan of zoos.
2 Well, I **will** / **would** say the opposite.
3 I mean, I'm **no** / **not** expert, but I think they do a lot to raise awareness about conservation and the plight of endangered species.
4 There are **some** / **few** things that I agree with about what they do, but I **only** / **just** think that they're an outdated concept.
5 I'm **guessing** / **thinking** it would be a big loss to science if we got rid of them.
6 **Obviously** / **Obliviously**, you've got to have some controls, but I think building zoos is going too far.
7 And the idea has a lot **going** / **gone** for it, but I don't think we'll have time to travel there in a weekend!

PRONUNCIATION

4A 🔊 **7.06** | **intonation when hedging and expressing reservations** | Listen to the sentences. Circle where the intonation rises, mark where there's a brief pause and underline where the intonation falls.

1 Well, maybe it's just me, but I'm not really a fan of zoos.
2 I'm no expert, but I think they do a lot to raise awareness.
3 Obviously you've got to have some controls, but I think building zoos is going too far.
4 The idea has a lot going for it, but I don't think we'll have time!

B 🔊 **7.06** | Listen again and repeat.

SPEAKING

5A 🔊 **7.07** | Complete the conversation with the phrases (a–f). Then listen and check.

A: I think the government needs to be building more houses. House prices have gone through the roof!
B: Well, ¹_____ me, but I'm not sure that's the solution. We've destroyed enough of the natural environment already.
A: So what is the solution?
B: ²_____, but there must be some sort of economic measure they can take.
A: I mean, ³_____ just build houses anywhere, but the fact is that there aren't enough houses for everyone.
B: ⁴_____ destroying natural habitats to make way for housing is a worrying problem.
A: Hmm, perhaps we need to start reducing our living space, so more flats and fewer houses.
B: Hmm, the ⁵_____ for it, but it's still going to mean we encroach further on habitats.
A: Well, I ⁶_____ at least it's a partial solution.
B: There are some things I agree with in relation to housing, but we urgently need to protect the environment.
A: Absolutely.

   a obviously, you can't   **d** idea has a lot going
   b would say   **e** I'm no expert
   c maybe it's just   **f** I just think that

B 🔊 **7.08** | You are B in Ex 5A. Listen and speak after the beep. Record the conversation if you can.

C Listen to your recording and compare it to Ex 5A.

D Repeat Ex 5B, without looking at the conversation in Ex 5A. Then repeat Ex 5C.

Speak anywhere — Go to the interactive speaking practice

50

Lesson 7D

LISTENING | consumer choice theory
READING | the problem with choice

LISTENING

1 🔊 **7.09** | Listen to a lecture on consumer choice theory. Does the lecturer agree or disagree with it?

2 🔊 **7.09** | Listen again. Are the statements True (T) or False (F), according to what you hear?
   1 The theory states that people think carefully about what they buy.
   2 Deciding what to buy might be based on price.
   3 Because of 'non-satiation', consumers will always be completely content with what they buy.
   4 The level of contentment resulting from what you buy stays the same for a long time.
   5 The theory allows businesses to set their prices according to demand.
   6 People aren't always logical when they buy things.
   7 What people buy may depend on what they have access to.
   8 Consumer choice theory accurately describes consumer behaviour rather than providing a general guide as to how consumers may act.

READING

3 Read the article quickly. Is the writer generally for or against us having so much choice?

4 Read the article again and choose the correct option (a or b) to answer the questions.
   1 Why does the writer mention their cat?
      a to explain how price comparison websites make their choice easier
      b to introduce the idea of the many options related to insurance
   2 How does the writer feel when faced with the options for pet insurance?
      a angry   b anxious
   3 How does the writer feel about notions of freedom and self-determination?
      a When in a hurry, they're not important.
      b They're not as important as quality products.
   4 The writer thinks that by providing so many options,
      a companies can match their customers' needs.
      b companies put customers off buying anything.
   5 The writer thinks that with having fewer things to choose from,
      a people will be more satisfied.
      b people will settle for less.
   6 What point does the writer make about private pension plans?
      a People will take them out at the wrong time because of the amount of choice.
      b People will take out the wrong type because of the amount of choice.

Too much choice?

We recently got a new pet, an eight-year-old rescue cat called Molly. She's a wonderful little ball of fluff and joy. Because she's getting on a bit, the first thing I did was to look up pet insurance. There are some wonderful price comparison websites out there which you would think make choosing the best pet insurance easy. But, as I'm sitting here reading about per-condition cover, lifetime or non-lifetime cover and type of excess, I can feel a bead of sweat running down my forehead. There are so many policies to choose from, I don't know where to begin.

The idea of having choice as a consumer represents values of freedom and self-determination. But when I've only got fifteen minutes left on my lunch break and I'm faced with rows and rows of different types of sandwiches, these values are most definitely not at the forefront of my mind. In a recent study carried out in a luxury jam shop, two groups were given a different choice of jams: one was offered six types of jam and samples; the other had twenty-four different types. In the first group, thirty percent of people made a purchase. In the second, just three percent bought something. This shows how too much choice can be overwhelming, causing us to baulk at the thought of trying to choose which we like most. By limiting choice, customers go from being 'utility maximisers' (people who make careful and calculated choices on what is best for them) to 'satisficers' (people who buy things which, for them, are 'good enough').

An important area where there's too much choice is that of private pension plans. Many young people don't see it as an urgent choice to make, and research shows that a lack of knowledge of the many different types of plans, coupled with this perceived lack of urgency, means that a lot of people defer making the choice until it's too late.

The plethora of options available may lead us into the false perception that there exists the perfect 'one' for us out there. So, when we do finally make that choice, we feel let down if it turns out not to be 'perfect'. Take TV, for example. Now, we have more and more streaming services, offering on-demand viewing for a fixed monthly subscription. These days, we're in the position of either paying more and enjoying the same range of shows or paying the same and enjoying fewer shows. Here, the streaming services at first create a false perception that we have more choice, but the number of subscriptions available actually limits that choice. And all of these factors are, well, just stressful. But, luckily, I have Molly, and she's a great de-stresser.

Lesson 8A

GRAMMAR | noun phrases
VOCABULARY | idioms and collocations: skills and abilities; compound adjectives
PRONUNCIATION | linking consonants

VOCABULARY

idioms and collocations: skills and abilities

1. Choose the correct word to complete the sentences.
   1. The government needs to get to _____ with the problems in the economy, not ignore them.
      a shape b zone c grips
   2. My sister has a particular _____ for remembering people's faces.
      a knack b drive c shape
   3. Ozbe has a(n) _____ gift for economics.
      a uncommon b rare c good
   4. I've had to overcome many _____.
      a talents b setbacks c grips
   5. I used to be _____ really good shape, but less so now.
      a in b on c at
   6. You'll need to show drive and _____ in order to succeed here.
      a shape b comfort c determination

2. Complete the text with the correct form of the verbs.

   | be get have overcome show step |

   The only thing stopping you from ¹_____ to grips with achieving your goals is the limits you impose on yourself. Of course, if it's a physical goal, such as running a marathon, you'll need to ²_____ in good shape, but even then you need to ³_____ determination when attempting to reach your goal. You'll also need to ⁴_____ the setbacks you'll face along the way, and even ⁵_____ outside your comfort zone, but if you ⁶_____ an aptitude for dealing with new challenges, this won't be a problem.

compound adjectives

3. Complete the compound adjectives.
   1. Our bread is baked in the same time-h_____ way that it has been for hundreds of years.
   2. These days it's a widely h_____ belief that some alternative medicines just don't work.
   3. The difference between the public and private sector is not always as clear-c_____ as people believe.
   4. There's a lot we still don't know about the long-t_____ effects of the virus.
   5. I thought her excuse was far-f_____. It wasn't very plausible at all.
   6. Have you finished the report for the upc_____ meeting with management yet?
   7. New investment in the sector will have far-r_____ consequences.
   8. It seems some people are born with language ability hardw_____ into their brains.

GRAMMAR

noun phrases

4. The sentences below have a mistake. Choose the best option to correct the mistake.
   1. The only thing is worse than wet weather is windy weather.
      a worse b which worse c that is
   2. This part of the river can be dangerous because of the flowing fast water.
      a flowed fast b fast flowing c fast flow
   3. The food discard by the side of the road was picked at by the birds.
      a discarded
      b was discarded
      c which discarded
   4. The time-honouring traditions of the villages go back years and years.
      a time-honoured
      b time-honour
      c honoured-time

5. Match the sentence beginnings (1–8) with the endings (a–h).
   1. Elaine does a highly
   2. I saw something
   3. I'm doing a course
   4. We have a mutual respect
   5. The impression you
   6. I need something to
   7. Put some grated
   8. The only one available

   a. make will last a long time.
   b. interesting outside earlier.
   c. cheese on top.
   d. is the display model.
   e. rewarding job.
   f. in food technology.
   g. for one another.
   h. hold these parts together.

PRONUNCIATION

6 A 🔊 8.01 | **linking consonants** | Listen and complete the sentences with one word in each gap.
   1. Nobody knows for certain what the _____-term effects will be.
   2. You might need to step outside your _____ zone.
   3. Do you think you're in _____ shape?
   4. She has a rare _____ for remembering people's faces.

B 🔊 8.01 | Listen again and repeat. Focus on how the words that fill the gaps in Ex 6A are linked to the next word in the sentence.

READING

7 Read the article and match numbers (1–8) with the things they refer to (a–h).

1 250,000
2 29
3 284
4 350
5 10,506.2
6 104
7 1,310
8 18

a the number of people who joined him on his 401st marathon
b the number of miles he intends to cycle
c the amount of money he hoped to raise with the 401 challenge
d the number of marathons he'd run when he had to stop for a few days
e the number of miles he ran
f the number of days he intends to complete his next challenge in
g the maximum age of children his virtual schools project is aimed at
h his age when he suffered a partial stroke

401 in 401

Back in 2015, Ben Smith, a marathon runner from Bristol, decided to step outside his comfort zone and set himself a unique challenge: to run 401 marathons in 401 consecutive days. Having experienced bullying himself as a child, and obviously being in good shape, he wanted to raise money for his chosen charities, which included a children's charity. And not just 'some' money: his target was to raise a quarter of a million pounds.

Ben had suffered with his mental health after being bullied at school, eventually leading to him having a partial stroke at the age of just twenty-nine. That's when a friend introduced him to running and he realised how good it was for mental well-being. Nowadays he only speaks about his earlier experiences to help kids who have their own issues.

And so it was that on 1 September 2015, he set off on his first marathon. Running a marathon is a huge challenge for anyone, but it seems Ben has a rare gift for pushing through to the end. This was highlighted in June 2016, after completing his 284th marathon, when he suffered an injury in the form of a hernia. It was then that he announced, with a heavy heart, that he would have to stop for ten days. But he showed real drive and determination when he managed to catch up in the days after that by running extra miles after each marathon, eventually completing his 401st marathon in October 2016. For this final marathon, he was joined by 350 other runners in a show of support.

On his way round Britain, he visited several schools and appeared on the news, spreading his message to kids that sometimes it's OK not to be OK. By the end of the challenge, not only had he covered 10,506.2 miles, he'd raised £330,000 for his chosen charities. He has since created his own charity, the 401 Foundation.

So, what next for this outstanding runner? His next challenge sees him travel across the pond to the USA, where he plans to cycle across the country in 104 days. The aim is to cover 14,000 miles in this time by competing in marathons in each state capital before cycling to the next, starting in Augusta, Maine. In total this will involve 12,690 miles of running and 1,310 miles of cycling. In so doing, he hopes to raise half a million pounds for his foundation, which provides grants to local groups who run projects to help build children's self-confidence and promote mental well-being. As part of this next gargantuan challenge, he's running a virtual schools project for students aged 5–18, where they'll complete the same distance, but over the length of the school year, through a range of school activities.

8 Read the blog post about Ben Smith and find six factual errors in it.

Runner of the year!

OK, so for most of us (even us seasoned runners), running a marathon is no mean feat, but can you imagine running them every day, for over a year? That's what Ben Smith achieved back in 2016, when he finished running 400 of them! OK, so he had to stop for ten days in the summer of 2016 when he developed a foot injury, but he was soon back on the road and finished in October, when he was joined by 350 people. And not only that, he raised a quarter of a million pounds for charity!

When he was at school, Ben was bullied, which caused him lots of mental health issues and eventually led to him having a heart attack at the age of 29. A friend suggested he take up running and, as it turns out, he had a particular aptitude for it. Not long after, he had the idea for the challenge.

It seems there's no stopping him now as he plans to cycle 14,000 miles across the USA this year, in 140 days. And this time he's thinking even bigger, aiming to raise half a million pounds for charity!

Lesson 8B

GRAMMAR | uses of *will* and *would*
VOCABULARY | adjectives to describe sensations and reactions; verbs to describe reactions
PRONUNCIATION | contracted *will*

VOCABULARY

adjectives to describe sensations and reactions

1 Choose the correct words to complete the sentences.
1. I always get a bit **hypnotic** / **nostalgic** when I smell freshly cut grass. It takes me back to my childhood.
2. The scream was so **shrill** / **tingling** it sent a shiver down my spine!
3. You might feel a slight **tingling** / **hypnotic** sensation in your hands for the next few days.
4. Dystonia is a condition which can cause **nostalgic** / **involuntary** movements.
5. Some scenes in the drama were **shrill** / **distressing**.

2 Complete the conversation using words from the box.

> comforting   distressing   hypnotic   involuntary
> nostalgic   shrill   soothing   unsettling

A: Have you ever tried a flotation tank?
B: Are they those things where you lie in water in a sort of pod, in the dark?
A: That's it. I used one last week. It was great. The water is nice and warm, so it feels ¹_____ and it's a very pleasant experience. Then they play this gentle, ²_____ music. I went into a sort of ³_____ state, not really focused on where I was.
B: It's definitely not for me! I'd find it a bit ⁴_____. I get really claustrophobic in small, confined spaces like that, so it would be a really bad and ⁵_____ experience!

verbs to describe reactions

3 Complete the text with the correct form of the verbs.

> clutch   flinch   gasp   grimace   set   squirm   wince

We had an amazing experience last week at a 4D cinema. When we arrived, they gave us 3D glasses so we could see the film. The film started quietly, but, then a spaceship seemed to fly out into the audience, and I think everyone ¹_____ as it felt like it was going to crash into us! You could hear everyone ²_____, too. There was another scene where they made it feel like you were inside a spacecraft, hurtling through the stars. I caught myself ³_____ the sides of the chair, and my friend said he saw me wriggle and ⁴_____ in my seat with fear. Because it's 4D, they pump smells into the theatre. One part of the film was in a market and it smelt awful. It made me ⁵_____ and it ⁶_____ my teeth on edge. During some scenes, the chair sprays water into your face and that made me ⁷_____ because some got in my eyes.

GRAMMAR

uses of *will* and *would*

4 Choose the correct description (a or b) of *will* or *would* in each sentence.
1. Every morning, he'll go round and say hello to everyone before starting work.
   a   future prediction
   b   present typical behaviour
2. I tried training my dog once, but he just wouldn't listen to me.
   a   being polite
   b   past refusal to do something
3. I think it'll be a nice day out for all of us.
   a   future prediction
   b   decision made while speaking
4. I would say we need to let her go from the company.
   a   being polite
   b   to soften something
5. Will you be meeting Pierre today?
   a   present refusal to do something
   b   part of a normal sequence of events
6. My grandmother would sit me on her knee and read me stories when I was little.
   a   past typical behaviour
   b   reported speech
7. I'm trying to call him, but he won't pick up his phone.
   a   typical behaviour
   b   present refusal to do something

5 Complete the sentences with *will* or *would* and the verbs in the box.

> help   go   make   not need   not start   win

1. However much I asked them not to, the children _____ a lot of noise while I was on the phone!
2. _____ you _____ me with this please?
3. Grrr! The car _____!
4. I _____ to the library on my way home tonight. Do you want me to get you anything?
5. Who do you think _____ the tournament?
6. Janice told me she _____ a lift in the morning, after all.

PRONUNCIATION

6A 🔊 **8.02** | **contracted *will*** | Listen to these sentences and add contracted *will* where it's used.
1. They have received the package by now.
2. They come in and leave mud all over the carpet!
3. You have to show me how to use it.
4. We need more time.

B 🔊 **8.02** | Listen again and repeat.

LISTENING

7 🔊 **8.03** | Listen to a podcast about a psychological condition. Is it a positive thing or a negative thing for people who have it?

8 🔊 **8.03** | Listen again and choose the topics (1–8) that are discussed.
1 feeling other people's pain
2 empathy
3 a traumatic experience
4 how common it is
5 an experiment
6 when it was first discovered
7 teaching people how to manage the condition
8 the link to genetics

9 🔊 **8.03** | Listen again. Are the statements True (T) or False (F), according to what you hear?
1 When explaining synaesthesia, Declan gives examples involving two of the five senses.
2 People with mirror-touch synaesthesia feel what they see.
3 We know that less than two per cent of the population have mirror-touch synaesthesia.
4 Research into the condition involves looking at pictures of people being touched.
5 People who have mirror-touch synaesthesia can be treated mentally and with drugs.
6 People with the condition are always born with it.

10 🔊 **8.04** | Listen to the recording and write what you hear. You will hear the sentences only once.
1 ....
2 ....
3 ....
4 ....

WRITING

a description

11 Read the description of a fictional character. Which is NOT given as an example to show why he's special?
1 He's on the autistic spectrum.
2 He's extremely talented in some subjects.
3 He's good with words.
4 He's very determined.

12 Read the description again and answer the questions.
In which paragraph (1–4) does the writer …
a describe what the main character is really good at?
b give the background to the story?
c describe difficulties the main character has?
d describes aspects of the personality of the main character, with examples?

13 Write a description of a fictional character you like. Write 250–300 words.

The Curious Incident of the Dog in the Night-Time

[1] I recently read and thoroughly enjoyed this book, in which a 15-year-old boy starts off carrying out an investigation into the death of his neighbour's dog and ends up going on a scintillating story of self-discovery. The boy in question is Christopher John Francis Boone and he's very special.

[2] Although it's never explicitly mentioned, it soon becomes clear that he's on the autistic spectrum. This means that he's hypersensitive to sounds, colours and so on. He also struggles to read facial expressions and takes language very literally. We can see this at the start when a policeman launches a barrage of questions at him about the dog, and all Christopher can do is groan in response as he's totally overwhelmed. This prompts the policemen to blurt out angrily, 'I'm going to lose my rag in a minute', which only serves to confuse Christopher further! Christopher himself acknowledges the difficulties he has recognising facial expressions, 'People do a lot of talking without words.' At another point, the writer expertly describes Christopher's first experience of a London Underground platform, as the train roars into the station in a cacophony of sounds which bombard his senses.

[3] However, despite the difficulties he has in a world not designed for those on the autistic spectrum, Christopher is extremely talented in both mathematics and astrology. He displays some of this aptitude when he's trying to explain to his befuddled father why the sky is dark at night, launching into a speech about how some stars are travelling away from us faster than the speed of light and so seem to disappear.

[4] The other thing you soon come to learn about Christopher is that he shows great drive and determination. The fact that he manages to travel to London by himself and eventually return to his hometown to take his A-level exam in maths at only fifteen are great examples of this.

Lesson 8C

HOW TO ... | explain the purpose and benefit of something
VOCABULARY | well-being
PRONUNCIATION | intonation in sentences containing contrasting ideas

VOCABULARY

well-being

1 **Choose the correct word to complete the sentences.**
   1 I can't start work in the morning until I've had some coffee. I need it to **leg- / kick- / punch-** start my brain.
   2 Growing plants and flowers can help **foster / advance / forward** a positive outlook on life.
   3 When you're feeling low, it can help to **expand / open / widen** up to others.
   4 During the Depression, they often sang songs to **hold / maintain / keep** their spirits up.
   5 If you're trying to lose weight, you can **offset / replace / switch** your food indulgences by planning ahead.
   6 At the end of a long day, I like to have a hot bath because it **substantiates / alleviates / mitigates** the symptoms of stress.

2 **Match the sentence beginnings (1–8) with the endings (a–h).**
   1 There are many things which can help to foster
   2 Adelina's taken up meditation as a way of alleviating
   3 I'm tired this morning. I need to kick-
   4 Thanks for talking to me. It's really helped keep
   5 If something's troubling you, it can help to open
   6 How can I best offset
   7 It's important that you take
   8 Doing yoga can really help

   a my spirits up in these difficult times.
   b loosen your muscles and joints.
   c the symptoms of stress she's been experiencing.
   d start my brain and focus somehow.
   e food indulgences?
   f a positive outlook, such as spending time with your family.
   g up to others.
   h time to unwind at the end of the day.

How to ...

explain the purpose and benefit of something

3 **8.05 | Listen to part of an interview with a gardener. Choose the topics (1–5) he mentions as benefits of gardening.**
   1 being able to wait calmly for things
   2 better concentration
   3 spending time in the sunlight
   4 a sense of achievement
   5 reduced blood pressure

4 **8.05 | Complete the extracts with one word in each gap. Listen and check.**
   1 It's just .... in so many ways.
   2 You've only got to .... at the fact that it's been really successful so far for so many people.
   3 I think a big .... for me is that it's taught me over the years to become a more patient person.
   4 ... it's not that you haven't done enough for them, it's .... that you have to simply leave them ...
   5 That's what I .... out of it, anyway.
   6 And another real .... about that is the things you've grown yourself always taste better.

PRONUNCIATION

5 A **8.06 | intonation in sentences containing contrasting ideas** | Listen to the sentences and decide if the intonation is higher in the first or second part.
   1 It's not that gardening is difficult, it's just that many people don't have the time.
   2 The point isn't to produce lots of vegetables, the point is to spend time outside.
   3 It's not about growing the best food, it's about caring for the plants.

B **8.06 | Listen again and repeat.**

SPEAKING

6 A **8.07 | Choose the correct words to complete the conversation. Listen and check.**
   A: What do you do to maintain your well-being?
   B: Crafting. I really like making things, especially 'upcycling' old things for a different purpose.
   A: And what things have you made?
   B: Not much so far! But it's not ¹**around / about** completing things for me. The ²**point / reason** is that it's something to focus on, and that helps reduce anxiety and alleviate the symptoms of stress. That's what I get ³**from / out** of it, anyway.
   A: Nice to have something to help focus your mind.
   B: Exactly. And it's just beneficial in ⁴**so / such** many ways. As well as helping me unwind, another ⁵**real / true** positive about upcycling is that it's good for the environment.
   A: Because you're repurposing things which would otherwise go to landfill, right?
   B: Exactly. You've only ⁶**got / have** to look at my latest project, where I turned an old car tyre into a seat. That's one less tyre they had to get rid of.

B **8.08 | You are speaker B in Ex 6A. Listen and speak after the beep. Record the conversation if you can.**

C Listen to your recording and compare it to Ex 6A.

D Repeat Ex 6B, without looking at the conversation in Ex 6A. Then repeat Ex 6C.

Speak anywhere Go to the interactive speaking practice

56

Lesson 8D

LISTENING | the Pratfall Effect
READING | mass hysteria

LISTENING

1 🔊 **8.09** | Listen to part of a programme about the Pratfall Effect. What is the surprise at the end?
  a People in the recordings spilt coffee on themselves.
  b The 'average' person only got a few of the trivia questions correct.
  c We can view two people very differently, even if they make the same mistake.

2 🔊 **8.09** | Listen again. Are the statements True (T) or False (F), according to what you hear?
  1 It's easier to like successful people who make errors.
  2 All the participants in the study listened to recordings of four people.
  3 The 'superior' person on the recording convinced the listeners of their superiority.
  4 The 'superior' person got more questions right than the 'average' person.
  5 Participants saw someone spill a drink over themselves.
  6 The participants thought less of the 'average' person after the mistake with the coffee.

Three times when mass hysteria baffled everyone

From 'the dancing plague' to sightings of mysterious animals, history is littered with examples of mass hysteria. These are times when large groups of people suffer the same delusions and even physical effects, but nobody seems to know why.

1 ....
In 1962 in a small community in Tanzania (then called Tanganyika), a schoolgirl erupted into a fit of laughter while at school. And then another one did. And another. These uncontrollable fits of laughter then started spreading to other communities as the girls passed the behaviour on to their parents. Soon, around a thousand people were affected. What's wrong with laughing, you might ask? Everyone loves a good giggle, surely? Except this wasn't your average run-of-the-mill laughter. It came in uncontrollable fits that lasted from a few hours to up to sixteen days in one instance. And it wasn't just laughter. Some people also found themselves running around aimlessly, fainting, having breathing problems and experiencing skin rashes. This went on for several months and forced fourteen schools to close.

2 ....
While the heading might suggest this event is related to food, it was actually the title of a popular soap opera in Portugal. In May 2016, many teenagers were facing the fast-approaching final-year exams when all of a sudden there was an outbreak of a virus – or so it seemed. Three hundred children in fourteen schools up and down the country complained of dizziness, and breathing difficulties, and some were admitted to hospital. Several schools closed as a precaution. However, doctors could find no underlying medical causes whatsoever. They were stumped. But then it transpired that the sick teens all had something in common: they'd all watched the same soap opera the night before and in that particular episode there had been an outbreak of a virus, with all the characters in the show falling victim to it. Did the teens all fake it to get out of taking their exams? It's unlikely, because of the completely different locations of the cases.

3 ....
In July 1980, 500 teenagers had travelled from different parts of England to Kirkby in Nottinghamshire to take part in a marching band competition. The excitement was tangible. But, then, suddenly, they all started to collapse, falling like dominoes. Some were also vomiting or had sore eyes or throats or headaches. Many were even taken to hospital. Thankfully, most recovered quite quickly, but nine of them had to stay in hospital overnight. Theories abounded as to what had happened. Was it water contamination? The water companies made stringent checks, but nothing was found. Radio waves? Nope. More sensible theories have attributed it to pesticide being sprayed on nearby fields, a type which has since been banned in the UK. In the end, however, it was labelled as another case of mass hysteria.

READING

3 Read the article below about mass hysteria and match the headings (a–c) with the paragraphs (1–3).
  a The fall of the march.
  b It's no joke!
  c 'Strawberries with sugar.'

4 Read the article again and choose the correct options (a and b) to complete the sentences.
  1 What happened in Tanzania was distressing
    a because the people couldn't help it.
    b because it spread so quickly.
  2 Each laughing fit lasted
    a several months.
    b for different lengths of time.
  3 The children in Portugal suffered the symptoms
    a at different times.
    b at an important time of the school year.
  4 People working in hospitals at the time
    a had no idea what caused it at first.
    b immediately had some idea of what caused it.
  5 The children in Kirkby
    a had different symptoms.
    b all had the same symptoms.
  6 At the end of the article, the writer suggests
    a nobody knows what happened.
    b there may have been a physical cause.

7–8 REVIEW

GRAMMAR

1 The sentences below have a mistake. Choose the best option to correct the mistake.

1 I speaking to Carla later, want me to ask her about the party?
   a I'm speak   b Speaking   c Am speaking
2 Did you hear Dan that might be losing his job?
   a hear Dan   b that hear Dan   c hear which Dan
3 I not sure. What do you think?
   a Not am sure   b Not sure.   c Am not sure
4 The house is featured in the painting still exists.
   a did feature   b featuring   c featured

2 Complete the text with the missing prepositions.

Even for those accustomed ¹_____ running long distances, running your first marathon will present a huge challenge. Without proper preparation, you'll stand little chance ²_____ succeeding ³_____ reaching your goal. Experts recommend a focus ⁴_____ starting to build your mileage at least a year before you enter a race. This is essential ⁵_____ building the muscle that you'll need properly, otherwise you run the risk ⁶_____ injuring yourself. You'll also benefit ⁷_____ paying close attention ⁸_____ your nutrition in the weeks leading up to the race, and being mindful ⁹_____ having a proper balanced diet. But it'll all be worth it when you cross the finish line and are immensely proud ¹⁰_____ yourself.

3 Underline the noun phrase in each sentence.
1 I've got something I need to talk to you about.
2 It was a totally unbelievable story.
3 We're looking for someone able to meet tight deadlines.
4 We're based in the high-rise building at the end of the street.
5 Poverty is a growing problem amongst the elderly.
6 The person who I admire most is my father.

4 Match the sentences (1–6) with the uses (a–f).
1 I said it's not a good idea, but she won't listen.
2 Tim told me he'd decide later.
3 It's 8.45, so he'll be on his way in now.
4 Carla wanted to have a party, but her parents wouldn't let her.
5 I'm hungry. I think I'll have a sandwich.
6 Would you open that window, please?

a refusal to do something in the past
b refusal to do something in the present
c a decision made while speaking
d reporting speech
e being polite
f expressing certainty

VOCABULARY

5 Complete the sentences with the words in the box. There are two extra words.

| ahhing   choice   fence   heels   quandary |
| resistance   sleep   thoughts |

1 I'm in a bit of a _____ over my choices. Could you help me?
2 If we don't accept their terms, they're just going to dig their _____ in and put up a fight.
3 We need to make a decision and stop umming and _____ over the choices.
4 I'm tempted just to take the path of least _____ and go with what they want.
5 Look at this buffet. We're spoilt for _____!
6 Why don't you _____ on it and decide tomorrow? There's no rush.

6 Choose the correct words to complete the sentences.
1 I know it's counter-intuitive, but you actually need to turn it **anti / pro**-clockwise to tighten it.
2 I don't really **sign up / subscribe** to the view that you should make random decisions.
3 We had a lovely Chinese take-**off / away** last night.
4 When **opposed / confronted** with so many choices, it's little wonder people are confused.
5 It looks like we're going **ahead / up** with implementation of the new system.
6 You should speak to Barbara. She has a lot of **clout / punch** with the local council.

7 Complete the text with one word in each gap. Some letters are given.

Many people think of reading as a fairly simple skill. But whether you're poring ¹o_____ a map, ²sk_____ the news headlines or ³d_____ into your favourite novel, there's a lot more to it than meets the eye (quite literally). Different types of texts require different types of reading skills, so, for example, you might carefully ⁴sc_____ the detail in an academic text when you're reading ⁵u_____ on a subject for university, whereas many people simply ⁶f_____ through a magazine.

8 Complete the sentences with the words in the box. There is one extra word.

| bookworm   cover   curl |
| die   heavy   hit   lost   nose |

1 Dan's such a _____. He's always got his _____ in a book.
2 I've never been much of a _____-hard book lover, but I really enjoyed this one.
3 I've read this book cover-to-_____.
4 Olga has no plans for this evening other than to _____ up with a good book on the sofa.
5 Big exam soon. Time to _____ the books!
6 It's a really good book, but I admit it's a bit _____-going in places.

REVIEW 7–8

9 Choose the correct word to complete the sentences.
1 Suzanne's recently become **functionally** / **actively** / **boldly** involved in the animal rights movement.
2 The topic of climate change is still one which is **coldly** / **warmly** / **hotly** debated, even today.
3 Measures such as these need to be **strictly** / **hardly** / **fast** enforced if they are to be effective.
4 The referendum has caused the nation to become **widely** / **deeply** / **trickily** divided.
5 Sorry, I was **fully** / **very** / **completely** oblivious to the fact you were waiting for me!
6 It's **patently** / **patiently** / **resourcefully** obvious that we need to control carbon emissions.

10 Choose the correct word to complete the sentences.
1 There are just so many .... to consider when buying a new car.
   a topics   b restrictions   c variables
2 I always try to .... the background of something before I buy it second-hand.
   a investigate b overwhelm   c think
3 I feel a bit .... when I have few options.
   a narrow   b restricted   c overwhelmed
4 My sister's so .... It takes her ages just to choose what to wear each morning.
   a various   b indecisive   c limited
5 We often .... and change topics in our English class. It makes it interesting, I think.
   a slice   b chop   c cut
6 Right, I've .... it down to these three options. What do you think?
   a narrowed   b slimmed   c widened

11 Complete the sentences with one word in each gap. The first letter is given.
1 Sometimes it takes a lot to s............... outside your comfort zone when trying something new.
2 Catherine has a particular a............... for sport in most of its forms.
3 We had to overcome a lot of s............... to get where we are today.
4 I'm impressed at how you showed such drive and d...............!
5 Let's get to g............... with this now and then we can relax later.

12 Complete the sentences with the words in the box. There are three extra words.

clear   far (x2)   hard   long   time   up   widely

1 The choices you make when you're young have ....-reaching consequences later in life.
2 The difference isn't as ....-cut as you think it is, I'm afraid.
3 It was once a .... held belief that the Earth was flat.
4 I'm sorry, but that all sounds a bit ....-fetched to me. I don't think it's true.
5 Would you like to join me in the ....-honoured tradition of fish and chips by the sea?

13 Match the adjectives in bold in the sentences (1–6) with the meanings (a–f).
1 The background music in this restaurant is **hypnotic**.
2 I have this slight **tingling** sensation in my hand.
3 Her **comforting** words made me feel a lot better.
4 You could hear her **shrill** voice very clearly.
5 I always get **nostalgic** about working in the bakery when I smell fresh bread.
6 I found his story rather **unsettling**, to be honest.

a making you feel tired or unable to pay attention
b feeling happy because you remember the past
c making you feel less worried or unhappy
d very high-pitched and unpleasant
e making you feel nervous or worried
f a very slight stinging feeling, especially on your skin

14 Choose the correct words to complete the sentences.
1 He didn't even **flinch** / **clutch** when the villain pulled out a gun.
2 I hate the sound of Velcro, it really **squirms** / **sets** my teeth of edge.
3 Everyone in the cinema **gasped** / **clutched** as the monster appeared.
4 Masha **set** / **started** at the sound of thunder.
5 I **clutched** / **winced** the door handle, worried about how fast he was driving.

15 Complete the text with the verbs in the box.

alleviate   keep   kick   loosen   offset   open   take

I love my walking group. We meet up every weekend in a different location and go for long walks in the countryside. First, we start with some simple stretching exercises to [1] .... up our muscles and joints, and then we get going. While I'm walking, I [2] .... the time to unwind and it's a great way to [3] .... the symptoms of stress. It also [4] ....-starts the brain and we have lots of good conversations with each other while we walk. We really [5] .... up to each other and it helps to [6] .... our spirits up while we walk. Not only does all this help me foster a positive outlook, but it can also [7] .... the food indulgences of the night before!

16 Match the sentence beginnings (1–5) with the endings (a–e).
1 Let me put
2 The same name keeps cropping
3 I don't want to push you
4 Pass it on to
5 The performer tried to mess

a the idea to them and see what they think.
b Liberty and see what she says.
c up in these reports. Has anyone met him?
d with our minds, but it didn't work.
e into a certain way of thinking

59

1-4 CUMULATIVE REVIEW

GRAMMAR

conditional forms

1 Choose the correct words or phrases.
1 **Should you** / **You should** be successful, we'll notify you by email.
2 If I **'m** / **were** to take over this company, I'd make some fairly big changes.
3 We'll be able to afford a new car **provided** / **unless** we save up.
4 But **to** / **for** your continual support, I would never have got the job.
5 I won't go to the party **without** / **unless** you want to come, too.
6 We'd always play football on Sunday, even **if** / **although** it was raining.

reporting

2 Put the words in the correct order to make sentences.
1 the book / thinks / amazing / Andressa / is / .
2 the decision / the / one / He / that / maintained / right / was / .
3 questioned / to govern / The journalist / ability / the minister's / .
4 the programme, / rise / inflation / mentioned / As / will / in / .
5 with / My teacher / satisfied / was / my explanation / .
6 it / food / to bring / We / if / wondered / OK / was / our / own / .

modal verbs and phrases

3 Complete the email with the words in the box. There are two extra words.

> aptitude   capable   chance   done
> given   highly   imperative   odds

Hi everyone!

Firstly, congratulations on securing the catering contract. Many thought it couldn't be ¹_____, but you managed it. The ²_____ are that this will bring in a lot of new business. You've really shown that you're ³_____ of working successfully as a sales team.

As a way of saying thank you, we would like to throw a party for staff at the end of the month. It's ⁴_____ likely that the weather will be good, so it's a ⁵_____ that we'll do something outside. We welcome all suggestions for activities, but it's ⁶_____ that everyone agrees, so once we've collated all the ideas we'll vote for the most popular ones.

Becky Stanton
Senior Sales Manager

continuous and perfect aspects

4 Complete the text with the correct continuous or perfect form of the verbs in brackets.

This time last year, I felt like I ¹_____ (stand) on the edge of the unknown. I ²_____ (just / decide) to start a rock choir, open to everyone, in my local community. I ³_____ (playing) guitar in a band for a while before then, but felt like I wanted to achieve more. On the day of the first rehearsal, lots of people ⁴_____ (wait) in the hall when I arrived, eager to join in and sing. Since then it ⁵_____ (be) a great success, with more and more people joining, and we ⁶_____ (find) a new place to rehearse. And this time next week, we ⁷_____ (perform) our first concert!

VOCABULARY

describing attitudes; idioms

5 Choose the correct alternatives.
1 What you said really **rung** / **struck** a chord with me.
2 You've made good progress on your course, it would be a shame to **throw** / **fly** in the towel at this stage.
3 It's **patently** / **sweepingly** not true that just because you know a subject you can teach it.
4 The company has been **doing** / **making** strides in developing medicines.
5 Politicians often **complete** / **trot** out these trite phrases to avoid really answering questions.
6 Try not to get too **hung** / **knocked** up about what Nathan said this morning.

creativity

6 Complete the sentences with the words in the box.

> blue   box   fertile   flash   spark

1 When planning a new approach, it's important to think outside the _____.
2 I think Charley's excuse was more a product of his _____ imagination than fact.
3 I had a sudden _____ of inspiration.
4 Sometimes, it takes hours to think of ideas, and sometimes they just come out of the _____.
5 What kinds of things _____ your imagination when you're writing?

summarising verbs; multi-word verbs for reporting

7 Complete the sentences with one word in each gap.
1 Sorry I missed the meeting. Please fill me _____ on what was decided.
2 Let me illustrate my _____ with a recent example.
3 I've been tipped _____ about a leak of information.
4 At yesterday's meeting, many residents _____ their concerns about the plans.
5 OK, you've talked me _____ it. Let's buy a new car.
6 I'd like to raise the _____ of the new working policy, if possible.

60

CUMULATIVE REVIEW 1–4

describing food

8 Choose the correct words to complete the text.

Last week we had a class party, and everyone brought a dish from their country. As soon as I walked in the room, I faced ¹**an assault / a take** on my senses, with a range of ²**redefining / intriguing** smells where my classmates had been creative and ³**topped / fused** different flavours together. My favourite dish was a Mexican ⁴**take / bring** on a bean salad, topped ⁵**with / by** cheese. It was delicious! I really like my classmates' ⁶**unique / culinary** cuisine.

collocations: job searching

9 Complete the sentences with the verbs in the box.

| identify   jeopardise   leave   play   spread   warrant |

1 I'm looking for a new job. Can you help me .... the word?
2 I think this CV might .... a second look. This candidate has a lot of useful experience.
3 Before you start your application, try to .... your strong selling points.
4 It's essential not to .... a problematic digital footprint when you're looking for a job.
5 Unfortunately, your lack of experience is likely to .... your chances of success.
6 I think working in IT will .... to my strengths.

collocations: politics

10 Match sentence beginnings 1–6 with endings a–f.

1 The government can take measures to help bridge
2 The union leader is chosen by secret
3 I'm so proud of the way you stood
4 Many countries have a hereditary
5 We'll do our best to enforce
6 Every employee will be able to cast

a monarch, but they don't have any real power.
b a vote on the new policy.
c ballot every four years.
d up for what you believe in.
e the gender pay gap.
f the regulations when they come in.

collocations: needing and giving; adjectives to describe people

11 Choose the correct words to complete the sentences.

1 We need to spend more time with Mum. She's **going / having** through a rough patch.
2 We all appreciate the truly **aloof / selfless** work you've done for our charity.
3 I'm not sure how I'm going to **make / do** ends meet this month. It's a real worry.
4 Well done everyone, the customers were **appreciative / enterprising** of how you helped them.
5 We're looking for local volunteers to **take / give** others a helping hand.
6 My sister's a really **intuitive / resourceful** person. She always seems to know what I'm thinking!

extinction

12 Complete the text with the words in the box.

| action   brink   grave   infinite   set   unprecedented |

In the past there existed a seemingly ¹................ number of Javan Rhinos throughout south-east Asia. But over time their numbers have declined at a(n) ²................ rate due to habitat loss and hunting. The ³................ impacts of these activities mean that the rhinos are now on the ⁴................ of extinction, ⁵................ to disappear completely. Unless immediate ⁶................ is taken, we could lose them forever.

How to …

manage interaction during a discussion

13 Complete the discussion with one word in each gap.

A: To get the ¹................ rolling, let's start with Anya. Where do you get your ideas for paintings from?

B: Everywhere, really, even a cup of morning coffee!

C: If I can ²................ in here, I often get ideas for song lyrics from overheard conversations. Sorry, I didn't mean to ³................ you off, Anya.

B: OK, but to go back to my earlier ⁴................, I don't think there's a 'magic pool' of ideas. It's a process of becoming aware of how you get them.

A: Interesting. I'd like to hear Jamie's thoughts ⁵................ this. Do you see it as more of a process?

C: I do. Let me pick ⁶................ on that. I need to be in the right mood to be creative …

maintain and develop interaction

14 Choose the correct words to complete the discussion.

A: Do you think people influence culture?

B: I think people not only influence, but create culture.

C: You're looking at things the wrong way ¹**along / round**, I think. Culture affects the way we behave.

B: That's a ²**relevant / respectful** point, of course. But ³**positively / surely** culture is a wholly human concept, and so humans are its greatest influence?

C: I get ⁴**who / where** you're coming from. But I think there's a ⁵**flaw / thaw** in your argument. Culture can influence future generations of a society.

A: It's clear you both have ⁶**big / strong** views …

check understanding by paraphrasing and summarising

15 Complete the sentences with the words in the box.

| correct   mean   not   put   words |

1 Please, ... me if I'm wrong, but are you saying we need a new leader?
2 Absolutely. That's exactly what I ....
3 OK, I'll .... it another way.
4 So, in other ...., you think it's a bad idea.
5 That's .... what I'm saying. I mean we need more resources.

61

5–8 CUMULATIVE REVIEW

GRAMMAR

giving emphasis: inversion, clefting, tailing, fronting

1 Match sentence beginnings 1–6 with endings a–f.
1 No sooner had I
2 What I love
3 It was the best I've ever studied,
4 So hot
5 What I'm going to cook
6 It was in 2021 when

a that course.
b got home than the phone rang.
c I have no idea.
d I started working here.
e about social media is that it keeps me connected.
f was the dish that I couldn't eat it.

adverbials

2 Complete the review with the words in the box.

horror   perfectly   remarkably
somewhat   unbelievably   utterly

Fans of rock band Benson were ¹_____ irritated last night as the band came on stage very late. After watching the ²_____ similar (in both music and appearance) warm-up band, fans had to wait even longer for Benson to arrive. ³_____, they then had to wait over an hour for the band to come on stage. To their ⁴_____, the band refused to play any of their classics. It soon became ⁵_____ clear that they were going to play a short set. However, this was fortunate as by this time most fans were ⁶_____ exhausted!

omitting words

3 Choose the correct words or phrases.
1 A: How was that book?
   B: **Haven't got** / **Not get** to the end of it yet.
2 The person **I** / **who** most look up to is my dad.
3 **I** / **Am I** invited to the party?
4 Everyone's saying **Liberty** / **which Liberty** might get promoted.
5 They **let** / **did let** you know your test results yet?

uses of *will* and *would*

4 Rewrite the sentences using the correct form of *will* or *would*.
1 'I'll be OK,' he said.
   He said he _____.
2 I can't get Jena to ask for help when she needs it.
   Jena _____.
3 It wasn't cold, so we didn't put the heating on.
   If it had been cold, we _____.
4 I sent the email yesterday. It's certain they received it.
   I sent the email yesterday so they _____.
5 Every night our dad told us stories while we fell asleep.
   Every night our dad _____.

VOCABULARY

collocations: first impressions; adjectives/adjectival endings

5 Complete the text with the words in the box.

bearing   effect   implausible   rapport
self-deprecating   unapproachable

How can we make a good first impression when we meet people? Well, there are several things which have a ¹_____ on whether you establish an immediate ²_____ or come across as ³_____ (so that people will avoid you). And first impressions can have a lasting ⁴_____ on future relationships. People like other people who are ⁵_____ (nobody likes a show-off), but not so much that it becomes ⁶_____ and people don't believe you.

persuasion; adjectives to describe presentations

6 Choose the correct words to complete the conversation.
A: What did you think of this morning's presentation?
B: I thought it was quite ¹**mediocre** / **assured**, to be honest. It didn't do much to capture my imagination. I mean if you're going to go to such extraordinary ²**widths** / **lengths** to convince people of your ³**image** / **credibility**, at least make it interesting!
A: Yes, it was a bit ⁴**long-winded** / **expressive**. I don't think it needed to go on for all that time. But I thought it was quite ⁵**cogent** / **muddled** in terms of content – it made a lot of sense to me.
B: I guess so. It would have been nice for the speaker to ⁶**bolster** / **gauge** people's reactions in that final part, though!

reacting to poetry and song

7 Complete the sentences with the words in the box. There are two extra words.

back   charged   confrontational   conjures
identify   lifts   melancholic   reduce

1 I can really _____ with the words in this song. It's almost like they're speaking to me.
2 A lot of his poetry is very _____. It often makes me cry!
3 This song _____ up images of the sea for me.
4 Wow, what an emotionally _____ piece!
5 Oh, this song takes me _____ to my school days!
6 It's quite a _____ poem, speaking out against the government at the time.

62

CUMULATIVE REVIEW 5–8

innovation

8 Match sentence beginnings 1–6 with endings a–f.
1 Early designs were far
2 My brother's company is at the cutting
3 This launched a new
4 But the best was
5 This all came
6 It was one woman's idea which set the

a edge of their industry.
b about while I was working on something different.
c ball rolling.
d era of public transportation.
e removed from what we know today.
f yet to come.

idioms for choices; connotation

9 Choose the correct words to complete the sentences.
1 Turn the handle **anti** / **wrong** -clockwise.
2 I can't decide right now. Is it OK if I **think** / **sleep** on it?
3 She doesn't **subscribe** / **concur** to your way of thinking, I'm afraid.
4 You can't just sit on the **quandary** / **fence**. What's your opinion?
5 Chantelle's **going ahead** / **embarking** on her new journey in life at university.
6 I was so sure it was the right thing to do, but now I'm having **spoilt** / **second** thoughts.

collocations: discussing issues

10 Complete the sentences with the words in the box.

| actively completely deeply |
| hotly patently strictly |

1 Would you ever become .... involved in an animal rights group?
2 Jonas seems .... oblivious to the fact that he upset them with his words.
3 Restrictions on hunting in this area are .... enforced.
4 The nation seems .... divided on the issue.
5 It seems .... obvious to me that this is wrong.
6 The issue of wildlife in big cities is often .... debated.

describing sensations and reactions

11 Choose the correct words to complete the text.

Last weekend I tried my first virtual reality experience. At first, they put the headset on me and I ¹**winced** / **clutched** as it was a bit too tight. They adjusted it comfortably and I looked around me. It was quite ²**tingling** / **distressing** as I was on top of a very tall building and I hate heights, so I ³**squirmed** / **gasped** out loud! I then chose another programme, walking through a magical forest. The ⁴**soothing** / **nostalgic** sounds of the birds and other magical creatures was very nice, and I relaxed. But then something terrible came out from a tree, making a ⁵**shrill** / **comforting**, screaming noise and I ⁶**set** / **started**!

thoughts and ideas

12 Match sentence beginnings 1–5 with endings a–e.
1 I love optical illusions. I really like the way they mess
2 I worry so much that I often pass my worries
3 Let me put it
4 One thing that keeps cropping
5 My teacher pushed

a on to people around me.
b me to try harder.
c with your mind.
d up is how well our brains have adapted.
e to you that this might be our best option.

How to …

use persuasive techniques in presentations

13 Choose the correct words to complete the sentences.
1 To be **perfectly** / **amazingly** honest, you couldn't do better than trying our product.
2 People will **lead** / **follow** you like sheep.
3 What have you been waiting **to** / **for**?
4 I would recommend this service without a moment's **hesitation** / **waiting**.
5 At no time in your life **you will** / **will you** feel as confident.

tell an anecdote

14 Match sentence beginnings 1–6 with endings a–f.
1 We had fruit and berries,
2 So, I was
3 He was like,
4 I looked up and there was this
5 It was really nice, you know
6 Last summer, I

a on my way to work when this happened.
b what I mean?
c think it was.
d 'Where were you?'
e cat sitting at my window.
f stuff like that.

hedge an opinion and express reservations

15 Complete the conversation with one word in each gap.

A: What's your take ¹............ this business of local councils letting green areas grow wild?
B: Hmm. Maybe it's ²............ me, but it all sort of looks messy, doesn't it?
A: Really? To me it makes a whole ³............ of sense. I mean, it's great for insects.
B: No one would disagree ⁴............ that. But ⁵............ at the facts. I think it's really just a way for councils to save money.
A: Well, that might be true to ⁶............ extent. But is that necessarily a bad thing?

63

1–8 CUMULATIVE REVIEW

GRAMMAR

nominal relative clauses

1 Choose the correct words to complete the text.

Edward Hughes scholarship

Great Northern University is pleased to announce the Edward Hughes scholarship, open to anyone ¹**is studying / studying** physics. In order to be considered, applicants must submit an application ²**explains / explaining** what they can bring to a course at this university in no more than 1,000 words. ³**Whatever / What** aspect of physics you are most interested in, all ideas ⁴**submitted / are submitted** will be considered. Innovation, motivation and diligence: these are ⁵**which / what** we're looking for. We want you to show ⁶**how / you** to put your ideas into practice. Please submit your application no later than 3rd June.

advanced ways of comparing

2 Match sentence beginnings 1–8 with endings a–h.
1 The exhibition was nowhere
2 You look a lot
3 It wasn't so much
4 The sequel wasn't
5 The theatre couldn't
6 The performance was so bad
7 To be honest, I'm more
8 His new book is nothing

a nervous than excited.
b a meeting as a get-together.
c have been more packed on the first night.
d like his previous novels.
e near as good as we were expecting.
f like your mum. Almost identical, in fact.
g a patch on the first film.
h as to be unwatchable.

passives

3 Complete the sentences with the passive form of the words in brackets, using the form given.
1 We've just heard that Janice _____ (fire) from the company. (present perfect)
2 It _____ (think) that the new development will create hundreds of jobs. (present simple)
3 He is hoping _____ (select) for the national team. (infinitive)
4 We _____ (replace / our windows) after the burglary. (past simple)
5 A decision _____ (need / make) soon. (present simple)
6 There's nothing more _____ (do). (infinitive)

verb patterns

4 Choose the correct option (a–c) to complete the sentences.
1 Did you persuade the boss _____ us the day off on Friday?
   a give   b to give   c giving
2 Upon _____ the room, Eva gave everyone a big smile.
   a to enter   b enter   c entering
3 Jake is always so meticulous about _____ his desk clean.
   a keeping   b keep   c to keep
4 I've got too much work _____ at the moment, can we speak later?
   a to do   b doing   c do
5 I definitely remember _____ my keys here, but I can't find them now.
   a put   b to put   c putting
6 Nobody can imagine _____ told they've won the lottery.
   a be   b being   c to be
7 There's no need _____ me, I know what I'm doing.
   a to help   b help   c helping
8 I'm inclined _____ for the second option, to be honest.
   a go   b to go   c going

participle clauses

5 Choose the correct words or phrases to complete the sentences.
1 Having **given / giving** it more thought, I'm not sure I like the idea.
2 **Affecting / Affected** by the floods, many people had to leave their homes.
3 Deniz ran towards the taxi, **shouting / shouted** for it to stop.
4 The money **was invested / invested** in the scheme proved to be too little, too late.
5 Having **told / been told** the joke, the room erupted with laughter.
6 **Known / Knowing** she could win, Katie gave it her all in the race.
7 Having **missed / been missed** his train, Harry knew he was going to be late.
8 **Planted / Planting** early enough, the flowers can grow to two metres tall.

64

CUMULATIVE REVIEW 1–8

narrative tenses review

6 Complete the text with the correct form of the verbs in brackets.

Last month I ¹_____ (join) a book club. I ²_____ (think) about joining for a while before a friend ³_____ (invite) me to come along. That month's book ⁴_____ (set) by the group three weeks before I joined the club, so I ⁵_____ (not have) much time to read it. During that week I ⁶_____ (have) a difficult time at work and kept putting off reading the book until the night before the meeting. Realising it was impossible to read it in time, I ⁷_____ (find) a summary online and decided to 'cheat' and hope for the best. But on the day of the meeting, it became clear to everyone in the room that I ⁸_____ (not read) it. So embarrassing! Never again will I try to 'cheat' at book club.

prepositional phrases

7 Complete the sentences with the correct prepositions.
1 There's a new training scheme that I think you might be eligible _____.
2 The food we offer will depend _____ people's preferences.
3 At the risk _____ sounding biased, my daughter is excellent at maths.
4 Good communication is essential _____ the smooth running of the team.
5 Emma has a real talent _____ making people do their best.
6 We're a bit concerned _____ the delay in finishing the project.
7 My brother's doing a course _____ microbiology.
8 I wasn't planning _____ going to the shop, but I can if you need me to.

noun phrases

8 Choose the correct words and phrases to complete the sentences.
1 Have you booked somewhere **staying / to stay** on holiday yet?
2 Arguing your point on social media can sometimes feel like a bit of an **echo / echoed** chamber.
3 Eat something **warm / is warm** when you get in.
4 I think all we can do is make an **educate / educated** guess.
5 Eating fresh fruit and veg is **high / highly** beneficial to your health.
6 The implications of the new guidelines **for / are for** us aren't too significant.
7 The impression **you make / you make which** will last a long time
8 Did you meet anyone **interesting / who interesting** at the conference?

How to ...

present survey results

9 Complete the sentences with the words in the box. There are two extra words

> assume   consensus   cite   contradict
> expressed   illustration   interest
> respondents   results   speaking

1 The _____ seems to be that people don't mind paying more for better quality.
2 This might lead us to _____ that it wasn't working.
3 Other results appear to _____ this.
4 Another _____ of this is the way people behave in public.
5 There was limited _____ in our other products.
6 People _____ a preference for more accessible software.
7 To _____ one example, an employee said he felt more productive afterwards.
8 Generally _____ though, most people want to give it their best.

explain the purpose and benefit of something

10 Decide if the sentences (1–8) are formal (F) or informal (I).
1 The reasoning behind my stance on this topic is that I want to prevent it happening again.
2 Without a doubt, it's the best thing for us to do.
3 You've only got to look at how popular it is with young adults.
4 With the benefit of hindsight, it becomes apparent that the purpose of this was to enhance her own career profile.
5 One pertinent example to support my stance on this topic would be that of the most recent rise in inflation.
6 That's what I get out of it, anyway.
7 Let me give a couple of examples here.
8 It's not that I don't think kids should have fun, it's just that they need to be supervised.

1–8 CUMULATIVE REVIEW

VOCABULARY

collocations: education; compound nouns

1 Match sentence beginnings 1–6 with endings a–f.
1 We always strive
2 Our new virtual
3 You should take the
4 This year's tuition
5 Most teachers aim to create a nurturing
6 Schools should teach more critical

a fees are very expensive.
b for excellence at the academy.
c initiative and create your own learning plan.
d thinking skills, in my opinion.
e learning environment is popular with students.
f environment for their students.

teaching and learning

2 Choose the correct words to complete the text.

On the first day of the course, the trainer talked us ¹**over** / **through** the basics of classroom management. For example, it's important not to just ²**feed** / **ask** students the answers to questions. You need to try and elicit information.

And it's important to ³**take** / **bring** into account that all students are different. This has an effect on the classroom ⁴**actions** / **dynamic**, of course. Once you know how your particular students learn best, you can ⁵**adjust** / **adopt** your teaching in order to ⁶**inspire** / **integrate** them on a personal level.

describing the impact of an action; binomials

3 Complete the sentences with the words in the box. There are two extra words.

benefits   break   detrimental   facilitate
harm   quiet   showcase   take

1 The exhibition will _____ the best local art.
2 It's so nice to have a bit of peace and _____.
3 Too much noise in the city can have a _____ effect on your ability to focus.
4 Our city is fifty years old, give or _____ a few years.
5 The aim is to _____ cultural development.
6 Some well-intentioned plans actually end up doing more _____ than good.

conventions/cultural heritage

4 Complete the sentences with one word in each gap.
1 Being late here is generally f_____ upon.
2 Our school has a long-s_____ tradition of mentoring between students.
3 Everyone has a deeply r_____ cultural heritage.
4 This way of drinking tea is c_____ in our country.
5 Certain behaviours are p_____ to our culture.

collocations and metaphors: work

5 Choose the correct words to complete the sentences.
1 We need to boost the **morale** / **moral** of our team.
2 Don't be such a **water** / **wet** blanket, come and have dinner with us.
3 Please don't **argue** / **aggravate** the problem.
4 Jo **poured** / **trickled** out her frustration to her mum.
5 I hate office politics. All it does is **alleviate** / **engender** distrust among staff.

workplace and work culture

6 Complete the text with the words in the box.

field   prioritise   shared   social   sound   toxic

Any company that wants to ¹_____ creating a healthy workplace culture needs to hire staff with ²_____ values. If employees value different things in their ³_____ of work, it can create a ⁴_____ culture. While having a ⁵_____ financial footing is important, employers should also consider the ⁶_____ aspect of working, which in turn will help it boost profits.

collocations: pioneers

7 Choose the correct words to complete the text.

How can we encourage people to make advances in society and allow people to ¹**raise** / **realise** their dreams? The most ²**suddenly** / **immediately** important thing is to ³**fuel** / **serve** people's motivation to embrace change. Many are ⁴**vehemently** / **infinitely** opposed to change. But to ⁵**back** / **push** the limits of what's possible, it's ⁶**wildly** / **blindingly** obvious that we need to go beyond the status quo.

money and economy

8 Complete the sentences with the words in the box.

finite   online   profit   umbrella   zero-

1 _____-driven solutions aren't always the best for certain industries.
2 We're a(n) _____ waste organisation.
3 'Organisation' is a(n) _____ term for private and public bodies.
4 We live in a world of mostly _____ resources.
5 The number of _____ transactions is greater than that of face-to-face transactions.

spreading misinformation

9 Choose the correct word to complete the sentences.
1 After giving an explanation of what actually happened, the rumour was **boosted** / **squashed**.
2 Don't **embellish** / **escalate** the details – just tell the truth.
3 Once the story was reported, it **escalated** / **swayed**.
4 After I posted the video, it went **ill** / **viral**.
5 The problem with social media is that it has a tendency to **distort** / **swipe** information.

CUMULATIVE REVIEW 1–8

role models

10 Match sentence beginnings 1–6 with endings a–f.
1 We always had an open
2 Think about how you present
3 I've decided to go down the same
4 I really respect the way my friend handles
5 I have a colleague who I always aspire
6 Think about the strengths you want to have and build them

a path as my parents and become a teacher.
b into your character.
c house when I was a child – all my friends used to come round.
d yourself to others.
e herself in a crisis.
f to be like.

describing literature and films

11 Complete the sentences with the words in the box. There are three extra words.

> breaking   fiendishly   grips   plunged
> resonate   revolves   sheer   turner

1 Alan Graceford is really _____ new ground with his latest novel.
2 That book was a _____ delight to read!
3 The themes of her stories really _____ with a lot of people.
4 The story takes a _____ clever turn towards the end.
5 From the start of the novel, we're _____ into a world of magical beasts and people.
6 The story _____ the reader from start to finish.

adjective–noun collocations: travel

12 Choose the correct words to complete the email.

Hi Cora

How are you? We're now half-way through our trip across South America. Last night we tried the fish-based dish, ceviche, which is a very ¹**authentic** / **indigenous** cuisine here in Peru. I have to say that the ²**undulating** / **opulent** dining here is amazing – so many flavours! It was the perfect end to the day's travelling through the ³**rugged** / **well-appointed** mountains until we ended up here by a perfect, ⁴**barren** / **pristine** beach. We plan to stay here a few days before heading down the coast into Chile. The road is beautiful, with ⁵**preserved** / **panoramic** views, different from the ⁶**dense** / **soaring** forest we've been travelling through until now.

I'll email in a few days to let you know how the journey went.

Speak soon,

Alma

ways of reading

13 Match sentence beginnings 1–6 with endings a–f.
1 Can you cast a
2 The novel's a bit heavy-
3 Take your time, I'll just flick
4 I can't wait to finish work and curl
5 You should read up
6 My brother's always got his nose

a going at the start, but it's worth sticking with it.
b on the company before your interview.
c quick eye over this email and check it's OK?
d in a book.
e through this magazine while I wait.
f up with a good book.

making choices

14 Complete the conversation with the words in the box. There are two extra words.

> chop   indecisive   investigate   limitations
> overwhelmed   narrow   restricted   variables

A: What are we going to get Mum for her birthday?
B: I have no idea. I feel a bit ¹_____ !
A: OK, let's not be ²_____. It's next week, so we don't have time to ³_____ and change.
B: Let's try to ⁴_____ it down to a few choices.
A: Well, what about these 'experience' days? It's like a day out, you know, for afternoon tea or something. Shall we ⁵_____ and see what's available?
B: Good idea! There's a wide range, so let's set ourselves ⁶_____ according to price.

idioms and collocations: skills and abilities; compound adjectives

15 Choose the correct words to complete the sentences.
1 I run a lot, so I'm in good **shape** / **knack**.
2 His excuse was a bit far- **reaching** / **fetched**.
3 I need to **have** / **get to** grips with the new rules.
4 Many athletes have a **hardwired** / **clear-cut** instinct to succeed.
5 We all fail sometimes, but it's what you do to **step** / **overcome** obstacles that counts.

well-being

16 Complete the sentences with the verbs in the box.

> keep   kick-start   loosen   open   unwind

1 We're going to start with a warm-up exercise to help _____ those muscles and joints.
2 We sang songs to _____ our spirits up.
3 It's important to take time to _____ at the end of a busy day.
4 I find a morning walk helps to _____ my brain.
5 When something's troubling you, you should _____ up to others.

67

AUDIOSCRIPTS

UNIT 1

Audio 1.01
1 If you have any questions, just let me know.
2 If it's not too expensive, let's do that course together.
3 If people properly check the facts, they would believe it.
4 If we leave now, we should make it.
5 If that rings true for you, then it probably is.
6 If it's not too difficult, let's give it a go.

Audio 1.02
1 We need to take the initiative here.
2 With us, you can fulfil your potential.
3 We're constantly striving for excellence.
4 We try to create a nurturing environment.
5 They have maintained rigorous standards for years.
6 All we're asking for is a bit of mutual respect.
7 Fostering good relationships is what our institution does best.
8 It's an excellent school with a quality curriculum in all subjects.

Audio 1.03
Terry: Good afternoon, I'm Terry Howell and I'm joined on the programme today by Kendra Lewis, an education professional who specialises in S-T-E-M – or STEM – education. In case you don't know what that is, it's a new way of thinking in curriculum development that strives for excellence in the way our children learn and develop the skills they need for the world of work. Kendra, tell us more about STEM education, and why it's important.
Kendra: Good afternoon, Terry, and thanks for having me on the show. So, this is all borne out of a mismatch between the skills and knowledge traditionally taught at school and those needed right across the board in a number of key industries. It's worth bearing in mind that we're trying to prepare children for jobs that don't yet exist. And with advances in technology lurching forward and unprecedented challenges in the world, this is becoming more of an issue at an increasingly fast rate. But with STEM learning, we can get to the heart of the issue and teach those skills which will be universally useful to people in the future, whatever profession they work in.
Terry: I see. So what is 'STEM learning', exactly, then?
Kendra: It involves the merger of four main educational disciplines: science, technology, engineering and mathematics (S, T, E, M). It's essentially an integrated curriculum that allows for the development of core skills that are useful, such as critical thinking and creativity in problem solving. But, in fact, delivering a quality curriculum involves more than that, and STEM education is now moving more towards a STEAM model. That's S-T-E-A-M.
Terry: STEAM? Let me guess – involving the arts?
Kendra: That's precisely what it is, that's spot on! It's essential that we embrace the fact that a lot of work in the future will be automated. So, whoever serves your burger or sells your cinema tickets will be replaced by technology. And that's a good thing in the long term, as companies can pass on savings to customers. But there are still a lot of areas that can't be fully automated, even with the use of AI (or artificial intelligence). You see, the thing that sets us humans apart is our creativity, especially in terms of creative solutions to problems. By adding the arts to the mix, we can further integrate existing curriculums into STEAM education. And by developing a nurturing environment across a range of disciplines, there are further possibilities for students to find their own path in the real world.
Terry: Fascinating. And so how do you see the way forward? Do you think schools will implement this approach to learning? What changes will need to be made?
Kendra: The starting point is to remember that it's an integrated approach. We as educators need to stop thinking of education as the transfer of knowledge within the distinct frameworks of school subjects. So the approach to education will need to establish clear connections between standards, assessments and teaching. Key skills to nurture are a sense of inquiry – which children are naturally equipped with – collaboration and a focus on process-based learning, not knowledge and facts.
Terry: I see, but what does that mean in more practical, day-to-day terms?
Kendra: Well, as I said …

Audio 1.04
1 It's essentially an integrated curriculum.
2 That's precisely what it is, that's spot on!
3 Do you think schools will implement this approach to learning?
4 The starting point is to remember that it's an integrated approach.

Audio 1.05
Terry: I see, but what does that mean in more practical, day-to-day terms?
Kendra: Well, as I said, the starting point is integration. So, in practical terms, that means teachers from different subjects getting together to plan lessons collaboratively. In some cases, a school will have a 'planning team', made up of teachers from different disciplines, looking at how they can integrate different strands of their courses.
Terry: That sounds like a lot of extra work.
Kendra: Actually, it's not – not in the long term, anyway. Many teachers I've spoken to find that the collaboration makes things easier, and they themselves learn a lot from each other. For educational managers, it's a case of adjusting timetables and the scheduling of classes to take account of the fact that different subjects have merged, and also developing a fully integrated curriculum, focusing on process, not product.
Terry: And I'm guessing staff will need training in this, right?
Kendra: Absolutely. Whoever decides to adopt STEAM learning will need full professional development. But, to be honest, it's not as drastic as it sounds. The resources and materials are there. It's more about changing the initial mindset towards one of fully integrated study.
Terry: Interesting.
Kendra: The last thing to consider is assessment. This really needs to be 'unpacked' and redesigned from scratch. Whereas traditional exams focus on knowledge of facts, STEAM assessments need to focus on skills. So, for example, an assessment might present a problem to be solved, and students are then assessed on how well they collaborate, what questions they ask, how creative their ideas are, that kind of thing. Again, the focus needs to be on the process, not the product.
Terry: So, solving the problem isn't as important as the way in which it's solved.
Kendra: That's exactly what I mean, yes.

Audio 1.06
Presenter: Welcome to today's programme, where we're discussing creativity. With me today are three creatives. We've got Daisy Pennant, a marketing manager, Eddie Kemp, who writes code and designs smartphone apps, and last but not least we have Ella Bowman, a journalist. To get the ball rolling, let's start with Eddie. Eddie, what exactly is creativity?
Eddie: Wow, what a question! Hmm, well, I guess it's sort of being able to have a lot of ideas, isn't it?
Daisy: If I can come in here, there's a commonly held view that while creativity does involve being able to have a lot of ideas, it also involves seeing them out to fruition. So, for example, I might have an idea for a marketing promotion, but being creative is about actually building that promotion and seeing it develop through a process of trial and error into a real, tangible campaign.
Presenter: So, sort of having lots of ideas build upon each other into something real?
Daisy: Yes, that's exactly what I mean.
Presenter: I'd like to hear Ella's thoughts on this. Ella?
Ella: I'm with Daisy on this. Creativity is so much more than just having ideas. And earlier you raised an important point, in that often it's a process of trial and error. You build on your initial idea with other ideas, try them out, take what works and build a solid picture. So creativity is more of a process …
Eddie: That's a really good point … sorry, I didn't mean to cut you off, but, yes, it is a process. I often find that the hardest part is having that first idea, so if I'm having trouble finding it, I might just start with something simple, knowing I won't end up using it, then that sort of gets the wheels in motion, so to speak, and other ideas follow. Sorry, Ella, you were saying …
Ella: No problem. I was just saying exactly that, really, that's it's more of a process than just a collection of ideas. It's what's often called the 'creative flow'.

AUDIOSCRIPTS

Presenter: Do you agree, Daisy?
Daisy: Absolutely. The creative flow's a bit like a fast river. Once you're in, the river will carry you in its flow, but sometimes that first piece of inspiration is the hardest, like jumping in the water, so to speak.
Presenter: Let me pick up on that, if I may. I know you probably get asked this all the time, but where do you get inspiration from? Daisy?
Daisy: That's the really big question, isn't it? And the answer, for me, is everywhere! I read, I watch videos, I watch people …
Ella: For me, if I'm trying to come up with ideas for a story, I almost always draw from my experience. I had an English teacher at school who always said, 'write about what you know.' And I think that's always guided my writing and made it feel more personal and engaging for my readers, something they can relate to, if you will.
Presenter: Interesting. If I can just bring Daisy back in, is that something you draw inspiration from, too?
Daisy: Well, what I started to say was that, yes, I soak up inspiration from everything, and that includes my own experience.
Eddie: I think, for me, when I'm trying to think of ideas is important, too, and, going back to what I was saying earlier, I think creativity is really all about getting the process started. As we mentioned before, it's like a river. And for me, I do this best first thing in the morning, that's when I can have that initial idea, then get things moving so that more ideas come to me.
Presenter: Interesting. Now, to go back to my earlier point about what exactly creativity is, do you think …

Audio 1.07
1 But surely it's not that simple.
2 But don't you think it's important to consider?
3 So you're saying we can draw ideas from anywhere.
4 Did you say 'a river'? What's that got to do with it?

Audio 1.08 and 1.09
A: To go back to my earlier point about what exactly creativity is, can we add anything to our definition? To get the ball rolling, let's start with Alison.
B: Well, I think there are two key concepts: novelty and value. Is it a new idea? Does it have value?
A: But surely an idea doesn't have to be completely new? Sorry, I didn't mean to cut you off, Alison. But take the work of a biographer, for example. They're telling a story that's already there. The novelty comes from the way that they tell it. Sorry Alison, you were saying …
B: Not at all, you're right. That's where novelty plays a part, in how you turn ideas into reality.
A: I'd like to hear Chris's thoughts on this.
C: I completely agree. And value is important, too. Does your idea have value to other people? Obviously everyone's different, and the more people it has value for, the more valuable it is.
A: Yes, and going back to what we were saying before, not all creative people are alike.

Audio 1.10
Ilsa: Yeah, so, a lot of the time when I was at school, I wasn't really into history as a subject, and I think that's mainly down to the way we were taught it. We read aloud long texts about what life was like during, say, the Tudor period, then we'd have to learn all these different important dates from history. I just couldn't really see the point of it all. But then I had this new teacher and he really loved the subject himself. And I think that passion for history just rubbed off on us as he was able to bring it to life. I remember, once, he told us to think about the very spot where we were sitting and consider all the people in the past who had walked over that same spot, how fascinating that was. I think that really inspired us on a personal level. After that, I started to find lessons really interesting. So, yeah, I think that was the best teacher I ever had.
Brayden: I had a French teacher when I was at secondary school, who I think was my favourite teacher. I learnt a lot with her. One of the reasons she was so good, I think, was that she encouraged risk-taking. So, if I made a mistake, rather than draw attention to that mistake, she'd praise me for making the effort. And she created this really sort of friendly, nurturing dynamic in the lessons, so that we felt secure and comfortable trying things out and not worrying too much about our errors. The other thing she did was help us to discover things for ourselves rather than just feed us answers. So instead of just lecturing us about a grammar point, she'd encourage us to work out the rules ourselves by looking at examples in context. She was great like that.
Joanna: I struggled a bit with maths at school. I was never very good at it because I just couldn't understand formulas and things like that. I think it was all a bit abstract for me. But I had this maths teacher who really helped me. She really went the extra mile by organising extra revision sessions after school when exams were approaching, and she'd painstakingly talk us through different concepts in a way which we could easily understand. Without those, I don't think I would have passed. Another way in which she went the extra mile was by creating these worksheets that were specifically designed to play to our strengths and interests. They were great worksheets and I suspect it took her ages to create them. They also allowed her to adjust her teaching style to suit us best. She really went above and beyond her basic role as a teacher, and I think I'll always be grateful to her for that.

UNIT 2

Audio 2.01
1 This chair's nowhere near as comfortable as my old one.
2 This feels a lot like being at home.
3 You can't drive any faster than you are.
4 I think she's more upset than angry, really.
5 This hill is nothing like as steep as I expected.

Audio 2.02
1 I always watch TV with the subtitles on, but my husband prefers watching without them.
2 His teacher thinks translation apps aren't very good, but Connor finds them quite useful.
3 While Scarlett thought writing subtitles would be quite easy, her boss knew this wasn't the case.

Audio 2.03
Presenter: Welcome to the programme. This week I'm looking into the often-overlooked world of subtitling. After a recent survey showed that most people who use subtitles when they watch TV aren't hearing-impaired in any way, we thought it would be interesting to look into the job of a subtitler. With me today is Lisa Weaver, a full-time subtitler. Lisa, what insights can you give us into your work?
Lisa: Thanks. Well … most people who get into subtitling work are translators by trade. And since I only work with English, I'm considered more of a scribe than a true subtitler, as I just convert the audio in films and TV programmes into the written word. However, that doesn't mean my work is without its own challenges.
Presenter: And what are some of the challenges you face?
Lisa: Oh, where to begin? I guess one of the first things we face is restrictions in terms of both space and time. We need to make sure the text doesn't cover up too much of the action in terms of screen space. We often work within very tight time limits, and if the actors are speaking fast and there's a lot of text, it can be quite tricky. We also need to balance how quickly the people on screen are speaking against how quickly the viewers can read the speech. And then there's what we call creative synthesis …
Presenter: What's that?
Lisa: Because of the time and space restrictions, we often find ourselves making decisions about what to include or whether to simplify the syntax to make it easier to follow. But in doing so, we have to always ensure we convey exactly the same meaning as what is said on screen. We also have to stay true to the character's style of speech, register and any eccentricities they might have.
Presenter: I had no idea there was so much to consider. But, yes, that all makes sense, how you describe it. What other considerations are there when subtitling or scribing?
Lisa: Well, there's also what we call 'reading flow conservation'. In other words – quite literally – each line of text needs to be a 'sense unit', so we can't split articles from nouns, collocations, that type of thing. And we also have to conserve the audio-visual rhythm. Speech in TV or films is often put together in a way to have maximum impact. We need to blend the text into this so that the subtitles almost appear invisible.

69

AUDIOSCRIPTS

Presenter: Is that something you work towards, then? The subtitles blending invisibly into the programme?
Lisa: Absolutely. This is our main aim whenever scribing text for subtitles. And we have a range of tools at our disposal to do so.
Presenter: Fascinating. It seems to me it's something of an art form.
Lisa: Indeed!
Presenter: Lisa Weaver, thanks very much. Now we turn to the subject of …

Audio 2.04

Interviewer: So, Deanna, how did you get into this line of work?
Deanna: It all started at home, really. When they were little, I used to read my kids a story when they went to bed at night. I'd been telling them a story, getting into each of the characters, when my husband walked past and stopped and listened. I think that's when I realised I had a talent for narration, so decided to pursue a career as a voiceover artist.
Interviewer: And how easy is it to get into?
Deanna: It's not as difficult as you might think. Basically, I search online for potential projects. These can be audiobooks, TV adverts, animated films, dubbing foreign-language videos, all sorts. Adverts will ask you to record a short piece of text as an audition, then you send it in. If they like it, you get the job. If not, you keep looking!
Interviewer: And what do you like about being a voiceover artist?
Deanna: Well, first of all, it's nice being able to choose what projects I take on, and being a freelancer means I can take on as much or as little work as I like. Though, to be honest, I always worry about not having enough work and usually end up taking on way too much! But also, there's a great community of people that you get to work with, and because the scope of projects is so varied, you end up making great contacts in a wide variety of fields.
Interviewer: Are there any downsides to the job?
Deanna: Well, it can be expensive to get started. You need to invest in some decent quality recording equipment. I'm lucky enough to have a home studio, otherwise I'd have to pay studio costs every day. Before I built that, I divided my time between working from home and working in the studio. You also need to be good at setting and sticking to a routine so you can not only get work done, but also plan for future work. It can all be a bit uncertain at times. And of course, working from home, you can feel a tad isolated. But when you manage to get behind the character you're voicing and express what they'd feel, it sort of makes it all worthwhile.
Interviewer: Fascinating, thanks for speaking to me today.

Audio 2.05

Wanda: I have to say, British people are way too polite sometimes. The other day I accidentally bumped into someone at the train station and they turned round to me and said, 'Sorry!', even though I was to blame!
Stacey: Yeah, I think I get where you're coming from, Wanda. We do go a bit overboard with the whole 'manners' thing sometimes, don't we, Nigel?
Nigel: But surely it's good to be polite like that? Otherwise we'd just be walking around being rude to each other all the time. That's not a society I'd like to live in.
Wanda: Obviously it's important to be civil to one another. But I just think people take it too far here sometimes.
Stacey: Ha, it's clear you both have strong views here. I have to agree with Wanda, though. I remember once when I was waiting at a bus stop, and a guy came rushing past, looking like he had to get somewhere quickly. So I stood back out of his way and he walked into the lamp post. His first reaction was to say sorry, which he said to the lamp post!
Nigel: OK, Stacey, I take your point. And you make a good point. When it gets to that stage, I think we've taken things too far. But I do think it's important to be nice to each other.
Wanda: Fair enough. But I think there's a flaw in your argument. I think often that politeness gets confused with the idea of polite language. So, for example, if I'm in my car, and a car coming in the other direction has to wait for me to pass, I'll give them a wave. That's polite, and good manners. But if someone's in my way at the bottom of a staircase, I'll say, 'Excuse me.' But if they then ignore me, I'll say, 'Would you please excuse me!' sort of aggressively. My language has become more polite, but the intent is more aggressive, if you see what I mean.
Stacey: Yeah, that's a relevant point. Formal, polite language doesn't always mean 'polite'.
Wanda: I find it odd, too, that often people are really polite, but actually not very friendly. In America, strangers always talk to each other in the street. But, here in England, for example, if I try to strike up a conversation at a bus stop, I can feel the other person getting uncomfortable and trying to avoid engaging with me.
Stacey: Ah, but you're looking at things the wrong way round. I think us Brits do have a reputation for being cold, but when you do get to know us, you'll find we're generally very warm and caring.
Wanda: I guess so. I mean, you two are good friends to me!

Audio 2.06

1 But surely it's good to be polite like that?
2 But surely that's the best way to behave?
3 But surely that's not a bad thing?
4 But surely you don't believe that?

Audio 2.07 and 2.08

A: I think it's fair to say that people's personalities are influenced by their culture.
B: I think there's a flaw in your argument there. People's personalities are made up of lots of things, not just culture.
A: No, no, I'm not saying that at all. I'm just saying that it's one of the influences, not the only one.
B: Ah – fair enough. I see what you mean. But surely other things are much more important? The experiences you have, education, for example.
A: Yes, but I think culture has a bigger impact than many people realise. The language, the way family is regarded, these are all part of culture.
B: I think I get where you're coming from. I guess these are things which affect us at a young age and seem less important as we get older.
A: You make a good point. The less relevant something is to us as we get older, the less aware of it we become, I guess.
C: It's clear you both have strong views on this.

Audio 2.09

Presenter: Traditional English food generally gets a bad rap round the world, with its beige colours and bland tastes. But in this week's episode, I'm travelling a bit further afield to sample some culinary delights from the UK's other nations. I'm going to be creating a three-course meal, with each course coming from one of the other nations which make up the UK: Wales, Scotland and Northern Ireland. First, I'm headed to Abergavenny in Wales for our starter, Welsh Rarebit.
So, I'm here in Abergavenny with local restaurant owner Dylan Williams, to try their modern take on a traditional Welsh dish, Welsh Rarebit. Dylan, can you tell us a bit about this dish?
Dylan: Yes, of course. So, originally this was called 'Welsh rabbit', but I can tell you now that rabbit has never been, and never will be an ingredient in this dish! What you have here is basically the world's most magnificent cheese on toast. It's common to use cheddar on the toast, but we're using a locally produced cheese called *Y Fenni*. Do you want to give it a shot?
Presenter: Go on then … Oh, that is superb! It's like it's redefining what I knew to be simple cheese on toast!
Dylan: I'm glad you like it. There's a variation on this called 'Buck Rarebit', which is basically the same thing, but topped with a fried egg.
Presenter: Well that's delicious, I have to say. OK, so now it's off to Northern Ireland for our main course.
Now a lot of food here in Belfast is, of course, influenced by Ireland, and there's possibly nothing more Irish than a plate of champ. It's creamy mashed potato, mixed with leeks and kale. With me is Tina Godfrey, who owns a trendy food truck here in Belfast, serving up the unique dish which is our main course. I can tell you now, it's an assault on the senses … so many intriguing smells in one dish! Tina, talk me through your Irish Champ.
Tina: Well, the key to getting it right is making the creamy mash, before we add the other vegetables. So, first we need to boil the potatoes thoroughly to make the mashing process easier. Then we serve it up on a plate to accompany meat or whatever.
Presenter: Well, I'm a vegetarian, so I'll just try it on its own. Oh wow, that's an enormous portion! OK, here goes … magnificent! Oh, that really is exquisite. So creamy!

AUDIOSCRIPTS

Tina: Ha, I'm glad you like it.
Presenter: Finally I'm here in Avonbridge in Scotland for the final course – dessert. I'm joined by Isla Bell, who is the current holder of the Clootie Dumpling World Championship. Isla, what's a Clootie Dumpling?
Isla: OK, as you can see it's a suet-based fruit pudding, a sort of fruitcake if you like. To the base, we add different types of spices and dried fruit.
Presenter: And where does it get its name from?
Isla: *Cloot* is Scots for 'cloth', and we bake it in a special cloth, which helps to fuse the flavours as it cooks.
Presenter: Mmm, it smells delicious. And I understand you're a champion baker, is that right?
Isla: Indeed! Every year the Clootie Dumpling World Championship takes place here in Avonbridge. I won last year. So, would you like to try my award-winning cake?
Presenter: I'd love to. Oh wow, that's delicious!
Isla: Thank you.

UNIT 3

Audio 3.01
1 The odds are that you'll be promoted.
2 Malia's bound to be late for the meeting.
3 It's guaranteed to succeed.
4 In all probability, we're not going to get funding.
5 I'm capable of completing it myself, thank you.

Audio 3.02
So, in the future, three main trends are going to affect how people look for jobs and how employers hire candidates. The first of these is one that is already starting to take off: the use of Artificial Intelligence, or AI. This is already becoming more and more prevalent in the use of applicant tracking systems, chatbots and screening systems. For some positions, the number of applicants is so high that it's simply impractical for employers to devote the necessary time to read each application and give it the attention it deserves. For example, one company in the Northeast of England recently had over 14,000 applications when it expanded. So, companies ask potential candidates to complete a form online in order to filter out applicants who are highly unlikely to reach interview stage at the first hurdle, using carefully constructed algorithms which match the job requirements. In the future, there's a strong likelihood that this trend will go even further, meaning job seekers will have to become more comfortable communicating with – even talking to – machines. A benefit of this for companies is that they'll be able to spend more valuable and productive 'human time' face-to-face with potential employees.

The second major trend in the future of job searching is what I call the 'consumerisation' of job hunting. At the moment, some aspects of job searching are similar to internet shopping, with applicants using multiple platforms to look for jobs. This will undoubtedly continue in the future. Another aspect of this is that people looking for a job will increasingly look into the reputation of the company as an employer, reading several peer-written reviews before they decide to apply … much as they would if they were an online customer looking to buy a product. Companies will need to rethink their branding so that they not only appeal to their customer base, but also to potential employees. This will also affect how job hunters search for jobs. Using the job title as a search term will, through the use of algorithms, throw up related jobs which require similar skillsets. So, for example, if you search for 'office administrator', results might also include something like 'hotel receptionist', which you may not have considered before. While beneficial for the person looking for a job, it's also beneficial for the company as it enables it to draw from a wider pool of potential employees.

The third major trend in the future of job searching relates to your online presence. Now, we all know that when you're looking for a job, it's important not to do anything which will leave a problematic digital footprint that might damage your online presence, but, in the future, you'll need to go further than this and build your own online brand. Companies are already starting to approach hiring in '3D' terms: that is, what you look like on paper, in person and online. So, you'll need to be constantly alert to this, even when you're not actively seeking employment. This might involve creating your own website, though the odds are that most people will use dedicated platforms to build their personal professional brand.

Audio 3.03
1 morale
2 exacerbate
3 divisions
4 aggravate
5 boredom
6 alleviate
7 engender
8 distrust

Audio 3.04
Interviewer: With me on the programme today is Lucy Bishop MP, the minister for industry. Welcome to the programme.
Lucy: Thank you.
Interviewer: Can I start by asking you about your new skills initiative? What will it mean for British industry?
Lucy: OK, so the problem many companies today are facing is two-fold: newly qualified workers are coming into the workplace at entry level with the necessary qualifications, but lacking the actual skills they need to do some jobs effectively. Secondly, not enough people from disadvantaged backgrounds are getting well-paid jobs.
Interviewer: So, in other words, they need to employ more people from the poorer sectors of society, even if they don't have the right skills?
Lucy: Not at all. What I said was that overall, newly qualified workers need to be better equipped with the skills they need for a job, and this needs to be across the board.
Interviewer: So, what you're basically saying is this needs to be dealt with in education.
Lucy: Mm-hmm. Absolutely, that's exactly what I mean.
Interviewer: Please, correct me if I'm wrong, but doesn't that just involve throwing money at schools? Will that really solve the issue?
Lucy: No, you've got it all wrong. Let me rephrase that. The aim of the new skills initiative is for industry leaders to work more closely with the Department of Education in order to have an influence on how they shape the curriculum.
Interviewer: Am I right in thinking that this means that there will be more of a focus in schools on business and economics?
Lucy: That's not what I mean. OK, I'll put it another way. We need to equip students with the necessary skills they need in most jobs. Things like critical thinking, communication skills, creativity. These are important skills in all jobs, and they fit into all school subjects. My point is these need to be implemented in all schools across the country, not just the leading academies and so on. And if we're successful at the next election, that is exactly what we intend to do.
Interviewer: OK. That's all we have time for, I'm afraid. Lucy Bishop MP, thank you.
Lucy: Thank you.

Audio 3.05
1 So, what you're basically saying is that we need more investment.
2 But isn't that the opposite of what you said before?
3 Am I right in thinking you need this to work?
4 What I said was it's important for everyone.

Audio 3.06 and 3.07
A: I was really impressed with Lucy Bishop's interview. Her skills initiative sounds like a great idea.
B: So, in other words, you think it will solve all the problems in industry?
A: Ha no, not at all. What said was I think it's definitely going to be a force for good, especially in helping to tackle inequalities.
B: Am I right in thinking inequality is simply caused by people not having the right skills?
A: No, you've got it all wrong. But it's a still a major contributory factor.
B: Let me rephrase that. Surely other things are more important. Like good quality housing.
A: OK, let me put it another way. This new initiative is important, but it's one of many important factors.
B: Absolutely. That's exactly what I mean.

71

AUDIOSCRIPTS

Audio 3.09

Eliana: I've been thinking about applying for this internship being offered at a company near where I live. Do you think it's a good idea?

Harry: I think it's an excellent idea. You know I did a summer internship at a bank when I was at university, don't you?

Eliana: Did you? What was it like?

Harry: It was a great way to get experience, as long as it's in the field of work you later want to work in. I would just say, look into the company a bit first, though. You want to do it at a company which prioritises staff development over profit, otherwise you're just going to end up being someone who gets the coffees, cleans up after others, that sort of thing.

Eliana: Right, that makes sense. So, what exactly did your work there involve?

Harry: So, the first day I started, I had to sign an NDA, because obviously the bank deals with a lot of sensitive and personal information about their clients.

Eliana: An NDA? What's that?

Harry: A Non-Disclosure Agreement. It's basically a document where you say you won't reveal any information about the bank or its customers.

Eliana: Got you.

Harry: Then I was placed with someone to shadow – a different person each week. I'd tag along with them while they were working, making notes, sometimes doing short tasks they set me. It was a great way to learn first-hand what the job entails in practical terms. And the person I was shadowing seemed to like it, too. They'd often bounce ideas off me while working – I enjoyed that as it made me feel useful and respected, like a proper employee.

Eliana: That does sound useful, yeah.

Harry: I also had a supervisor, a bit like a sort of line manager. We'd meet up at the end of each week and review what I'd learnt that week. I could ask questions about anything I wasn't sure of, and she'd ask me questions about what I might do differently. She also asked me how I could use what I'd learnt that week in the following week. That was a great way of reviewing and learning everything.

Eliana: I think I'm going to go for it, then. It sounds really useful. Any advice for a successful internship?

Harry: Let me think … Well, I guess the first thing to keep in mind is to dress and act professionally at all times. Don't fall into the trap of thinking that you're not a real employee. You essentially are, and you're doing real work.

Eliana: Yes, of course.

Harry: Also, don't take on more work than you can handle. When I first started, I didn't want to seem 'difficult' so I took on all the tasks I was given and it nearly burnt me out! Don't be afraid to say 'no' sometimes.

Eliana: OK.

Harry: And don't be afraid to make mistakes. Remember that it's all new for you at first, so you're bound to get some things wrong. Everyone makes mistakes sometimes. The point is to try and learn from them. That's the real learning process.

Eliana: Thanks, Harry. You've definitely persuaded me!

UNIT 4

Audio 4.01

1 We need to think about how to raise funding.
2 Who's going to back our project?
3 I've always wanted to pursue my ambition.
4 Wow, they're really pushing the limits!
5 It's interesting, but I don't see how it serves science.
6 I just wanted to satisfy my curiosity, really.

Audio 4.02

1 Can you help me spread the word about our organisation?
2 Some mornings I just don't feel like I can face the day.
3 Some people in society struggle to make ends meet.
4 Why not give them a helping hand?

Audio 4.03

Presenter: Some of the biggest challenges modern charities face, especially in these uncertain times, include that of how to raise funding and spread the word about what they're trying to do. I'm joined today by two enterprising people who work for charities, to share their innovative ideas. First up is Caleb Ward, who works for the charity ScotKids, which helps disadvantaged children in Scotland. Caleb, you've created an app, is that right?

Caleb: Yes, that's right. We always get requests from donors asking to see how their donations are spent. With this in mind, we always try to post success stories on our website and social media. But then, one day a while back, I thought to myself, why not go one step further? I have a background in computer science – I worked in IT before I joined the charity – so I decided to make an app which enables users to track in real time where their money's being spent.

Presenter: Wow! So how does that work?

Caleb: It's actually very simple. When someone makes a donation, that money is assigned a tracking number as it goes into our account. Whenever money is withdrawn or spent, the tracking number follows it, and the user gets a notification on their app, showing how much has been spent and exactly what on. It's great because it makes for more transparency within our organisation. This then has a knock-on effect on how people perceive us. They become more appreciative of our work and they're encouraged to donate more. So far, the app's been downloaded nearly a thousand times, so it's popular, too.

Presenter: That sounds amazing, thank you Caleb! Next, we turn to Megan Lamb, founder of ImpactVest, which has been described as 'the human face of investment'. Megan, tell us about your organisation.

Megan: Yeah, so we've been around for a while now. In fact by early next year, we'll have been running for ten years. What we aim to do is match people in third-world countries with people in this country who want to invest ethically and in a way which has a direct impact on people's personal lives in those places. And there are a whole range of business types waiting for investment, from comedians and musicians working in the entertainment industry to small shop owners.

Presenter: So how does it work, exactly?

Megan: Let's say you have someone in South America who owns a small hairdressers. Business is going well and they want to expand to a bigger place and hire more staff, but they don't have the funds to do it. They post on our website, answering questions about their business plan. Investors can browse these posts on our site, pick one they like the look of, and then invest part or the whole of the sum required. Once they've invested, they get regular updates on how the money's being spent and what their returns are. It's sort of venture capitalism, I guess, but on a smaller, more human scale.

Presenter: It sounds wonderful! And I guess it works well, since you've been running it for so long?

Megan: It's been incredibly successful, yes. It's great for the people who need the investment capital and great for people to see the good that their money is doing in real, practical terms.

Audio 4.04

On the whole, most respondents tended to agree with some form of compulsory community service for 16-year-olds. Having said that, many people expressed a concern that this shouldn't go too far. To cite one example, one respondent stated that this should by no means include military service. Generally speaking, though, most people thought community service was a good idea in principle and some element of it should be included as part of educational life. Their interest presumably reflected the fact that they feel young people should do more to help strengthen local communities while learning important lessons about life. Our impression was simply that this idea is perceived as a positive thing.

The consensus seems to be that young people should be made to do things like run errands for elderly residents or tend community gardens. One might speculate that this could be during school hours, and form part of their means to gain a general secondary education certificate. The overall picture was one of approval, but with some key reservations, as mentioned earlier.

Audio 4.05

1 Having said that, many people expressed a concern that this shouldn't go too far.
2 To cite one example, a respondent stated that this should by no means include military service.
3 Generally speaking though, most people thought community service was a good idea.

AUDIOSCRIPTS

Audio 4.06 and 4.07
When asked if they would make use of young volunteers, the overall picture was one of enthusiasm. To cite one example, an elderly respondent stated that she would welcome help collecting her medication from the chemist. Another illustration of this was a respondent who said he would like to see young people out picking up litter during school hours. Their interest presumably reflected the fact that not only would they appreciate the help, but it would be useful for the young people themselves. One might speculate that they believed young people would learn the value of community relationships. The consensus seems to be that this idea would be good for everyone.

Audio 4.08
I'm near the town of San Felipe, on the Baja California peninsula in Mexico. We're hoping to see the world's rarest animal, the *Phocoena sinus*, or what's locally called the vaquita, an affectionate name meaning 'little cow'. It is, of course, nothing like a cow, as this cute little mammal is a porpoise which closely resembles a dolphin, with a large dark ring around its eyes and a dark grey hue over its top surface. Females grow up to 150 cm long, whereas their male counterparts grow to around 140 cm long. This makes it the smallest of all cetaceans, a group which includes whales, dolphins and other porpoises.

The vaquita roams the very top end of the Gulf of California, and loves the warm, shallow waters with its abundance of smaller fish, crustaceans and squid. An unfortunate disadvantage of this lifestyle, however, is that living so close to the shoreline makes it susceptible to pollution from land run-off. It will swim away quickly, though, if disturbed, so we're playing a bit of a waiting game as quietly as possible. However, the main culprit for its decline is the illegal fishing industry, as the vaquita is often caught up and drowned in gillnets, huge vertical nets which sort of sweep up everything they encounter.

Vaquita numbers have fallen drastically in recent years, and sadly it's now on the brink of extinction. Having only been discovered in 1958, by 1997 there were an estimated 567 left in this bay. By 2007, this number had fallen to around 150. Eleven years later, there were only 19, and today there are believed to be fewer than ten in the wild. They truly are set to disappear, which is heart-breaking.

Attempts to breed them in captivity have failed miserably. In 2017 one captured female was so traumatised that she died. So it ended up doing more harm than good. Alas, as the sun begins to set over these shallow waters, we haven't been able to see any vaquita today. But tomorrow brings a new dawn and a fresh opportunity for us to get a glimpse. Let's just hope there are fresh opportunities for this beautiful, but dwindling population in the future, too.

UNIT 5

Audio 5.01
1 What I hate most is when people lie to me.
2 Under no circumstances should you attempt to lift this without help.
3 It felt like the longest ever, that meeting.
4 That customer you were talking to, what did she want?
5 All I needed was a bit more time.
6 When I'm going to have time to finish this, I have no idea.

Audio 5.02
1 Having lost the game, the team walked off the pitch miserably.
2 Being an experienced salesperson, Talita knew how to win customers round.
3 Produced by Paul Simmons, the film was a roaring success.
4 Having shut my computer down, I remembered that I needed some important files from it.

Audio 5.03 and 5.04
Man: They took everything, my life savings. I feel so stupid for falling for it and don't know if I'll ever get any of it back.
Presenter: Every year, innocent people in the UK have stories to tell about how they have fallen prey to scammers, a crime which costs the country millions. And their tactics are becoming ever more duplicitous as they distort information to achieve their goal. So what are the types of scams they're using, and how can we protect ourselves? With me today is Dorian Price, founder of moneysafe.com, which helps people avoid the worst of these scams. Welcome, Dorian.
Dorian: Thank you. Well, maybe I can start by telling your listeners about some of the most common scams out there at the moment.
Presenter: Yes, please.
Dorian: So one of the most common is what are called authorised push payments, or APP for short, when fraudsters get you to move your money. What happens is, contacting you by phone, they claim to be from your bank, saying that you've been a victim of fraud and your account details have been compromised. They then ask you to urgently move your money to another account to keep it safe, when, in fact, …
Presenter: It's not a safe account.
Dorian: Exactly. You're basically just paying it directly to them. A lot of people have experienced this type of scam happening when they're about to make a large payment, say, for example, a deposit for a house or a new car, something like that. Having intercepted your payment details, they're able to redirect the money to their account via a phone call or a false website.
Man: I was in the process of buying a new car when they called. It all seemed so legit, so real. Before I knew it, they'd cleared out my account.
Presenter: Ouch. So what can people do to avoid this?
Dorian: Well, for a start, the law here changed recently and banks now have to provide what's called a Confirmation of Payment service. This means whenever you make a bank transfer, they check the name of the payee and that it's a real account. But you shouldn't rely on banks and other organisations to protect you. If you get a phone call and you feel uneasy or even have the slightest inkling that it's not legit, it's important that you phone the people who supposedly called you straight away, whether it's the bank or property developer or whoever, and verify the call you've just received was actually from them. Avoid contacting them by email as these can easily be intercepted.
Presenter: Sage advice there.
Dorian: So, another common scam we hear about is what's called synthetic identity fraud. Looking to obtain a loan or other funds under false pretences, scammers will create an entirely fictional identity, made up from a mix of credentials from different real people, with some embellished details. So, for example, they might use your email address and a made-up name. This can come back to bite you as your address will then be associated with bad credit.
Woman: I didn't find out until it was too late. I went to take out a new contract from an internet provider and got refused. It turns out, when I requested my credit report, there were several black marks against my name. I'm at a complete loss as to how they managed it.
Presenter: So what can people do?
Dorian: The main thing is to use strong passwords. Most browsers will invent very strong passwords for you, and remember them. And don't use the same password for everything. Also, make use of two-step authentication where possible when you log in.
Presenter: That's where you get an additional, temporary password sent to your phone, right?
Dorian: Yep, that's the one.
Presenter: Any other advice to stay safe from scams?
Dorian: Yes. Check your credit report every month for any unusual signs. And when doing anything financial online, always check the URLs carefully. Often sites which mimic others look very similar, but will have one or two minor differences. And, finally, the first time you buy from a website, do a search for reviews of the site. Let's say a travel site is offering a really good deal on flights. Before you click 'buy now', check how they've dealt with customers in the past. You may well just see a ream of comments saying 'avoid at all costs!'
Presenter: Dorian Price, thank you.

Audio 5.05 and 5.06
Thanks for coming today, and showing an interest in Better Presentations Ltd. To be perfectly honest, you couldn't do better than taking one of our courses on presenting. Just consider for a moment the benefits of being able to bring people round to your way of thinking. You'll give a great presentation and people will come up to you at the end and say things like, 'That was awesome!' and you'll feel like a cat that's just got a big old plate of cream. After doing one of our presenting courses, there'll be no last-minute panic before you get up on stage, no cold sweats the night before, no fear of forgetting what you're going to say. Not only will you be able to present more calmly, you'll also be more likely to sell your idea. So what are you waiting for? Nothing, that's what! And when it's time to give your next presentation, you'll be cool, calm and collected.

AUDIOSCRIPTS

Audio 5.07
1 The software is robust, reliable and rapid.
2 Our product is cool, creative and captivating.
3 The walk is barefoot, bewildering and beautiful.
4 The film is magnificent, mysterious and magical.

Audio 5.08
Presenter: Today I'd like to tell you about virtual reality games. Perhaps you've played them with the kids, or with friends. But just consider for a moment the benefits they could bring to the workplace. Not only would VR games be a good way to let off steam, but they could also help build strong bonds between members of your team. If it were up to me, and I ran a company, I would definitely give them a try. VR games can be seen as a huge opportunity and a huge breakthrough when it comes to the team-building exercises you can do without anyone needing to leave the office. So come on, what have you been waiting for? VR is a way to get your staff doing something cool, collaborative and creative.

Audio 5.09
Cora: When I grew up in California, my parents weren't really around much. They struggled with their own issues career-wise and often didn't have time for me. I was constantly passed around to different family members and had this deep sense of being a burden to them. That was until I met my friend Tamra, and she took me to her house for dinner one day and I met her mom. She was just this big, warm, friendly woman who took an instant shine to me, I think. She always had an open house for me and made me feel loved. She knew about my home situation – or lack of it – and always cooked me meals, even bought me clothes and presents on my birthday. She also took me on vacation with her family a few times. It was just awesome. As I grew up, I started to realise more and more how kind she really was. Nothing ever seemed to upset or faze her. She could handle herself well in any situation, no matter how bad, and, more than anything, she always put me and Tamra first. She's definitely been the biggest role model to me in my life, and I hope when I have children I go down the same path as her, in the way she treated us.

Ed: I think my biggest role model career-wise was an ex-boss of mine. When I first came to work at that company, we clicked straight away. I think she saw something in me that I didn't see in myself. She not only supported me, but also pushed me to do things I didn't think I could do. Like, one time there was an opportunity for one of our teams to speak at a national conference. Being the youngest, least experienced member of the team, I didn't for one minute think it was something I could – or should – do. You can imagine my shock, then, when she came and asked me to do it. My first reaction was just to say, 'Look, I don't think I have enough experience', but she insisted that I was the best person for the job. Over the coming weeks, we had regular meetings where I'd run my ideas past her and she'd offer feedback, so that, in the end, I felt confident in giving the talk. It went well and I felt really proud of myself. I'd achieved something I didn't think was possible. Years later, we work at different places, but we're still in touch and she helps me out sometimes when I need ideas or have to solve problems at work. I think of her as kind of like my mentor. It's great to have that support when I need it.

UNIT 6

Audio 6.01
1 He thinks he's going to have an easy day, but it's actually the worst of his career.
2 When he arrives at the museum, the squid is nowhere to be seen.
3 He thinks she loves him, but actually she's in love with another.
4 After all the twists and turns in the story, we find out it was Edmonson all along.

Audio 6.02
1 Some people love their work, and some people hate it.
2 Some days he's quite unwell and others he's remarkably healthy.
3 Last week was absolutely hectic, but this week it's relatively quiet.
4 The meaning of songs can be quite complex or perfectly clear.

Audio 6.03 and 6.04
Presenter: I'm lucky enough to be joined on today's show by Kyle Luma and Luke Allen, two members of Red Shift, the popular jazz fusion band with their rich sound emboldened by their brilliant lead vocalist, Katy Dumas, and drummer Steffi Boateng – one of the best in the business in my opinion. Guys, you've obviously had a lot of success recently, and I have to say your music is so emotionally charged that it sometimes reduces me to tears! Kyle, what advice would you have for any new bands out there? What can they do to make it?

Kyle: I think the simple answer is you need to get lucky! It's an incredibly difficult business to break into, so you need an opportunity to get yourself heard by as many people as possible.

Presenter: Of course, yes. But it's more than just luck, though, isn't it? I mean, you need to have some substance to what you create. Do you agree, Luke?

Luke: Yeah, Kyle's right, though, you do need luck. With any type of success you've got to have something that's worth sharing, something people can relate to. You need to take a good look at where music is today and get a feel for the direction it's heading in. So, we all met at college, and we soon discovered we had a mutual love for the type of punchy, rousing sound that we play. I could already play the saxophone and so we got the idea of putting a band together.

Presenter: And how did that happen? Kyle?

Kyle: I think that brings us on to another point. The really crucial, key thing that makes up a band is its members. I realise that sounds obvious, but it's not just about how well people in your band can play, it's about how well you play together. That's the thing about music: it's more than the sum of its parts. When good musicians get together and they're a good fit, what they produce is poignant and beautiful.

Luke: And not just in the music. It's important to get on socially, too. If you don't all click, it will show in the music. Luckily, we all get on really well in the band, and I think that's really a key part of our success. When we get together to rehearse, it doesn't feel like work. We all just really have a lot of fun.

Presenter: So, how did you create your unique sound?

Luke: When we first started we just played covers of songs we all really like and can relate to. I think that's an important first step in a new band. You need the real sense of direction that brings. And more than that, it gives you a real feel for playing the type of music you eventually want to get to. Nowadays, we even play the odd cover as a warm up, or just for fun. But, these days, the song writing mainly comes from Kyle. The man's a genius!

Kyle: I don't know about that. But it's true that I do most of the writing. Occasionally, we'll just be together in the studio and jamming together and an idea will be born out of that. But most of the time I get an idea when I'm at home, just mucking about on a keyboard or something, and develop words and a melody out of that. I'll bring it to the next band practice and then other people will add little riffs here and there, and, then, before we know it, we end up with a new hit.

Presenter: Kyle and Luke, really great to talk with you. And congratulations on your latest album.

Audio 6.05
A while back I spent a few years living in Rio de Janeiro in Brazil, teaching English. I'd not been there very long when some friends I had in another city invited me over to visit them for the weekend. They were like, 'It's easy, you can get a cheap flight over on Friday night after work, then fly back Sunday evening.' Being new to the country, I wasn't that sure about travelling to somewhere even newer, you know what I mean? But I thought to myself, yeah, why not? And booked myself a return flight.

So, on the Friday afternoon, I left work with a pre-packed bag and headed to the bus stop to get a bus to the airport. Funny, I hadn't really thought about this part of the journey, as I was more concerned about the flight and getting to my friends. I suddenly realised I didn't have a clue which bus to get. Buses in Rio are great, there are so many of them you can get pretty much anywhere quite easily, but that also makes them a bit confusing when you're new to the city. So, I stopped someone on the street with my very basic Portuguese and I was like, 'Um … aeroporto? Bus?' And they told me to get the number 40 and

AUDIOSCRIPTS

where to catch it from. When I got to the bus stop, up pulled a number 40. My luck was in … or so I thought.

Rio's a beautiful city, but I didn't want to get lost in it. The bus wound its way through the busy streets for a while, but then it headed into some remote area of the city I didn't recognise at all. There wasn't anything like an airport in sight. It was one of those moments when you realise you've made a mistake and that bad feeling sinks in. We pulled into what looked like a bus station, so I thought, great, I can get off here and change to the right bus.

So, I got off and the bus drove away. I was left in this sort of eerily quiet bus station, feeling totally lost! That was when this friendly stranger came rushing up to me and he was like, 'where are you trying to go?' in English. I said the airport and that's when he said, 'That bus there! Quick!' I looked up and saw the bus that was just about leave. It was a number 14.

Audio 6.06
1 I always like to be active on holiday – climbing, cycling, running, stuff like that.
2 She turned round and she was like, 'Why don't we rent a car?'
3 It was sort of smooth and chocolatey.

Audio 6.07
A few years ago, I was on holiday with a friend in Turkey and one day he suggested we hire a car and see a bit of the countryside and mountains, stuff like that. I wasn't sure at first, but then he was like, 'Come on, it'll be an adventure.' So, we went into town and found this little car rental place. We told them where we wanted to go and the guy working there suggested we hire this sort of mini jeep thing. We agreed.

It wasn't long before we were racing along beautiful rugged country roads, and it really was truly beautiful, you know what I mean? Gradually the road started to twist and turn, and climb up a hill. We got to this one corner and started to really climb the hill, but it just got steeper and steeper, and the car got slower and slower, until it came to a stop. It was one of those moments when you start to panic, and, as I felt the car engine grind, I was like, 'Do you know what? I think you need to get out, sorry!' So, my friend hopped out and I was able to get the car under control and move it. After that, we turned around and went back. That was enough adventure!

Audio 6.08
Presenter: Welcome to *All About Design*. I'm joined on the podcast today by Professor Mandy Baker, professor of design at Manningford University. Professor Baker, welcome to the show.
Mandy: Thanks for inviting me. And call me Mandy, please.
Presenter: Thank you. So, Mandy, what can you tell us about the future of design?
Mandy: Well, it seems pretty clear to me that the biggest development in design in the future – and it's happening already – is the use of Artificial Intelligence, or AI. This is going to make more people become designers alongside their usual job, and traditional designers by profession won't hold the monopoly on skills.
Presenter: And how will that work?
Mandy: Well, to understand the role of a designer, you first have to look at their core skill set. It includes empathy, problem-framing, creativity in problem-solving, negotiation and persuasion.
Presenter: That sounds a bit like the role of a good manager.
Mandy: Exactly! And so, more and more, I think we're going to see managers take on design roles as the software becomes available to help them do so.
Presenter: So, does that mean us designers are going to be out of a job?
Mandy: In fact, it's going to create more work for you, but in a different way!
Presenter: How so?
Mandy: So, the AI software that exists now is able to harness clever algorithms which can churn out hundreds of variations on a design in an instant. It's used in video games, which are able to create entire vast universes while you play them.
Presenter: I see. I've seen some games like that, where you explore space, for example.
Mandy: Yes, that's it. So, in future, the role of a designer will be to set that up, if you like. They'll set the goals, parameters and constraints, then review and fine-tune what the AI supplies them with.
Presenter: Fascinating. So rather than creating design, it's more like they'll be there to curate it?
Mandy: Exactly. And because designers will be able to explore huge numbers of alternatives in a fraction of the time it takes them today, they'll be able to massively upscale their productivity.
Presenter: Wow, I see. That's actually quite exciting.
Mandy: That's right, so don't worry, your job's safe!
Presenter: Phew!

UNIT 7

Audio 7.01
1 I don't want to sit on the fence.
2 It's time to stop umming and ahhing.
3 You need to dig your heels in.
4 It's easy to just take the path of least resistance.
5 I'm in a bit of a quandary over this.
6 Ooh, we're really spoilt for choice!

Audio 7.02
1 Don't just skip to the end!
2 No need to obsess about it.
3 Do you give in?
4 This will help protect you against illness.
5 We need to set aside some time to talk.
6 I'm going to comment on this article.

Audio 7.03 and 7.04
Presenter: With me today on the programme is Professor Gwen King, professor of neurology at Northern University. Professor King, one of the things we've been talking about on the show this week is people's changing reading habits. Recent studies have shown that many people now prefer listening to audiobooks rather than reading books, whether that's online or print copies. At the same time, people often feel a little embarrassed by this, as they feel like they're 'cheating'. Are they right to feel like this?
Gwen: Well, that's a common misconception. The truth is, both reading the printed word and listening to audiobooks are both beneficial to the brain, but in slightly different ways.
Presenter: How so?
Gwen: So, when you read, a number of parts of your brain are involved. Reading involves cognitive processing, attention, reasoning, language comprehension, memory, visual processing and motor control of your eyes. So, poring over text, even if it's not particularly heavy-going, is a good, if you like, 'work out' for different parts of your brain. In fact, some studies have even shown that regular reading can increase your lifespan.
Presenter: That's fascinating. So, what about listening to stories?
Gwen: Well, listening has exactly the same benefits, except for, obviously, visual processing and motor control of your eyes.
Presenter: The visual skills.
Gwen: Precisely. And both reading and listening to stories benefit your brain in terms of making sense of the plot of the story. But we use different parts of our brain when we process speech to those for written words. However, listening to stories comes with its own benefits. When we listen to a performance, we can feel the emotions of the characters instead of having to imagine them, so it can help us develop empathy.
Presenter: I guess you can multitask, too. I often listen to audiobooks while I'm driving or pottering around in the garden, something like that.
Gwen: Indeed, but that's where books also have an advantage.
Presenter: In what way?
Gwen: Well, books are better at holding our attention, and paying attention is another skill we use when reading. Also, if you do get distracted, it's easier to get back to the place where you left it.
Presenter: Of course. I sometimes find my mind wandering to other things I'm doing when I listen to an audiobook, and it can be tricky getting back to the exact spot. Or the doorbell goes and I forget to pause it or something. When I'm reading, I might find I've just read a paragraph and not really taken it in, but then it's easy to go back and find my place.
Gwen: Yes, and, also when you're reading, turning each page gives your eyes a tiny sort of break, which allows your brain to process what you've just read. But, either way,

AUDIOSCRIPTS

the most important skills involved in both reading and listening to books are the ones to do with processing content, and they're the highest-level skills. This, in effect, means that both reading and listening to books are good for your brain.

Presenter: I can just imagine the sighs of relief from our listeners at hearing that! Professor King, thank you.

Audio 7.05 and 7.06

A: My sister's coming to stay this weekend, with her kids. I was thinking of taking them to the zoo. What do you reckon?
B: Well, maybe it's just me, but I'm not really a fan of zoos. I think they're a bit cruel if I'm honest.
A: Really? Well, I would say the opposite. I mean, I'm no expert, but I think they do a lot to raise awareness about conservation and the plight of endangered species.
B: Yeah, there is that I suppose. There are some things that I agree with about what they do, but I just think that they're an out-dated concept. And not all of the animals are endangered, are they?
A: True, but what about the research they do into animals at zoos? I'm guessing it would be a big loss to science if we got rid of them.
B: Yeah, but I think it's much better to observe animals in their natural environment.
A: Of course, but in the wild some animals are vulnerable to poaching, forcing them to the brink of extinction.
B: Obviously, you've got to have some controls, but I think building zoos is going too far. If you watch animals in the wild, on something like a safari, then you see them behave more naturally.
A: I get you. And the idea has a lot going for it, but I don't think we'll have time to travel there in a weekend!
B: Ha! No, of course not!

Audio 7.07 and 7.08

A: I think the government needs to be building more houses. House prices have gone through the roof!
B: Well, maybe it's just me, but I'm not sure that's the solution. We've destroyed enough of the natural environment already.
A: So what is the solution?
B: I'm no expert, but there must be some sort of economic measure they can take.
A: I mean, obviously you can't just build houses anywhere, but the fact is that there aren't enough houses for everyone.
B: I just think that destroying natural habitats to make way for housing is a worrying problem.
A: Hmm, perhaps we need to start reducing our living space, so more flats and fewer houses.
B: Hmm, the idea has a lot going for it, but it's still going to mean we encroach further on habitats.
A: Well, I would say at least it's a partial solution.
B: There are some things I agree with in relation to housing, but we urgently need to protect the environment.
A: Absolutely.

Audio 7.09

Good morning everyone, I trust you all had a good weekend. Today we're going to start by taking a look at consumer choice theory. The basic foundation for this theory is that consumers buy things in order to achieve the most satisfaction possible. Now, there are three assumptions to this, which you can see on this slide. The first of these is what's called utility maximisation. This means that customers make calculated choices based on what they perceive will make them happiest. This might mean buying a more expensive version of something because they feel the quality is better, or perhaps the cheapest because spending less will make them happier. The second principle is that of non-satiation. This assumes that no matter what consumers opt for, they'll never be totally satisfied. So, taken with the first principle, consumers aim to be as happy as possible, but they'll never be fully satisfied with what they purchase. The third assumption behind the theory is known as decreasing marginal utility. This states that the amount of satisfaction you gain from a purchase decreases gradually over time.

This theory is useful for companies, especially during times of boom or bust, as it allows them to calculate the relationship between what prices to set and the state of the economy at any given time, which as you all know, is termed 'the demand curve'.

However, in recent years consumer choice theory has come in for a lot criticism, for a number of reasons. The primary assumption, utility maximisation, makes the mistake of assuming that consumers always act rationally. But they don't. An example of this is impulse buying, which is something most retailers try to take advantage of. Perhaps people might be in a hurry and not have time to make the best choice. Or they might simply be feeling overwhelmed at the amount of choice available, so they just pick the first or nearest product. Perhaps a certain product makes a consumer think of a happier time, or they're feeling down and want to buy something to cheer themselves up. Or perhaps the item that a consumer really wants to buy isn't available so, rather than skip the purchase – if it's a small one – they might look for a quick substitute. The point is, consumer choice theory is now regarded as too simplistic. In effect, rather than looking at how consumers behave, it portrays a somewhat idealistic view of how customers *should* behave. And with that, we're going to move on to the next topic: behavioural economics.

UNIT 8

Audio 8.01
1 Nobody knows for certain what the long-term effects will be.
2 You might need to step outside your comfort zone.
3 Do you think you're in good shape?
4 She has a rare gift for remembering people's faces.

Audio 8.02
1 They'll have received the package by now.
2 They come in and leave mud all over the carpet!
3 You'll have to show me how to use it.
4 We'll need more time.

Audio 8.03 and 8.04

Presenter: With me on the podcast today is Declan Howard, a professor of psychology. We're going to be discussing the rare condition known as mirror-touch synaesthesia. So, what is it exactly, Declan?
Declan: Well, as you probably know, synaesthesia involves the mixing of two or more senses, that aren't usually connected, so people with synaesthesia might see sounds as colour, or even taste sounds.
Presenter: Right.
Declan: With mirror-touch synaesthesia, people feel sensations that other people feel. So, for example, if they see someone stub their toe, they'll feel that pain.
Presenter: Oh, that sounds quite distressing.
Declan: Yes, it can be, for obvious reasons. But it's not just unpleasant sensations. One person I spoke to said that whenever she saw someone else being hugged, she felt like she was getting a hug, too.
Presenter: So, it's a bit like empathy?
Declan: Um, yes, a bit, except it sort of goes further than that. These are real sensations, so if you were to, say, see someone grasp another person's arm, you'd actually feel like your arm was being grasped, too.
Presenter: We know it's a rare condition, but just how rare?
Declan: According to several studies carried out here and in the US, it's estimated that it affects between 1.6% and 2.5% of the population.
Presenter: You mention studies into the condition. How are they carried out?
Declan: Well, different studies take different forms. In one of them, people are touched on different cheeks while they watch an assistant being touched on their cheeks. In what's known as a congruent study, the participants are touched on the same cheeks as the assistant that they're looking at. In an incongruent study, participants are touched on different cheeks to that of the assistant, and asked to report back which cheek they feel being touched. If it's a different one to where they were actually physically touched, then it's likely they have the condition.
Presenter: And is there any treatment available for sufferers of the condition?
Declan: Treatment mainly involves therapy, and might include things like imagining there's an invisible wall separating the synaesthete from the person they're looking at. In some cases, prescription medicines normally used to treat anxiety and depression can be effective. But that's all assuming the person wants to be treated.
Presenter: Why might they not want to be treated? It all sounds quite overwhelming to me!
Declan: Well that brings me back to a word you mentioned earlier – empathy. It mostly occurs in people who have – as you'd imagine – higher levels of empathy towards others, and many see that as a good thing.
Presenter: And is it a condition people are born with?

AUDIOSCRIPTS

Declan: It can be, but it can also be acquired. It's a bit more common in people who have had a limb removed. Quite a few amputees complain of feeling pain in missing limbs, when they see other people experiencing pain in that limb.
Presenter: Fascinating! Thanks, Declan. Join us again next week and don't forget to subscribe!

Audio 8.05
Presenter: It's recently been reported that doctors have been prescribing gardening or even just spending time in nature to help with anxiety and depression. Well on today's programme I'm joined by TV gardening personality Gerald Butler to discuss exactly that. Welcome, Gerald. So, is gardening really helpful?
Gerald: Absolutely. It's just beneficial in so many ways. You've only got to look at the fact that it's been really successful so far for so many people, not just in alleviating the symptoms of stress and anxiety.
Presenter: In what ways, specifically?
Gerald: I think a big plus for me is that it's taught me over the years to become a more patient person. You do everything you can for young plants and they don't seem to grow much at first, and then you realise it's not that you haven't done enough for them, it's just that you have to simply leave them and wait. Nature is an incredibly powerful force that affects everyone, and sometimes you just have to wait for it to do its magic. That's what I get out of it, anyway.
Presenter: Well yes, and a successful career, of course!
Gerald: Yes, of course! Ah, well, it's not about that for a lot of people, it's about what goes through your mind when you're nurturing – tending to – your plants. And studies show that as well as providing the ideal conditions for you to unwind, gardening can also kick-start your brain and help you focus on things. I get some of my best ideas when gardening. The point is that you're spending time with living things. You care for them, protect them. It really is a labour of love.
Presenter: And then you get to reap the rewards come harvest time.
Gerald: Absolutely, you really feel like you've accomplished something. And another real positive about that is the things you've grown yourself always taste better. Whether they actually do or whether it's just a psychological effect isn't really important, but food always tastes better when you know you've grown it yourself. And looking at all the benefits, of course doctors are prescribing it to help people's mental well-being.
Presenter: Well, you've convinced me. Time to don my gardening gloves, I think!

Audio 8.06
1 It's not that gardening is difficult, it's just that many people don't have the time.
2 The point isn't to produce lots of vegetables, the point is to spend time outside.
3 It's not about growing the best food, it's about caring for the plants.

Audio 8.07 and 8.08
A: What do you do to maintain your well-being?
B: Crafting. I really like making things, especially 'upcycling' old things for a different purpose.
A: And what things have you made?
B: Ha, not much so far! But it's not about completing things for me. The point is that it's something to focus on, and that helps reduce anxiety and alleviate the symptoms of stress. That's what I get out of it, anyway.
A: Nice to have something to help focus your mind.
B: Exactly. And it's just beneficial in so many ways. As well as helping me unwind, another real positive about upcycling is that it's good for the environment.
A: Because you're repurposing things which would otherwise go to landfill, right?
B: Exactly. You've only got to look at my latest project, where I turned an old car tyre into a seat. That's one less tyre they had to get rid of.
A: Fantastic!

Audio 8.09
Presenter: With me today is Sara Lin, an expert in psychology. She's just written a book on psychological illusions and effects. Sara, your book makes for very interesting reading, I must say.
Sara: Thank you.
Presenter: One idea that kept cropping up in the book is that of the Pratfall Effect. Can you tell us a bit about that?
Sara: Sure. So, the basic principle is that highly competent or successful people – or at least those who we view as such – become more likeable when they make a mistake, or 'pratfall'.
Presenter: I see. So, for example, if a famous actor slips up on the red carpet when arriving at an awards ceremony, we like them more, feel empathy for them?
Sara: Yes, that's a good example. And you feel it more when it's someone like that than when it's your average Joe on the street.
Presenter: Right.
Sara: So, this effect was first studied by the social psychologist Elliot Aronson in 1966. What he did was to gather together a group of forty-eight participants and organise them into four groups, and then play a different recording to each group. The first group listened to someone, perceived as 'superior' by the participants, answering a series of trivia questions.
Presenter: How did he get them to think the person was superior?
Sara: At the start of the recording, the person would introduce themselves, saying things like 'I was a high school honours student, I was on the school track team', that kind of thing.
Presenter: Got it.
Sara: Yeah, so that was the first group. And the person answered ninety percent of the trivia questions correctly. The second group was played a recording of someone answering the same trivia questions, but this person was perceived to be 'average' and only answered thirty percent of the questions correctly.
Presenter: And was that seen as the 'pratfall'?
Sara: Ah, no, here comes the interesting bit. The third and fourth groups listened to the same recordings, but the actor on them announced at one point, 'Oh no, I've spilled coffee all over my new suit!'
Presenter: Ah, I see.
Sara: So, then, after listening to these recordings, the participants in each group answered a series of survey questions, and it turns out that the 'superior' person seemed more attractive to the group which heard the announcement about the coffee.
Presenter: Interesting.
Sara: Indeed, but not just that. The person seen as average actually became less attractive to the group which heard the announcement about the coffee.
Presenter: Oh! That's fascinating Sara. Now I wonder if I could ask you about another …

77

ANSWER KEY

UNIT 1

Lesson 1A
VOCABULARY
1. 1 b 2 c 3 c 4 a 5 a 6 b 7 a 8 b
2. 1 towel
   2 tack
   3 up about
   4 knock
   5 flies
   6 making
   7 along
   8 give
   9 out for
   10 fair

GRAMMAR
3. 1 c 2 b 3 a 4 b
4. 1 Provided that
   2 But for
   3 Without knowing
   4 If I were to
   5 Unless
   6 Should
5. 1 to take your ID, you won't be able to get in
   2 my teacher's help/the help of my teacher, I would have failed the exam
   3 we miss our flight, we can just take the next one
   4 slow driving, we would have been on time
   5 spent more time studying, you would have got better grades
   6 Were Lily to prepare the meal, everyone would love it

PRONUNCIATION
6A 1 If you have
   2 If it's not
   3 If people properly
   4 If we leave
   5 If that rings
   6 If it's not

READING
7. b
8. 1 Tod Ibarra ('absolute twaddle'; 'If I were to trot out these trite inspirational phrases'; 'a complete fallacy')
   2 Roman Hughes ('The whole idea of success is a very personal thing, and obviously success means different things to different people.')
   3 Tod Ibarra ('Being successful is about getting results. If my team doesn't get results, my company won't survive. It's as simple as that.')
   4 Isla Boyer ('And that's why I make sure I do my best – with every word I write.')
   5 Roman Hughes ('In order to be successful, you first need to define what success means to you.')
   6 Isla Boyer ('I'm talking about how people feel after they've read my stories. If the words have moved them in some way, then I know I've done my job, more so if that effect remains with them.')
9. 1 F ('That's the key, I think. In order to be successful, you first need to define what success means to you.')
   2 T ('So in that sense, the conventional wisdom definitely rings true.')
   3 F ('If I were to trot out these trite inspirational phrases … we wouldn't be where we are today.')
   4 T ('Doing your best is obviously important … but in the adult world of business it's patently not true.')
   5 T ('It might appear on the face of things that being a successful author is a clear-cut thing to measure – you get your book published. But to me, it's more complex than that.')
   6 T ('I think you have to be lucky and get a break at some point, but it's what you do with that luck that counts.')

Lesson 1B
VOCABULARY (collocations: education)
1. 1 striving
   2 find
   3 maintain
   4 deliver
   5 develop
   6 focusing
   7 take
   8 fulfilling
2. 1 quality
   2 rigorous
   3 nurturing
   4 mutual
   5 good

PRONUNCIATION
3B 1 <u>take</u> the <u>in</u>itiative
   2 ful<u>fil</u> your po<u>ten</u>tial
   3 <u>striv</u>ing for <u>ex</u>cellence
   4 <u>nur</u>turing en<u>vi</u>ronment
   5 <u>rig</u>orous <u>stan</u>dards
   6 <u>mu</u>tual re<u>spect</u>
   7 <u>fos</u>tering good re<u>la</u>tionships
   8 a <u>qual</u>ity cu<u>rri</u>culum

VOCABULARY (compound nouns)
4. 1 learning
   2 environment
   3 loan
   4 thinking
   5 training
   6 fees
   7 learning
   8 assessment
   9 accreditation
   10 assessment

GRAMMAR
5. 1 c 2 a 3 a 4 a 5 c 6 b
6. 1 whatever
   2 what
   3 how
   4 whenever
   5 what
   6 Whichever

LISTENING
7. b, c, e, f, h
8. 1 a ('So, this is all born out of a mismatch between the skills and knowledge traditionally taught at school and those needed right across the board in a number of key industries.')
   2 b ('But with STEM learning, we can get to the heart of the issue and teach those skills which will be universally useful to people in the future, whatever profession they work in.')
   3 b ('It's essentially an integrated curriculum that allows for the development of core skills that are useful, such as critical thinking and creativity in problem solving.')
   4 c ('You see, the thing that sets us humans apart is our creativity, especially in terms of creative solutions to problems.')
   5 a ('We as educators need to stop thinking of education as the transfer of knowledge within the distinct frameworks of school subjects.')
   6 a ('Key skills to nurture are a sense of inquiry – which children are naturally equipped with – collaboration and a focus on process-based learning, not knowledge and facts.')
9. 1 It's essentially an integrated curriculum.
   2 That's precisely what it is, that's spot on!
   3 Do you think schools will implement this approach to learning?
   4 The starting point is to remember that it's an integrated approach.

ANSWER KEY

WRITING

10
1. begins
2. compares
3. points
4. gives
5. accepts
6. focuses
7. goes
8. cites

12 Sample answer
In this extract about STEAM learning, the presenter begins by asking Kendra Lewis what implementing a STEAM model of education means in practical terms for education staff. She then outlines how teachers should work together to plan lessons and explains that there might be a dedicated team looking at how different courses can be integrated. The presenter points out that this might cause extra work, but Kendra compares it to individual planning and cites teachers that she's spoken to who says that they've learnt a lot from the process. She goes on to talk about the role of educational managers and gives information on how they need to plan the curriculum and timetable carefully to allow for the integration of subjects. She then goes on to talk about the training educational staff will need and focuses on the importance of professional development. She also points out that it won't be a huge task as they can make use of the materials and resources that already exist. Finally, she talks about the role of assessment and compares it with traditional assessment which focuses more on knowledge of facts. She gives an example of what STEAM assessment might look like, and states that it needs to focus more on the process than the product.

Lesson 1C

VOCABULARY

1
1. fertile
2. box
3. sparked
4. raw
5. flash
6. novel

2
1. inspiration
2. blue
3. innate
4. outside
5. up
6. intuitive

How to …

3 1 c 2 e 3 a 4 f 5 b 6 d

4 1 a 2 d 3 f 4 g 5 b 6 e 7 c

PRONUNCIATION

5 2 and 3

SPEAKING

6A
1. point
2. rolling
3. cut
4. saying
5. like
6. what

Lesson 1D

LISTENING

1 1 B 2 J 3 I

2
1. Brayden ('The other thing she did was help us discover things for ourselves rather than just feed us answers.')
2. Ilsa ('… when I was at school, I wasn't really into history as a subject …')
3. Joanna ('I struggled a bit with maths at school, I was never very good at it because I just couldn't understand formulas and things like that.')
4. Joanna ('Another way in which she went the extra mile was by creating these worksheets that were specifically designed to play to our strengths and interests. They were great worksheets and I suspect it took her ages to create them.')
5. Ilsa ('I remember, once, he told us to think about the very spot where we were sitting and consider all the people in the past who had walked over that same spot, how fascinating that was.')
6. Brayden ('And she created this really sort of friendly, nurturing dynamic in the lessons, so that we felt secure and comfortable trying things out and not worrying too much about our errors.')

READING

3 1 c 2 b

4
1. T ('… and daily life is dominated by the overwhelming stench of the tip.')
2. F ('When teacher, musician and environmental technician Favio Chávez visited the area as part of a state recycling project, he was shocked at the conditions these families were living in.')
3. F ('Enlisting the help of former carpenter Don Cola Gomez, they set about creating musical instruments from the material they found in the dump.')
4. F ('Up to three-quarters of the children's families were living in motels.')
5. F ('She then set about launching a national campaign to raise funds by asking businesses and organisations across the country to donate money.')
6. T ('As a result the students' scores in all subjects greatly improved.')

UNIT 2

Lesson 2A

VOCABULARY

1
1. profile
2. facilitating
3. bring
4. than
5. detrimental
6. up

2
1. tangible
2. boost
3. harm
4. stuck
5. showcase

3
1. bustle
2. large
3. about
4. parcel
5. learn
6. dried

4
1. peace and quiet
2. First and foremost
3. make or break
4. slowly but surely / sooner or later
5. slowly but surely / sooner or later
6. give or take

GRAMMAR

5 1 b 2 c 3 b 4 a 5 c 6 b

PRONUNCIATION

6A
1. as, as
2. a
3. than
4. than
5. as, as

They all have the same weak schwa sound.

READING

7
1. sister cities
2. (an) international (relationship)
3. (to develop) trade
4. (the) mid-20th century

79

ANSWER KEY

8 1 a ('exotic-sounding place you've never heard of and have no intention of finding out about')
2 b ('This was intended as a way of opening up lasting channels of communication between cities after years of conflict between warring nations.')
3 b ('the two previously warring cities of Paris and Rome became exclusively twinned. This sisterhood of great cities carries the motto, 'Only Paris is worthy of Rome; only Rome is worthy of Paris.')
4 a ('But, decades on, much has now changed in these industries. So is there much point in them being twinned?')
5 a ('... such as exchange programmes where teenagers get to visit the other town and stay with a family.')

Lesson 2B
VOCABULARY
1 1 a 2 c 3 c 4 b 5 b 6 a 7 c

2 1 cited   4 echoed
   2 acknowledged 5 questioned
   3 pondered   6 called

3 1 for   4 off
   2 into 5 in
   3 off   6 up

GRAMMAR
4 1 a 2 b 3 b 4 c

5 1 called   5 opinion
   2 claimed   6 pointed
   3 echoed   7 ability
   4 confident 8 need

PRONUNCIATION
6A The second part of the sentences gives a contrasting view. The intonation is higher on the names or descriptions of the people with the contrasting view.

LISTENING
7 The correct order is b, d, a, e, c.

8 1 F ('And since I only work with English,')
2 F ('However, that doesn't mean my work is without its own challenges.')
3 T ('I guess one of the first things … We need to make sure the text doesn't cover up too much of the action in terms of screen space.')
4 T ('... and if the actors are speaking fast and there's a lot of text, it can be quite tricky.')
5 F ('Because of the time and space restrictions, we often find ourselves making decisions about what to include or whether to simplify the syntax to make it easier to follow.')
6 T ('We also have to stay true to the character's style of speech, register and any eccentricities they might have.')
7 T ('each line of text needs to be a 'sense unit', so we can't split articles from nouns, collocations …')
8 T ('We need to blend the text into this so that the subtitles almost appear invisible … That is our main aim whenever scribing text for subtitles.')

WRITING
9A Suggested answers:
1 audiobooks, TV adverts, animated films, dubbing foreign-language videos
2 They search online, record an 'audition' and send it off.
3 Pros: you can choose your work (and how much work you take on), there's a great community of people, you make contacts in a wide variety of fields.
Cons: can be expensive to get started, need to set and stick to a routine to be able to manage the work, uncertainty about future work, can be lonely

9B Suggested answers:
Both texts refer to radio advertisements in addition to the areas of work mentioned in the recording in 9A.
1 Morning – non-vocal work, e.g. search for new jobs, send emails and invoices; Afternoon – vocal work in studio: record auditions to warm up then work on main client's jobs; Evening – take a walk and rest voice.
2 organised (needs to set a routine to manage the different tasks involved to keep on top of things, can't rush things), ability to understand meaning behind the script, reading fluency, ability to work to deadlines, good timing.

10 Sample answer:
A voiceover artist usually works as a freelancer. They record for a range of media such as audiobooks and radio and TV adverts. They search online for jobs and when they find one they like the look of, they record an audition and submit it. The advantages of the work are being able to choose which projects to work on and how much work to take on. They are part of an interesting community of people who work in a wide range of different fields. On the other hand, it can be expensive to get started and it can be a bit lonely, working alone all the time. Voiceover artists also need to be organised and able to set and stick to a routine. On a typical morning, one voiceover artist does administrative work such as emailing and sending invoices, then afternoons are spent in the studio recording auditions and projects she's working on, before resting her voice in the evening by going for a walk. As well as having organisational skills, voiceover artists need to be able to understand meaning behind scripts and have reading fluency and good timing.

Lesson 2C
VOCABULARY
1 1 frowned   4 irrespective
   2 commonplace   5 peculiar
   3 long-standing

2 1 stereotypical 4 standing
   2 irrespective   5 peculiar
   3 rooted   6 upon

How to ...
3 1 Wanda ('The other day I accidentally bumped into someone at the train station and they turned round to me and said, 'Sorry!', even though I was to blame!')
2 Omar ('But surely it's good to be polite like that? Otherwise we'd just be walking around being rude to each other all the time.')
3 Stacey ('I remember once … a guy came rushing past, looking like he had to get somewhere quickly … and he walked into the lamp post. His first reaction was to say sorry, which he said to the lamp post!')
4 Omar ('And you make a good point. When it gets to that stage, I think we've taken things too far.')
5 Wanda ('I think often that politeness gets confused with the idea of polite language … My language has become more polite, but the intent is more aggressive, if you see what I mean.')

ANSWER KEY

6 Wanda ('In America, strangers always talk to each other in the street. But, here in England, for example, if I try to strike up a conversation at a bus stop, I can feel the other person getting uncomfortable and trying to avoid engaging with me.')

4   1 But   4 Fair
    2 take   5 point
    3 make   6 way

PRONUNCIATION

5A 1 b 2 a 3 d 4 c

SPEAKING

6A 1 e 2 b 3 c 4 d 5 a 6 f

Lesson 2D
LISTENING

1   1 A 2 C 3 C

2   1 unpopular   4 with something else
    2 isn't   5 the way it's baked
    3 cheese   6 competition

READING

3   All except 2, 5 and 8 are mentioned

4   1 fish tacos   5 sample
    2 (small fried) fish   6 (three) different parts
    3 unique cuisines   7 convenience
    4 hygiene

REVIEW 1–2
GRAMMAR

1   1 If I'd known about the dress code, I would have dressed smartly.
    2 Unless you check, you won't have the full picture.
    3 But for my parent's support, I wouldn't have gone to university.
    4 If I were to go out tonight, I'd regret it tomorrow.
    5 Had you studied more, you would have passed the exam.
    6 We'll be there on time providing (that) we leave early.

2   1 Whoever   4 whatever
    2 how   5 what
    3 exactly   6 this

3   1 b 2 c 3 b 4 a

4   1 hopeful   5 cited
    2 to   6 echoed
    3 acknowledged   7 ability
    4 implored   8 have

VOCABULARY

5   1 spot on   4 vacuous comments
    2 struck, chord   5 ring true
    3 complete fallacy   6 sweeping statement

6   1 up   4 nothing
    2 in   5 out
    3 in   6 making

7   1 blended   5 potential
    2 virtual   6 critical
    3 rigorous   7 path
    4 nurturing   8 tuition

8   1 fertile   4 sparked
    2 box   5 raw
    3 out of

9   1 answer/answers   4 level
    2 through   5 account
    3 adjust

10 1 b 2 a 3 a 4 b 5 a 6 b

11 1 b 2 b 3 a 4 c 5 a 6 c

12 1 acknowledged   4 illustrate
    2 reeled   5 fill
    3 raised   6 echoed

13 1 deeply-rooted   4 frowned
    2 irrespective of   5 commonplace of
    3 stereotypical   6 peculiar

14 1 b 2 c 3 b 4 c 5 a

UNIT 3
Lesson 3A
VOCABULARY

1   1 warrant   4 spread
    2 identify   5 jeopardise
    3 leave

2   1 word   4 success
    2 selling   5 second
    3 footprint   6 strengths

GRAMMAR

3   1 unimaginable   5 a requirement
    2 essential   6 bound
    3 capable of   7 may
    4 an aptitude   8 a chance

4   1 c 2 a 3 c 4 b 5 b 6 a

PRONUNCIATION

5A 1 are   4 all
    2 to   5 of
    3 to

LISTENING

6   2, 3 and 5

7   1 b ('For some positions, the number of applicants is so high that it's simply impractical for employers to devote the necessary time to read each application and give it the attention it deserves.')
    2 b ('A benefit of this for companies is that they'll be able to spend more valuable and productive 'human time' face-to-face with potential employees.')
    3 b ('Companies will need to rethink their branding so that they not only appeal to their customer base, but also to potential employees.')
    4 a ('So, for example, if you search for 'office administrator', results might also include something like 'hotel receptionist', which you may not have considered before.')
    5 b ('… you'll need to be constantly alert to this, even when you're not actively seeking employment.)

WRITING

8   1 F (*you're, I've, I'm, That's, I'd, haven't, you'd*)
    2 F (*Hope you're well. I really like the look of this job. I think I'd fit the bill! … good at the job. Let me know*, etc.)
    3 T
    4 F (Is he actually formally applying for the job or just wanting to find out if he's a 'good fit'?)
    5 F
    6 F (He hasn't attached his CV.)

81

ANSWER KEY

9 Sample answer
Dear Mr Wilkley
I am writing to apply for the role of sales and marketing executive as advertised on the job seekers website. Your company has an excellent reputation in the industry and I was particularly impressed with your recent *Homes for all* campaign.
Aspects of my background which I consider relevant include the following:
- I hold a first-class degree in marketing from the University of Birmingham.
- During my five years' experience in my current sales and marketing role, I have consistently met or exceeded my monthly sales targets, often working calmly under pressure.

During my time here, I have also worked within a small sales team and have helped integrate new members into the team as well as participated in team-based activities to build strong relationships. In addition, I have led workshops on developing communication skills with clients. I am passionate about my career and see myself working long-term with the right company. I feel that my experience, expertise and skills would be a real asset to your company.
I am attaching my CV, which includes further details and references. Please do not hesitate to contact me should you require any further information. Thank you in advance for your consideration.
Kind regards,
Chris Pennington

Lesson 3B
VOCABULARY
1 1 ease, stress 5 strengthen, bonds
   2 engender, distrust 6 boost, morale
   3 exacerbate, divisions 7 alleviate, boredom
   4 aggravate, problem

2 1 c 2 a 3 a 4 b 5 b 6 c

PRONUNCIATION
3A 1 mo<u>rale</u> 5 <u>bore</u>dom
   2 ex<u>a</u>cerbate 6 al<u>le</u>viate
   3 di<u>vi</u>sions 7 en<u>gen</u>der
   4 <u>a</u>ggravate 8 dis<u>trust</u>

GRAMMAR
4 1 got 6 to have been
   2 it was 7 to be learnt
   3 must 8 have been
   4 had 9 is
   5 being 10 having

5 1 b 2 a 3 b 4 c

READING
6 b (In text A: '… it was down to the very fact that I didn't have those interruptions. This meant that I wasn't taking the odd break. The fact that I was so focused and able to concentrate meant I was working much harder.'; In text B: 'That there are fewer distractions from other people so you can focus better and get your work done more quickly, leaving you free for the rest of your day to go and sit in the park or whatever else takes your fancy.') (Point a is mentioned in text A and point c is mentioned in text B.)

7 1 B ('But not all social interaction is healthy (think of the crowded daily commute …')
   2 A ('Except, I soon started to realised that if I do dress up for the office every morning it really motivates me to get started and put my work 'hat' on (changing it from my home 'hat'), and helps me focus on my work more easily.')
   3 B ('… it's been shown that people with emotional stability and good self-discipline work best at home.')
   4 B ('… they often find they end up working longer hours in order to fill the day.')
   5 A ('I had a comfortable place to work (in front of a big window overlooking the park – always work near a window if you can: another top tip!)')
   6 B ('But this really isn't true, as, when working remotely, people often feel more of a need not to waste each other's time.')
   7 A ('So I started using a timer to force myself to take a break every thirty minutes, no matter what I was doing. I felt much better at the end of each day.')

8 1 A (The writer talks directly to the reader: 'If you follow my blog, you'll know, …', etc. while in A the writer takes a more formal and impersonal approach.)
   2 B (The writer uses paragraphs signposted by linkers, such as 'Firstly', 'Another common fallacy' and contrasting language, for example, 'There are some health advantages …, however'. The paragraph in Text B also have an identifiable introduction and conclusion, while in Text A the structure seems to reflect the writer's thoughts on the topic as they develop.)
   3 A ('Big plus!', etc.)
   4 B (The writer generally uses longer sentences, passive forms, more formal language, more technical and 'higher level' language.)

Lesson 3C
VOCABULARY
1 1 enforce 4 stand
   2 encouraging 5 shape
   3 eliminate 6 allocate

2 1 wing 5 cast
   2 manifesto 6 hereditary
   3 exit 7 constitution
   4 head 8 spin

How to …
3 1 F (She thinks they have the necessary qualifications, but don't have the right skills.)
   2 T ('The aim of the new skills initiative is for industry leaders to work more closely with the Department of Education in order to have an influence on how they shape the curriculum.')
   3 F (This is what the interviewer suggests, but the politician rejects this suggestion: 'That's not what I mean.')
   4 T ('We need to equip students with the necessary skills they need in most jobs. Things like critical thinking, communication skills, creativity. These are important skills in all jobs, and they fit into all school subjects.')

4 1 So, what you're basically saying is that we need more investment.
   2 But isn't that the opposite of what you said before?
   3 Am I right in thinking you need this to work?
   4 What I said was it's important for everyone.

ANSWER KEY

SPEAKING

6A
1 words
2 What
3 right
4 got
5 rephrase
6 put
7 exactly

Lesson 3D
LISTENING

1 1 a 2 d 3 g 4 h 5 e 6 b 7 c 8 f

2 1 b ('It was a great way to get experience, as long as it's in the field of work you later want to work in.')
2 a ('You want to do it at a company which prioritises staff development over profit, otherwise you're just going to end up being someone who gets the coffees, cleans up after others, that sort of thing.')
3 a ('So, the first day I started, I had to sign an NDA, because obviously the bank deals with a lot of sensitive and personal information about their clients … It's basically a document where you say you won't reveal any information about the bank or its customers.')
4 b ('We'd meet up at the end of each week and review what I'd learnt that week. I could ask questions about anything I wasn't sure of, and she'd ask me questions about what I might do differently. She also asked me how I could use what I'd learnt that week in the following week.')
5 a ('Don't fall into the trap of thinking that you're not a real employee. You essentially are and you're doing real work.')
6 a ('When I first started, I didn't want to seem 'difficult' so I took on all the tasks I was given')
7 b ('The point is to try and learn from them. That's the real learning process.')

READING

3 1 h 2 c 3 d 4 a 5 f 6 g

4 1 T ('Employees should have sufficient space and the capacity to allow them to personalise their own space, too.')
2 F ('Some studies suggest … Whether you buy into all that or not …')
3 F ('There are many aspects to this, such as …')
4 T ('… it's important to provide quiet spaces where staff can go when they need to concentrate, or just have some quiet time.')
5 T ('… unless everyone's fully involved and contributing, it's going to be wasting time that could be much better spent.')
6 F ('It seems that most people have a sense of duty and knowing that they don't need to be in the office helps them work more productively when they are.')

UNIT 4

Lesson 4A
VOCABULARY (verb–noun collocations)

1 1 a 2 c 3 b 4 b 5 a 6 c

2 1 satisfy
2 Fuelled
3 back
4 raise
5 push
6 pursuing
7 realised

PRONUNCIATION

3A 1 <u>fun</u>ding
2 <u>pro</u>ject
3 am<u>bi</u>tion
4 <u>li</u>mits
5 <u>sci</u>ence
6 curi<u>os</u>ity

VOCABULARY (adjective–adjective collocations)

4 1 infinitely
2 ludicrously
3 significantly
4 blindingly
5 immediately
6 vehemently
7 wildly
8 gravely

GRAMMAR

5 1 c 2 c 3 a 4 a 5 b 6 c

READING

6 1 submit a proposal/submit proposals
2 Philadelphia
3 intelligent automation

7 1 c
2 b
3 a

8 1 F ('Technology which can read human brainwaves isn't new …')
2 F ('This technology is a way off from being universally developed, as everyone's brain signals are different …')
3 T ('However, the software developed by the team features a form of AI that learns how to distinguish different signals as it goes on, learning the correct functions over time.')
4 T ('They're building a hub for delivery drones and flying taxis …')
5 F ('The whole hub and its vehicles are powered by hydrogen and are carbon neutral with zero emissions … In fact, it doesn't need to be connected to the national energy grid at all.')
6 F ('Using a mixture of sand, gel and bacteria …')
7 T ('It can also draw in dangerous toxins from air pollution …')

Lesson 4B
VOCABULARY

1 1 patch
2 ends
3 hand
4 effect
5 word

2 1 rough
2 meet
3 face
4 helping
5 knock
6 spread

3 1 compassionate
2 enterprising
3 aloof
4 appreciative
5 intuitive
6 resourceful
7 conscientious
8 selfless

PRONUNCIATION

4A 1 word
2 day
3 meet
4 hand

GRAMMAR

5 1 had been looking
2 's living
3 've been helping
4 have received
5 has finally implemented
6 've lost
7 'd forgotten
8 've had

6 1 b 2 a 3 c 4 b

LISTENING

7 b and c

83

ANSWER KEY

8
1 T ('We always get requests from donors asking to see how their donations are spent.')
2 F ('I worked in IT before I joined the charity.')
3 T ('This then has a knock-on effect on how people perceive us, they become more appreciative of our work and they're encouraged to donate more.')
4 F ('So far the app's been downloaded nearly a thousand times, so it's popular, too.')
5 F ('In fact by early next year we'll have been running for ten years.')
6 T ('What we aim to do is match people in third-world countries with people in this country who want to invest ethically.')
7 F ('and then invest part or the whole of the sum required.')
8 T ('It's sort of venture capitalism, I guess, but on a smaller, more human scale.')

WRITING

9A a

9B 1 c 2 e 3 a 4 b 5 d

10 Sample answer
<u>Small scale, but a big difference</u>
People invest for all sorts of reasons. While everyone wants to see a good return on their investment, there are a whole host of other motivations, such as making a difference to people's lives or protecting the planet. ImpactVest allows you to not only do that, but also see the positive effects of your money.
So, what makes investing with ImpactVest different? Well, unlike other investment companies which promise higher returns the higher the risk, the aim of this organisation is to get the money exactly where it's needed on a small scale. Not only that, but you can see who it's giving a helping hand to and how.
The way it works is simple. For example, someone in a developing country might have a small business which is doing well, and wants to expand. So they post the amount needed and their business plan on the website. Potential investors can then browse the website and choose how much they want to invest. They can invest part or all of the required amount. They then receive regular updates on how the business is doing.
This is a great way to invest ethically, so if you want your money to do some good in the world as well as bring you a return, this is the organisation for you.

Lesson 4C
VOCABULARY

1 1 a 2 c 3 b 4 a 5 c 6 b

2 1 c 2 e 3 f 4 b 5 a 6 d

How to ...

3 b

4 1 whole   4 speaking
   2 Having   5 presumably
   3 To   6 impression

PRONUNCIATION

5A
1 Having said that, // many people expressed a concern that this shouldn't go too far.
2 To cite one example, // one respondent stated that this should by no means include military service.
3 Generally speaking, though, // most people thought community service was a good idea.

SPEAKING

6A 1 picture   4 reflected
     2 cite   5 might
     3 Another   6 seems

Lesson 4D
LISTENING

1 b ('It is of course, nothing like a cow, as this cute little mammal is a porpoise which closely resembles a dolphin, with a large dark ring around its eyes and a dark grey hue over its top surface.')

2
1 female (Females grow up to 150 cm long, whereas their male counterparts grow to around 140 cm long')
2 (a group of mammals including) whales, dolphins and porpoises ('This makes them the smallest of all cetaceans, a group which includes whales, dolphins and other porpoises')
3 (at the very top end of) the Gulf of California ('The vaquita roams the very top end of the Gulf of California …')
4 smaller fish, crustaceans and squid ('… loves the warm, shallow waters with its abundance of smaller fish, crustaceans and squid.')
5 the illegal fishing industry ('However, the main culprit for its decline is the illegal fishing industry …')
6 567 ('… by 1997 there were an estimated 567 left in this bay.')
7 fewer than ten ('… today there are believed to be fewer than ten in the wild.')
8 She died. ('In 2017 one captured female was so traumatised that she died.')

READING

3 Yes.

4
1 a ('Wondering what a bird of prey is doing in such an urban environment,')
2 b ('Their appearance as a bird of prey created an impression of them as a harbinger of doom, something dark and to be feared.')
3 b ('In Wales, however, … they were afforded some semblance of protection over the next hundred years.')
4 a ('That came in the unprecedented form …')
5 b ('From their new home, they started to spread out westwards along the corridor of the M40 motorway, feeding on carrion found there.')
6 a ('a truly magnificent and awe-inspiring creature that has gone from being on the brink of extinction in Britain to numbers there now forming nearly ten percent of the world's population …')

REVIEW 3–4
GRAMMAR

1
1 It's a given that he'll get the job.
2 It seems totally unimaginable that they'd fire her.
3 We aren't supposed to wear trainers at work.
4 This needs to be sorted out immediately.
5 That must have been the client on the phone.
6 The odds are that we'll get homework tonight. / The odds are that tonight we'll get homework.

2 1 thought   4 got
     2 having   5 be done
     3 being   6 to have been

ANSWER KEY

3
1 Solving
2 doing
3 to fix
4 engaging
5 to get
6 to pull

4
1 've never tried
2 lived / was living
3 'll be travelling
4 've been
5 'll have been working / 'll have worked
6 'd been waiting

VOCABULARY

5
1 plays
2 footprint
3 jeopardise
4 selling
5 warrant

6
1 engender
2 aggravate/exacerbate
3 exacerbate
4 alleviate
5 strengthen
6 boost

7
1 freezes
2 head
3 blanket
4 flooded
5 trickling

8
1 tackle
2 enforce
3 shape
4 allocate
5 encourage

9
1 exit
2 head
3 ballot
4 views
5 constitution
6 manifesto

10
1 share
2 aspect
3 field
4 toxic
5 footing

11
1 realise
2 back
3 raise
4 push
5 serve
6 pursue

12
1 vehemently
2 ludicrously
3 blindingly
4 significantly
5 wildly
6 gravely

13
1 patch
2 hand
3 effect
4 meet
5 face
6 word

14
1 conscientious
2 aloof
3 compassionate
4 enterprising
5 resourceful
6 intuitive

15
1 profit
2 zero
3 umbrella
4 finite
5 transactions

16
1 taken
2 grave
3 global
4 set
5 brink

UNIT 5

Lesson 5A
VOCABULARY

1
1 up
2 have
3 project
4 preconceptions
5 adopt
6 establish
7 lasting
8 taint

2
1 dishevelled
2 bereft
3 gullible
4 self-deprecating
5 distinctive
6 susceptible
7 unfavourable
8 implausible

3
1 reassuring
2 pompous
3 unapproachable
4 disconcerting
5 unperturbed

GRAMMAR

4 1 b 2 b 3 c 4 b

5
1 her brother's an electrician
2 was my workload last month that
3 I love about my new job
4 was the best I've seen in ages
5 was Jan who took your mug

PRONUNCIATION

6A
1 What I hate <u>most</u> is when people lie to me.
2 Under no <u>circumstances</u> should you attempt to lift this without help.
3 It felt like the longest <u>ever</u>, that meeting.
4 That customer you were <u>talking</u> to, what did she want?
5 All I <u>needed</u> was a bit more time.
6 When I'm going to have time to <u>finish</u> this, I have no idea.

READING

7 The correct order is: b, d, a, c.

8
1 a ('We unwittingly size them up by their posture, eye gaze, tone of voice, body language and facial expressions.')
2 b ('… appearance counts. If we see something we don't like, it taints our impression.')
3 b ('They try to project themselves in a certain way, even adopting mannerisms that they believe will help them succeed.')
4 a ('A lot of our expressions come from our eyebrows. In monkeys, raised eyebrows are a sign of aggression, but with us it's the opposite.')
5 b ('… perhaps not the best advice, as people do it in a split-second and without thinking.')

Lesson 5B
VOCABULARY

1
1 went
2 sway
3 escalate
4 abound
5 boost
6 embellished

2 1 c 2 b 3 a 4 b 5 a 6 c

3
1 distort
2 sway
3 boost
4 embellish
5 go
6 escalates
7 abound
8 quashed

GRAMMAR

4 1 b 2 b 3 a 4 c 5 c 6 a

5
1 Having forgotten
2 approaching
3 Designed
4 having/having had
5 Having run
6 Cooked

PRONUNCIATION

6A
1 lost
2 Being
3 was
4 Having

LISTENING

7 a and c

85

ANSWER KEY

8   **1** F ('And their tactics are becoming ever more duplicitous as they distort information to achieve their goal.')
     2 T ('contacting you by phone, they claim to be calling from your bank, saying that you've been a victim of fraud and your account details have been compromised.')
     3 T ('A lot of people have experienced this type of scam happen when they're about to make a large payment, say, for example, a deposit for a house or a new car, something like that.')
     4 F ('But you shouldn't rely on banks and other organisations to protect you.')
     5 F ('And, finally, the first time you buy from a website, do a search for reviews of the site.')

9   **1** What are the types of scams they're using?
     2 Contacting you by phone, they claim to be from your bank.
     3 You shouldn't rely on banks and other organisations to protect you.
     4 Check your credit report every month for any unusual signs.

WRITING

10   **1** aim   **6** few
     2 on   **7** proportion
     3 minimise   **8** large
     4 consensus   **9** worrying
     5 cited   **10** points

11   Sample answer

Introduction
The aim of this report is to summarise the positive and negative effects of businesses having a social media presence, based on a survey of 50 companies. It will go on to offer recommendations on how companies can minimise any negative effects.

Positive effects
There was widespread agreement among those interviewed that it is generally expected these days. A frequently mentioned reason was that it can help improve the company's image online. A significant proportion of those interviewed said it helps them interact with customers directly, by answering questions or responding to complaints. A few businesses also said that they use social media to promote their services and launch new products. Companies with links to the local community can use social media to communicate initiatives and activities directly to local people.

Negative effects
On the other hand, an overwhelming number of businesses mentioned the risk to the company's image. They mentioned that if complaints aren't dealt with quickly, they can be amplified. A substantial percentage cited the need to keep the account information up to date to avoid creating a negative impression among customers. A worrying number of companies stated the cost of constantly monitoring social media for the business is sometimes prohibitively expensive. However, companies which had a dedicated member of staff or trained their staff in social media management reported fewer risks to their image.

Recommendations
After considering these points, I recommend that businesses should be advised to:
- have a social media presence
- monitor and update their social media as much as possible
- respond to queries and/or complaints as quickly as possible
- train staff in social media management skills

I believe that a social media presence has more positive than negative effects for businesses and so should be used, but managed carefully.

Lesson 5C

VOCABULARY

1   **1** own   **4** come
     2 bring   **5** convince
     3 gauge

2   **1** a   **2** b   **3** c   **4** a   **5** c   **6** b   **7** a   **8** b

HOW TO …

3   a

4   **1** perfectly   **5** Not
     2 like   **6** for
     3 like   **7** calm
     4 no

5   **a** 2   **b** 1   **c** 6   **d** 3   **e** 4   **f** 5   **g** 7

PRONUNCIATION

6A It rises on each word except the last one, when it falls.

SPEAKING

7A   **1** just consider   **4** huge breakthrough
     2 Not only   **5** waiting for
     3 to me   **6** cool, collaborative

Lesson 5D

LISTENING

1   2, 5

2   **1** Cora   **5** Ed
     2 Ed   **6** Ed
     3 both   **7** Cora
     4 Cora   **8** Ed

READING

3   **1** b   **2** e   **3** f   **4** a   **5** d   **6** g

4   **1** T ('On the one hand, when faced with problems, try to keep things in perspective and look at the whole picture.')
     2 F ('Achieving these will put you in a good frame of mind, which will rub off on others.')
     3 T ('…but you'll also be demonstrating that things can actually be done.')
     4 F ('I think everyone admired him for doing that.')
     5 F ('If you try to be something or someone you aren't, it might make other people suspicious.')
     6 T ('Even if you don't agree with what they say, the act of hearing them will make them feel like what they're saying is important.')
     7 T ('Pay attention to people's actions and when you notice something that's been done successfully, compliment them and make a bit of a song and dance about it.')
     8 F ('But, in arguments over a polarising issue, how often does one side actually 'win' and convince the other? That's not something I've ever experienced.')

ANSWER KEY

UNIT 6

Lesson 6A
VOCABULARY

1. **1** c **2** c **3** b **4** b **5** a **6** a

2. **1** set **4** revolves
   2 seen **5** resonated
   3 plunged **6** devoted

3. **1** sheer **5** riveting
   2 style **6** debut
   3 plotted **7** fiendishly
   4 grips

GRAMMAR

4. **1** b **2** a **3** c **4** b

5. **1** 'd been steadily getting
   2 liked
   3 went
   4 followed
   5 were gently running
   6 felt
   7 woke
   8 had fallen

PRONUNCIATION

6A The stress increases and the intonation is higher.

READING

7. **1** T ('there has to be something learnt in the story, whether that's a lesson in life or a resolution to a conflict.')
   2 T ('Remember that, when writing, you don't have to begin at the start. You can start to relay the narrative from the middle, or even the end. But a clear structure will allow you to do so without confusing the audience.')
   3 F ('Bear in mind that the reader has allowed you to venture into their time, and so if your offering is too difficult to follow, they'll just give up.')
   4 F ('Once you've got the message and structure in place, it's time to explore your characters and scenarios.')
   5 F ('I was always told to write about what I know, but there's no harm in throwing in a few surprises for your reader.')
   6 T ('It's easy to build short bursts of writing into your daily schedule.')

8. **1** a **2** a **3** b **4** b **5** a **6** a

WRITING

9. **1** b **2** d **3** e **4** a **5** c

10. Sample answer
    Neverwhere by Neil Gaiman
    It's London, but not as you know it. This fiendishly clever tale is set against the backdrop of a murky underworld, deep in the belly of England's capital. The protagonist, Richard Mayhew, having moved to London from his native Scotland, finds himself in a dead-end job and a failing engagement. One night, he chances upon a girl in the street looking completely wretched, as though she'd just been attacked. He stops to help her when they are whisked through a door into a magical kingdom full of mythical people and beasts, a whole subterranean world which, though it exists before our very eyes, we're blissfully unaware of.

The girl's name is Door, which is ironic as Richard went with her through an actual door into this world. What follows is a rollercoaster ride of an adventure through 'London Below' to aid Door in escaping assassins and to locate whoever was responsible for her family's deaths and avenge them. Here, everything is aptly named, of course. As they travel through the world, they meet shepherds at Shepherd's Bush, a baron at Baron's Court, and a band of black friars at Blackfriars. And who do you think they meet at Earl's Court? That's right, it's the Earl himself!
The story itself is absolutely amazing and quite brilliant. Gaiman is a true storyteller and, with his ability to make the completely absurd seem plausible, a proper entertainer. It's well worth a read. It'll open up a whole new world to you that you never knew existed, just like it does for the protagonist himself.

Lesson 6B
VOCABULARY

1. **1** confrontational **5** simplistic
   2 melodic **6** emotionally charged
   3 poignant **7** melancholic
   4 rousing **8** punchy

2. **1** find **4** nothing
   2 back **5** relate
   3 conjures

3. **1** e **2** a **3** f **4** c **5** d **6** b

GRAMMAR

4. **1** b **2** b **3** c **4** b **5** a **6** c **7** c **8** a

5. **1** f **2** b **3** c **4** g **5** a **6** h **7** d **8** e

PRONUNCIATION

6. It rises in the first part in bold, and falls on the second.

LISTENING

7. B

8. 1, 2, 4, 6 and 7

9. **1** a ('I think the simple answer is you need to get lucky! It's an incredibly difficult business to break into, so you need an opportunity to get yourself heard by as many people as possible.')
   2 c ('You need to take a good look at where music is today and get a feel for the direction it's heading in.')
   3 c ('So, we all met at college, and we soon discovered we had a mutual love for the type of punchy, rousing sound that we play.')
   4 b ('… but it's not just about how well people in your band can play, it's about how well you play together. That's the thing about music, it's more than the sum of its parts. When good musicians get together and they're a good fit, what they produce is poignant and beautiful.')
   5 a ('It's important to get on socially, too.')
   6 b ('When we first started we just played covers of songs we all really like and can relate to.')
   7 c ('But these days, the songwriting mainly comes from Kyle … But it's true that I do most of the writing.')
   8 a ('I'll bring it to the next band practice and then other people will add little riffs here and there and then, before we know it, we end up with a new hit.')

ANSWER KEY

10   **1** It's an incredibly difficult business to break into.
     2 You need to have some substance to what you create.
     3 You've got to have something that's worth sharing.
     4 When we get together to rehearse, it doesn't feel like work.

Lesson 6C
VOCABULARY
1   **1** d   **2** e   **3** i   **4** a   **5** f   **6** g   **7** c   **8** j   **9** b   **10** h

2   **1** rugged   **4** rugged
     2 rambling   **5** pristine
     3 dense   **6** barren

How to …
3   **1** c   **2** g   **3** a   **4** d   **5** e   **6** b   **7** f

4   **1** like   **4** those
     2 mean   **5** this
     3 Funny

PRONUNCIATION
5A   Yes, they are.

SPEAKING
6A   **1** stuff   **5** know
       2 like   **6** those
       3 this   **7** like
       4 sort

Lesson 6D
LISTENING
1   b

2   **1** c   **2** d   **3** a   **4** f   **5** e   **6** b

READING
3   **1** c   **2** a   **3** d   **4** e   **5** b

4   **1** a   **2** a   **3** b   **4** a   **5** a   **6** b

REVIEW 5–6
GRAMMAR
1   **1** The source of the misinformation we
     2 What I really hate is
     3 It's very popular round the world, this
     4 It was this story which
     5 All we need is
     6 That article you shared, where

2   **1** the rumour was false, Kevin spread it anyway.
     2 I read last week was fascinating.
     3 discussed the matter at length, we've agreed it's not viable
     4 convinced by the story, Sonja decided to check it.
     5 by Liam, the article was later proved to contain falsehoods.
     6 slowly, the onions taste best.

3   **1** were talking   **4** hadn't even started
     2 'd been working   **5** didn't know
     3 were you doing   **6** walks

4   **1** perfectly   **4** distinctly
     2 utterly   **5** fully
     3 horror   **6** Difficult

VOCABULARY
5   **1** e   **2** c   **3** a   **4** d   **5** b

6   **1** industrious   **4** reassuring
     2 disconcerting   **5** dishevelled
     3 unintelligible   **6** unperturbed

7   **1** sway   **4** embellished
     2 go   **5** distorted
     3 boosting

8   **1** come   **5** convince
     2 bring   **6** go
     3 gauge   **7** bolster
     4 own

9   **1** mediocre   **4** muddled
     2 long-winded   **5** assured
     3 stiff   **6** inappropriate

10   **1** e   **2** c   **3** a   **4** d   **5** f   **6** b

11   **1** resonated   **4** breaks
      2 addresses   **5** devoted
      3 set

12   **1** riveting   **4** grips
      2 plotted   **5** debut
      3 sheer   **6** fiendishly

13   **1** emotionally   **4** nothing
      2 melancholic   **5** relate
      3 conjures   **6** reduced

14   **1** c   **2** a   **3** e   **4** f   **5** b   **6** d

15   **1** farmhouse   **4** beach
      2 forest   **5** mountains
      3 room

16   **1** b   **2** e   **3** c   **4** a   **5** d

UNIT 7

Lesson 7A
VOCABULARY (idioms for choices)
1   **1** spoilt   **4** take
     2 umming   **5** second
     3 quandary   **6** sit

PRONUNCIATION
2A   **1** I'm trying not to sit on the <u>fence</u>.
      2 It's time to stop umming and <u>ahh</u>ing.
      3 You need to dig your <u>heels</u> in.
      4 It's easy to just take the path of least re<u>sist</u>ance.
      5 I'm in a bit of a <u>quand</u>ary over this.
      6 Ooh, we're really spoilt for <u>choice</u>!

VOCABULARY (connotation)
3   **1** b   **2** c   **3** a   **4** b   **5** b   **6** c

4   **1** embarking upon   **4** vexing
     2 subscribe to   **5** anti
     3 Confronted   **6** out

GRAMMAR
5   **1** c   **2** a   **3** c   **4** a   **5** b   **6** c

6   **1** c   **2** f   **3** a   **4** g   **5** d   **6** e   **7** b

READING
7   The correct order is: b, d, a, c.

8   **1** F ('… but that doesn't mean we can't apply those techniques in our daily lives.')
     2 T ('This is linked to the next step, generating multiple solutions, or suggestions in our case. Then we need to evaluate each option.')

ANSWER KEY

3 F ('Quite simply, what you do is write all your ideas on separate sticky notes or cards and stick them to a wall or a board.' Only the ideas are written on paper, not the whole diagram.)
4 T ('The idea behind this is that when you're spoilt for choice and have many different options and factors, you organise them into sense groups, which lead you more easily towards making a decision.')
5 T ('… especially if we're looking to make a large purchase such as a new car.')
6 F ('These methods involve making decisions that are good enough, though possibly not the best.')

9
1. affinity diagram
2. heuristics
3. seven-step model
4. heuristics
5. seven-step model
6. cost/benefit analysis

10
1. ('So, what are some of these techniques?')
2. ('Finally, we get to select the option based on our evaluation … and implement it …')
3. ('Let's say it's a relative's birthday coming up, and you need to decide what to buy them and how to celebrate.')
4. ('… but deciding what to have for dinner isn't as important a decision as how to allocate thousands of pounds …')
5. ('This might involve ambling around the supermarket to see what's on offer, or looking up a recipe online.')
6. ('When deciding what to have for dinner, we might feel hungry, or just be planning ahead to the evening.')

Lesson 7B
VOCABULARY
1
1. cast
2. scrutinise
3. plough
4. skim
5. pore

2
1. perusing
2. skipped
3. up
4. dip
5. pored
6. skim
7. flick
8. cast

3
1. bookworm
2. die
3. curl
4. heavy
5. lost
6. nose
7. cover
8. hit

GRAMMAR
4 1 a 2 c 3 c 4 a 5 c 6 a
5 1 d 2 e 3 a 4 g 5 c 6 h 7 f 8 b

PRONUNCIATION
6A
1. skip
2. obsess
3. in
4. protect
5. aside
6. comment

The verbs are stressed when followed by a dependent preposition, while particles (prepositions or adverbs) are stressed in the phrasal verbs.

LISTENING
7 c

8
1. L ('At the same time, people often feel a little embarrassed by this, as they feel like they're "cheating".')
2. B ('Reading involves cognitive processing, attention, reasoning, language comprehension, memory, visual processing and motor control of your eyes. … Well, listening has exactly the same benefits except for, obviously, visual processing and motor control of your eyes.')
3. B ('And both reading and listening to stories benefit your brain in terms of making sense of the plot of the story.')
4. R ('When we listen to a performance, we can feel the emotions of the characters instead of having to imagine them …')
5. L ('I guess you can multitask, too. I often listen to audiobooks while I'm driving or pottering around in the garden, something like that.')
6. R ('Well, books are better at holding our attention, and paying attention is another skill we use when reading.')
7. L ('I sometimes find my mind wandering to other things I'm doing when I listen to an audiobook, and it can be tricky getting back to the exact spot.')
8. B ('But either way, the most important skills involved in both reading and listening to books are the ones to do with processing content, and they're the highest-level skills.')

9
1. When you read, a number of parts of your brain are involved.
2. Regular reading can increase your lifespan.
3. Both reading and listening to stories benefit your brain.
4. Indeed, but that's where books also have an advantage.

WRITING
10 1 F 2 A 3 F 4 A 5 F 6 A

11 Sample answer
There's nothing worse than one of your colleagues or employees having problems with grammar and spelling, especially on important or promotional documents. Hearing someone say, 'You should of done that' really grates. But how do you broach the subject with them? It has been suggested that the solution to the problem may lie in employers providing grammar and spelling 'lessons' or directing employees to online courses, to avoid any embarrassment.
Supporters of the idea argue that learning grammar and correct spelling helps with other key skills, such as the ability to communicate clearly and social interaction. And having all employees undergo the training together will help strengthen bonds and encourage teamwork. It can even help people when they want to learn other languages by providing a framework for the way the language is structured.
Those who disagree with the idea, though, suggest it's perhaps a waste of time, and that it's time that could be spent much more usefully on the job at hand. And I guess it depends on the job, too. I mean, does a plumber really need to be able to tell the difference between the past continuous and the past perfect, or spell words that they will probably never need to write?

ANSWER KEY

Personally, I agree with this argument: I don't think it's that important for many jobs. I mean, of course, for certain professions that involve a lot of communication, such as marketing or publishing, it's important, but you'd expect people in those professions to have already been trained in such matters.

Lesson 7C
VOCABULARY
1 1 b 2 a 3 c 4 c 5 a 6 b

How to …
2 1 b 2 e 3 a 4 d 5 c

3
1 maybe
2 would
3 no
4 some, just
5 guessing
6 Obviously
7 going

PRONUNCIATION
4A Rising intonation is shown in bold below. Falling intonation is shown with the underlined words.
1 Well, maybe **it's just me**, / but I'm not really a fan of <u>zoos</u>.
2 **I'm no expert**, / but I think they do a lot to raise <u>awareness</u>.
3 Obviously you've got to **have some controls**, / but I think building zoos is going too <u>far</u>.
4 The idea has a lot **going for it**, / but I don't think we'll have <u>time</u>.

SPEAKING
5A 1 c 2 e 3 a 4 f 5 d 6 b

Lesson 7D
LISTENING
1 She disagrees.

2
1 T ('This means that customers make calculated choices based on what they perceive will make them happiest.')
2 T ('This might mean buying a more expensive version of something because they feel the quality is better, perhaps buying the cheapest because spending less will make them happier.')
3 F ('This assumes that no matter what consumers opt for, they'll never be totally satisfied. So, taken with the first principle, consumers aim to be as happy as possible, but they'll never be fully satisfied with what they purchase.')
4 F ('This states that the amount of satisfaction you gain from a purchase decreases gradually over time.')
5 F ('… as it allows them to calculate the relationship between what prices to set and the state of the economy at any given time.')
6 T ('The primary assumption, utility maximisation, makes the mistake of assuming that consumers always act rationally. But they don't.')
7 T ('Or perhaps the item that a consumer really wants to buy isn't available, so rather than skip the purchase – if it's a small one – they might look for a quick substitute.')
8 F ('In effect, rather than looking at how consumers behave, it portrays a somewhat idealistic view of how customers *should* behave.')

READING
3 They are against too much choice.

4
1 b ('But, as I'm sitting here reading about per-condition cover, lifetime or non-lifetime cover, size and type of excess …')
2 b ('I can feel a bead of sweat running down my forehead.')
3 a ('But when I've only got fifteen minutes left on my lunch break and I'm faced with rows and rows of different types of sandwiches, these values are most definitely not at the forefront of my mind.')
4 b ('This shows how too much choice can be overwhelming, causing us to baulk at the thought of trying to choose which we like most.')
5 b ('By limiting choice, customers go from being 'utility maximisers' (people who make careful and calculated choices on what is best for them) to 'satisficers' (people who buy things which, for them, are 'good enough').')
6 a ('… and research shows that a lack of knowledge of the many different types of plans, coupled with this perceived lack of urgency, means that a lot of people defer making the choice until it's too late')

UNIT 8

Lesson 8A
VOCABULARY
1 1 c 2 a 3 b 4 b 5 a 6 c

2
1 getting
2 be
3 show
4 overcome
5 step
6 have

3
1 honoured
2 held
3 cut
4 term
5 fetched
6 coming
7 reaching
8 wired

GRAMMAR
4 1 a 2 b 3 a 4 a

5 1 e 2 b 3 f 4 g 5 a 6 h 7 c 8 d

PRONUNCIATION
6A
1 long
2 comfort
3 good
4 gift

READING
7 1 c 2 h 3 d 4 a 5 e 6 f 7 b 8 g

8
1 400 (should be 401)
2 a foot injury (should be hernia)
3 a quarter of a million pounds (should be £330,000)
4 heart attack (should be a partial stroke)
5 cycle 14,000 miles (most of this distance will be covered by running marathons, only 1,310 miles of cycling)
6 140 days (should be 104 days)

Lesson 8B
VOCABULARY
1
1 nostalgic
2 shrill
3 tingling
4 involuntary
5 distressing

2
1 comforting
2 soothing
3 hypnotic
4 unsettling
5 distressing

3
1 flinched
2 gasp
3 clutching
4 squirm
5 grimace
6 set
7 wince

ANSWER KEY

GRAMMAR
4 **1** b **2** b **3** a **4** b **5** b **6** a **7** b

5 **1** would make **4** 'll be going
2 Would (you) help **5** will win
6 won't start **6** wouldn't need

PRONUNCIATION
6 **1** They'll have received the package by now.
2 Contracted *will* is not used.
3 You'll have to show me how to use it.
4 We'll need more time.

LISTENING
7 There are both positive and negative things about it.

8 1, 2, 4, 5 and 7

9 **1** F ('synaesthesia involves the mixing of two or more senses, that aren't usually connected, so people with synaesthesia might see sounds as colour, or even taste sounds.' The examples involve three senses: hearing (sounds), sight and taste.)
2 T ('With mirror-touch synaesthesia, people feel sensations that other people feel. So, for example, if they see someone stub their toe, they'll feel that pain.')
3 F ('in the US, it's estimated that it affects between 1.6% and 2.5% of the population.')
4 F ('In one of them, people are touched on different cheeks while they watch an assistant being touched on their cheeks.')
5 T ('Treatment mainly involves therapy and might include things like imagining there's an invisible wall separating the synaesthete from the person they're looking at. In some cases, prescription medicines normally used to treat anxiety and depression can be effective.')
6 F ('It can be, but it can also be acquired.')

10 **1** She felt like she was getting a hug, too.
2 We know it's a rare condition, but just how rare?
3 Is there any treatment available for sufferers of the condition?
4 It all sounds quite overwhelming to me!

WRITING
11 3

12 **a** 3 **b** 1 **c** 2 **d** 4

13 Sample answer
One of my favourite fictional characters is very well-known: Forrest Gump. He's the main character of the 1986 novel of the same name by Winston Groom (as well as the 1994 film). In the story, we soon come to learn that he's compassionate, optimistic and determined as he manages to overcome a number of major setbacks through a combination of luck and a steely desire to help others.
At an early age, Forrest is diagnosed with polio, which means that, while he has strong legs, he has a crooked spine. He therefore has to wear thick metal leg braces in order to help him walk. Due to his innocent nature and low IQ, coupled with the unsightly leg braces, Forrest is bullied at school. One day, walking home from school with his friend Jenny, some bullies appear and start to chase him. Jenny then blurts out the famous line, 'Run, Forrest, run!' and that's exactly what he does. His steel and determination show themselves here, when he runs so fast, and with such strength that his leg braces come off and he's able to make good his escape.
What follows is a series of robust challenges he faces as he makes his journey through life, all of which he's able to deal with in his own unique way. These include war, shrimp fishing, running across America, meeting presidents and rock stars and much, much more. By the end of the story, you'll come to love Forrest just as much as I did, I'm sure!

Lesson 8C
VOCABULARY
1 **1** kick- **5** offset
2 foster **6** alleviates
3 open
4 keep

2 **1** f **2** c **3** d **4** a **5** g **6** e **7** h **8** b

How to …
3 1, 2 and 4

4 **1** beneficial **4** just
2 look **5** get
3 plus **6** positive

PRONUNCIATION
5A The intonation in the first part of each sentence is higher.

SPEAKING
6A **1** about **4** so
2 point **5** real
3 out **6** got

Lesson 8D
LISTENING
1 c

2 **1** T ('highly competent or successful people – or at least those who we view as such – become more likeable when they make a mistake, or 'pratfall'.')
2 F ('What he did was to gather together a group of forty-eight participants and organise them into four groups, and then play a different recording to each group.')
3 T ('At the start of the recording, the person would introduce themselves, saying things like 'I was a high school honours student, I was on the school track team', that kind of thing.')
4 T ('And the person answered ninety percent of the trivia questions correctly. The second group was played a recording of someone answering the same trivia questions, but this person was perceived to be 'average' and only answered thirty percent of the questions correctly.')
5 F ('The third and fourth groups listened to the same recordings, but the actor on them announced at one point, 'Oh no, I've spilled coffee all over my new suit!'')
6 T ('The person seen as average actually became less attractive')

READING
3 **1** b **2** c **3** a

4 **1** a ('What's wrong with laughing, you might ask? Everyone loves a good giggle, surely? Except this wasn't your average run-of-the-mill laughter. It came in uncontrollable fits …')
2 b ('It came in uncontrollable fits that lasted from a few hours up to sixteen days in one instance.')

ANSWER KEY

3 b ('many teenagers were facing the fast-approaching final-year exams when all of a sudden there was an outbreak of a virus – or so it seemed.')
4 a ('… doctors could find no underlying medical causes whatsoever. They were stumped. But then it transpired that the sick teens all had something in common: they'd all watched the soap opera the night before and in that particular episode there had been an outbreak of a virus …')
5 a ('Some were also vomiting or had sore eyes or throats or headaches.')
6 b ('More sensible theories have attributed it to a type of pesticide being sprayed on nearby fields, a type which has since been banned in the UK.')

REVIEW 7–8

GRAMMAR
1 1 b 2 a 3 b 4 c
2 1 to 2 of 3 in 4 on 5 for 6 of 7 from 8 to 9 of 10 of
3 1 I've got <u>something I need to talk to you about</u>.
   2 It was <u>a totally unbelievable story</u>.
   3 We're looking for <u>someone able to meet tight deadlines</u>.
   4 We're based in <u>the high-rise building at the end of the street</u>.
   5 Poverty is a growing problem <u>amongst the elderly</u>.
   6 <u>The person who I admire most</u> is my father.
4 1 b 2 d 3 f 4 a 5 c 6 e

VOCABULARY
5 1 quandary   4 resistance
   2 heels   5 choice
   3 ahhing   6 sleep
6 1 anti   4 confronted
   2 subscribe   5 ahead
   3 away   6 clout
7 1 over   4 scrutinise
   2 skimming   5 up
   3 dipping   6 flick
8 1 bookworm, nose 4 curl
   2 die   5 hit
   3 cover   6 heavy
9 1 actively   4 deeply
   2 hotly   5 completely
   3 strictly   6 patently
10 1 c 2 a 3 b 4 b 5 b 6 a
11 1 step   4 determination
    2 aptitude   5 grips
    3 setbacks
12 1 far   4 far
    2 clear   5 time
    3 widely
13 1 a 2 f 3 c 4 d 5 b 6 e
14 1 flinch   4 started
    2 sets   5 clutched
    3 gasped
15 1 loosen   5 open
    2 take   6 keep
    3 alleviate   7 offset
    4 kick
16 1 a 2 c 3 e 4 b 5 d

CUMULATIVE REVIEW 1–4

GRAMMAR
1 1 Should you   4 for
   2 were   5 unless
   3 provided   6 if
2 1 Andressa thinks the book is amazing.
   2 He maintained that the decision was the right one.
   3 The journalist questioned the minister's ability to govern.
   4 As mentioned in the programme, inflation will rise.
   5 My teacher was satisfied with my explanation.
   6 We wondered if it was OK to bring our own food.
3 1 done   4 highly
   2 odds   5 given
   3 capable   6 imperative
4 1 was standing   5 's/has been
   2 'd/had just decided 6 've found
   3 'd/had been playing 7 'll/will be performing
   4 were waiting

VOCABULARY
5 1 struck   4 making
   2 throw   5 trot
   3 patently   6 hung
6 1 box   4 blue
   2 fertile   5 spark
   3 flash
7 1 in   4 voiced
   2 point   5 into
   3 off   6 issue
8 1 an assault   4 take
   2 intriguing   5 with
   3 fused   6 unique
9 1 spread   4 leave
   2 warrant   5 jeopardise
   3 identify   6 play
10 1 e 2 c 3 d 4 a 5 f 6 b
11 1 going   4 appreciative
    2 selfless   5 give
    3 make   6 intuitive
12 1 infinite   4 brink
    2 unprecedented   5 set
    3 grave   6 action

How to …
13 1 ball   4 point
    2 come   5 on
    3 cut   6 up
14 1 round   4 where
    2 relevant   5 flaw
    3 surely   6 strong
15 1 correct   4 words
    2 mean   5 not
    3 put

CUMULATIVE REVIEW 5–8

GRAMMAR
1 1 b 2 e 3 a 4 f 5 c 6 d
2 1 somewhat   4 horror
   2 remarkably   5 perfectly
   3 Unbelievably   6 utterly

ANSWER KEY

3
1 Haven't got
2 I
3 Am I
4 Liberty
5 let

4
1 'd/would be OK
2 won't ask for help when she needs it
3 'd/would have put the heating on
4 'll/will have received it
5 would tell us stories while we fell asleep

VOCABULARY

5
1 bearing
2 rapport
3 unapproachable
4 effect
5 self-deprecating
6 implausible

6
1 mediocre
2 lengths
3 credibility
4 long-winded
5 cogent
6 gauge

7
1 identify
2 melancholic
3 conjures
4 charged
5 back
6 confrontational

8 1 e 2 a 3 d 4 f 5 b 6 c

9
1 anti
2 sleep
3 subscribe
4 fence
5 embarking
6 second

10
1 actively
2 completely
3 strictly
4 deeply/completely
5 patently/completely
6 hotly

11
1 winced
2 distressing
3 gasped
4 soothing
5 shrill
6 started

12 1 c 2 a 3 e 4 d 5 b

How to …

13
1 perfectly
2 follow
3 for
4 hesitation
5 will you

14 1 f 2 a 3 d 4 e 5 b 6 c

15
1 on
2 just
3 lot
4 with
5 look
6 some

CUMULATIVE REVIEW 1–8

GRAMMAR

1
1 studying
2 explaining
3 Whatever
4 submitted
5 what
6 how

2 1 e 2 f 3 b 4 g 5 c 6 h 7 a 8 d

3
1 has been fired
2 is thought
3 to be selected
4 had our windows replaced
5 needs to be made
6 to be done

4 1 b 2 c 3 a 4 a 5 c 6 b 7 a 8 b

5
1 given
2 Affected
3 shouting
4 invested
5 been told
6 Knowing
7 missed
8 Planted

6
1 joined
2 'd/had been thinking
3 invited
4 had been set
5 didn't have
6 was having
7 found
8 hadn't read

7
1 for
2 on
3 of
4 for/to
5 for
6 about
7 in
8 on

8
1 to stay
2 echo
3 warm
4 educated
5 highly
6 for
7 you make
8 interesting

How to …

9
1 consensus
2 assume
3 contradict
4 illustration
5 interest
6 expressed
7 cite
8 speaking

10 1 F 2 I 3 I 4 F 5 F 6 I 7 I 8 I

VOCABULARY

1 1 b 2 e 3 c 4 a 5 f 6 d

2
1 through
2 feed
3 take
4 dynamic
5 adjust
6 inspire

3
1 showcase
2 quiet
3 detrimental
4 take
5 facilitate
6 harm

4
1 frowned
2 standing
3 rooted
4 common/commonplace
5 peculiar/particular

5
1 morale
2 wet
3 aggravate
4 poured
5 engender

6
1 prioritise
2 shared
3 field
4 toxic
5 sound
6 social

7
1 realise
2 immediately
3 fuel
4 vehemently
5 push
6 blindingly

8
1 Profit
2 zero-
3 umbrella
4 finite
5 online

9
1 squashed
2 embellish
3 escalated
4 viral
5 distort

10 1 c 2 d 3 a 4 e 5 f 6 b

11
1 breaking
2 sheer
3 resonate
4 fiendishly
5 plunged
6 grips

12
1 authentic
2 opulent
3 rugged
4 pristine
5 panoramic
6 dense

13 1 c 2 a 3 e 4 f 5 b 6 d

14
1 overwhelmed
2 indecisive
3 chop
4 narrow
5 investigate
6 limitations

15
1 shape
2 fetched
3 get to
4 hardwired
5 overcome

16
1 loosen
2 keep
3 unwind
4 kick-start
5 open

93